INDONESIAN

BORNEO

KALIMANTAN

Text and Photographs by

KAL MULLER

Edited by David Pickell

PERIPLUS
EDITIONS
BERKELEY - SINGAPORE

Kalimantan

This book divides Kalimantan into six regions. Use the color coded bars to refer to the appropriate region.

THE EAST COAST

THE APOKAYAN

THE MAHAKAM RIVER

SOUTH KALIMANTAN

CENTRAL KALIMANTAN

WEST KALIMANTAN

© 1990 by Periplus Editions, Inc., U.S.A.
ALL RIGHTS RESERVED
Printed in the Republic of Singapore
ISBN 0-945971-09-5

Periplus Editions, Inc.
1442A Walnut Street #206
Berkeley, California 94709

Distributor in UK/Europe (except Holland)
Robertson McCarta Ltd.
122 Kings Cross Road
London WC1X 9DS

Distributor in Indonesia
C.V. Java Books
P.O. Box 55 JKCP
Jakarta 10510

Publisher: Eric Oey
Designer: Peter Ivey
Production and cartography: David Pickell

Author Kal Muller has explored, photographed and written about Indonesia for over 15 years. His work has appeared in dozens of books, as well as in the pages of *National Geographic*, *Geo*, and many other magazines. Muller now spends half the year in Indonesia, and the other half at his home in Mexico.

Cover: *Hudoq* dancer in the upper Mahakam.
Frontispiece: A woman of Ben Hes village and her grandchildren.
Pages 4-5: The *hudoq* dance.
Pages 6-7: Exploring the upper Kayan River.

Periplus Indonesia Travel Guides

BALI
Island of the Gods

INDONESIAN NEW GUINEA
Irian Jaya

SPICE ISLANDS
The Moluccas

JAVA
Garden of the East

INDONESIAN BORNEO
Kalimantan

SULAWESI
The Celebes

SUMATRA
Island of Adventure

EAST OF BALI
From Lombok to Timor

UNDERWATER INDONESIA
A Guide to the World's Best Diving

The name PERIPLUS derives from the Greek, meaning "to circumnavigate." One of the earliest classical texts to mention Southeast Asia was the *Periplus of the Erythrean Sea*, an Alexandrian sailing manual dating from the first century A.D. Periplus Editions, founded in 1988 by Eric Oey, specializes in the arts, cultures and natural history of the Malay archipelago—making authoritative information on the region available to a wider audience.

Contents

PAGE 43

PAGE 174

**To my brother Anthony,
and in memory of our parents,
Apci and Dini**

With special thanks to: Pak Budiarjo of the Samarinda Tourism Department; Herman Diener, the founder and former manager of the splendid Benakutai Hotel in Balikpapan, and his successor Udo Döring; and travel companions Irene and Phil Reid. Also to anthropologist Bernard Sellato, who contributed greatly to the Dayak sections and read the manuscript for errors. This book would have been impossible without the open hospitality of the many Dayaks who shared their houses, meals and life with me.

PART I

Introducing Kalimantan

Borneo has always had a special place in the imagination of the West. Brooding and fecund, teeming with strange creatures and unimaginably huge forests, it was the exotic and unruly antithesis of ordered and seemly Europe. The people of Borneo, the Dayaks, were blood-thirsty and naked, and well into the 19th century reports straightforwardly noted that the forest nomads of the interior were "possessed of a caudal appendage."

Such things belong to literature, of course, of a particular and thankfully dated kind, but the island still has the power to fire the imagination. (One even occasionally hears about the Punan's tails.)

A huge island

Kalimantan, which means "River of Diamonds" in Indonesian, is the name Indonesia gave to her two-thirds of the huge island of Borneo. It is a rugged land of thick rainforests, through which flow tremendous rivers: the Kayan, the Mahakam, the Barito, the Kahayan, the huge Kapuas, and many others. The region is abundant in natural resources, many of which are still untapped, and is covered by one of the world's largest stretches of tropical rainforest.

Borneo is the world's third largest island (after Greenland and New Guinea) covering 746,309 square kilometers (288,150 sq. mi.)—bigger than Texas and Oklahoma combined and five times the area of England and Wales. The northern section of Borneo holds the East Malaysian states of Sarawak, (the former kingdom of James Brooke, the famous "White Raja,") and Sabah as well as the tiny, oil-rich, independent sultanate of Brunei, which has the world's highest per-capita income.

Although the region is home to just 5 percent of Indonesia's population, Kalimantan's 549,032 square kilometers (211,981 sq. mi.) represents 28 percent of the nation's land mass. Kalimantan is further divided into four provinces—Kalimantan Timur (East), Kalimantan Selatan (South), Kalimantan Tengah (Central), and Kalimantan Barat (West). These provinces are usually called Kaltim, Kalsel, Kalteng and Kalbar.

The people of Kalimantan

The Dayaks of Kalimantan never did have tails, and although they were some of the world's fiercest head-hunters, today their traditional swords—*mandau*—are no longer used to collect grisly trophies. Still the Dayaks have a varied and rich culture, and some groups continue to maintain their traditional ways of life.

It is still possible to visit longhouses, huge huge structures on stilts that house an entire village. The stilts were originally a measure of protection against marauding head-hunters. Most Dayaks still hack their rice fields out of the jungle, burning the brush to provide nutrients to the generally poor soil. The men hunt with blowguns and fish Kalimantan's many rivers with cast nets. The women weave baskets of rattan using age-old patterns and techniques.

With proper timing and some luck, you can witness traditional agricultural and funerary rituals in which water buffalos are sacrificed (formerly slaves) and bones placed in special carved coffins. On a less spectacular scale, you can observe a spirit-medium use sacred chants and animal sacrifice to cure the sick or dedicate a new house.

But a word of caution before your expectations surpass reality: The days of loincloth-wearing head-hunters are gone. Just about all Dayaks, even those of the remote interior, wear cheap, serviceable, Western clothing.

Opposite: *A Kenyah Dayak chief. If this warrior's regal bearing were not itself enough to communicate his status, the tattoo motifs, leopard skin poncho, hornbill feathers and other decorations would mark him as an aristocrat.*

Christianity, both Catholic and Protestant varieties, has made great inroads into Kalimantan, and the majority of the Dayaks have adopted this new faith—with the usual result for their traditional culture.

Most travelers, in a hurry to head upriver to see the Dayaks, skip the predominantly Muslim cultures of the coastal areas. But there are fine old mosques to visit as well as a splendid new one in Banjarmasin. You just follow proper etiquette—remove your shoes and dress decently, arms and legs covered and, for women, a scarf. You can visit a mosque on your own or, if it is locked, find a local guide who can locate the keeper.

History buffs will want to visit the sultans' palaces and tombs, which in several areas are well-preserved. Ask around about any circumcisions or weddings coming up. Bring a present if you attend and, if you are well dressed, you might become one of the guests of honor. There will be plenty of food but no alcoholic beverages. These events can include splendid costumes, stately dances and gamelan music.

Life of the rainforest

Although the orangutan is the most celebrated inhabitant of Kalimantan's forests, the region is home to many fascinating creatures—ranging from the beautiful Argus pheasant, a relative of the peacock and just as well-dressed, to the king cobra, an up to five-meter-long monster that has been reported to attack man.

Many of the island's creatures have adapted to the conditions of life in the rainforest canopy. Some have evolved the ability to fly, or really glide, from tree to tree to escape predators—there are flying lizards, lemurs, frogs, squirrels and even three species of flying snakes. To frustrate the many birds, insects have developed intricate camouflage—resembling a leaf, a twig or fungus—or are poisonous.

The island's jungle houses some animals that are just plain weird: the proboscis monkey, the male of which is blessed with a most peculiar and disproportionate nose, the archer fish, which can bring down an insect from two meters above the surface with a startlingly accurate missile of water, and a crab spider that has reached an evolutionary pinnacle of sorts—it bears a striking resemblance to a glob of bird dung.

Perhaps the most interesting of the island's 600 species of birds are the hornbills, which play an important role in native mythology. One hornbill's call—hoots followed by whooping chuckles building to maniacal laughter—has led locals to call it the "chop-down-your-mother-in-law bird."

Plant life includes 70-meter (230 ft.) trees, some of which do not even branch until the 30-meter mark, and an incredible variety of exotic species including carnivorous pitcher

ALAIN COMPOST

al travel agencies in both Balikpapan and Samarinda, some of which can custom design tours, including ones to the remote interior.

South Kalimantan—Kalsel—is also well organized for visitors. Banjarmasin is the only city in Kalimantan worth a visit for its own sake. It has an interesting floating market and nearby river islands with gibbons and shy proboscis monkeys. Nearby, diamonds are dug out of primitive shafts and traditional cutting and polishing readies them for sale in Martapura. Banjarmasin, in the Loksado

plants, bioluminescent mushrooms and many subtly colored orchids—including the rare black orchid. The largest flower in the world is found here. The blossom of the rafflesia is huge, but instead of the perfumy scent of other flowers, it attracts pollinating insects by approximating the smell of rotten meat.

The Tanjung Puting nature reserve in Central Kalimantan is relatively easy to reach and is a rewarding place to view wildlife. The reserve maintains two rehabilitation centers where orangutans which have been kept as illegal pets are readapted to to jungle life. This center is the only place where you are guaranteed to see orangutans. Elsewhere, it is a matter of patience and luck to see these huge apes and other shy exotics—which have a most healthy fear of man.

Visiting Kalimantan

East Kalimantan—Kaltim—receives the greatest number of tourists, thanks to an infrastructure built for the petroleum industry and area promotion. The Balikpapan airport is one of the busiest in Indonesia, and the city has Kalimantan's only really international class hotel. The Mahakam River and its tributaries reach far inland in Kaltim, providing access to relatively remote Dayak villages. Tourism here has developed to the point where guided tour groups out of Samarinda to Tanjung Isuy sometimes have to wait in line for the "traditional" welcome-and-dance show. As a general rule, the further upriver one goes in Kalimantan, the more traditional the Dayaks.

To get a good taste of the Dayak way of life, we suggest traveling to the area around and above Long Iram on the Mahakam, the area around Long Segar on the Kedang Kepala River, and to the Apokayan. The Kutai Game Reserve, although lacking in facilities, provides an opportunity to see orangutans and other wildlife. For those with little time or knowledge of Indonesian, there are sever-

area, is a good spot from which to make treks into Dayak-inhabited regions. There is one good travel agency in Banjarmasin and plenty of freelance guides, some quite experienced.

Central Kalimantan—Kalteng—has few facilities for tourism, although the regional capital, Palangkaraya, offers decent accommodations. This is the least visited region in Kalimantan, and trips up the various rivers in Kalteng, on your own or with a guide, can be fascinating. Many of the Dayaks in Kalteng follow the traditional Kaharingan faith whose spectacular funerary rituals, lasting for weeks, are open to visitors. This event is only recommended for those with a genuine interest in the culture and a willingness to put up with village living conditions.

West Kalimantan—Kalbar—and its capital, Pontianak, are low on most visitors' agendas, at least partly because there is so little information available on the area. Travel agencies, which once limited their tours to coastal areas, are finally beginning to organize inland trips. From Pontianak it's easy to fly or take a riverboat up the Kapuas River to outposts from where you can visit the Dayaks of the interior.

Opposite: *A boy and his family show off their family pet.* **Above, left:** *A pretty Bahau Dayak girl from East Kalimantan.* **Above, right:** *Logging brings considerable income to Kalimantan, but its long-term environmental impact may be grim.*

GEOGRAPHY

Mighty Rivers and Vast Rainforests

A great network of rivers flows from the mountainous center of Borneo to the coasts. These are the island's highways, along which most of the population and commerce is concentrated. Most are easily navigable only to the beginning of the highlands, after which the current picks up and stretches of rapids can force overland portage. Past this transition, they become navigable again. In the past, the rapids provided some protection against head-hunting marauders from the coast, but today they serve only to increase the price of fuel and trade goods to sometimes exorbitant levels.

In the north, where the coasts are closer to the mountains, the rivers rush down to the sea, slowed only by a relatively narrow coastal plain. At the island's widest part, two basins drain into Borneo's greatest rivers: the Mahakam, flowing east, and the Kapuas, the longest river in all of Indonesia, flowing west. In the south, several almost parallel rivers flow through extensive lowlands and swamps before emptying into the Java Sea.

Off northern Kaltim, the Sulu Sea becomes the Sulawesi Sea and finally the Straits of Makassar running down the east coast. Off South Kalimantan is the Java Sea, and the west is separated from mainland southeast Asia by the South China Sea. Despite the long coastlines, there are no good natural harbors in Kalimantan. Much of Borneo is barely above sea level, and tidal fluctuations affect river levels far inland.

A mountainous interior

Borneo's highest mountain ranges lie on a roughly north–south axis, beginning close to the sea in Sabah and heading towards the island's center where the mountains spread out laterally. Individual summits seldom exceed 1,500 meters (5,000 ft.), but the black granite peak of Mount Kinabalu in Sabah rises to a respectable 4,100 meters (13,455 ft.)—the highest point on the island and, indeed, all of Southeast Asia.

West Kalimantan is decorated with spectacular, near-vertical limestone outcroppings. The highest of these, Mount Mulu, reaches 2,377 meters (7,798 ft.). These unusual formations have haunting shapes, and are thought by the people to be the abode of spirits.

The island first emerged from the sea only some 15 million years ago, well after the Age of the Dinosaurs. Various shifts in the earth's sea level during the Ice Ages alternately submerged sizeable chunks of the island, then raised Borneo so that it was joined by land to Sumatra, Java and peninsular Malaysia. Channels formed by the great rivers rushing down from Sumatra's mountains towards Malaysia and Borneo still score the ocean floor. Tectonic upheavals of sedimentary rock formed the mountain chains.

During the height of the Ice Ages, shorelines around the world dropped some 150 meters (500 ft.). At that time, Borneo's coast came within 40 kilometers (25 mi.) of Sulawesi. When the climate warmed and the ice melted, the seas rose and all life capable of locomotion retreated inland. Today, similar and unique species of freshwater fish are found in Sumatra and Borneo, but not in Sulawesi, which was never connected by land.

Rich natural resources

If, geologically speaking, Borneo fails to reach the volcanic excitement of the crater-strewn "ring of fire" which sets out in Sumatra and continues to Java, Bali and beyond into the Pacific, there is plenty on the island to keep exploration geologists gainfully employed. Some 4.5 million years ago, volcanic fireworks and folding shaped Borneo. Then sedimentation and erosion put the finishing touches on the island's mineral riches.

Borneo first gained international fame thanks to her diamonds, followed by a Chinese gold rush into the alluvial deposits in Kaltim. Today, gold mining is an international business, and small-scale entrepreneurs pan for the scraps. Recently, uranium deposits have been discovered. Indonesia's coffers have also been enriched through the export of liquified natural gas to Japan's power-starved electrical plants.

Large-scale coal mining began in the late 19th century, followed by a series of oil booms. Tiny Brunei, sitting on a fortune in oil, generates the world's highest per capita

Opposite: *A river cuts through the lowland forest of East Kalimantan. Nipa palms line the water.*

income. East Kalimantan has been a producer of oil since the first decade of this century.

The most important gold-bearing veins lie in the primary deposits of the mountains. The veins are broken down by intensive weathering into auriferous clay, which is carried downstream by the tropical downpours. Back-breaking labor and luck can result in gold bits, many of which reach an unusual purity—23 to 24 carats.

Equatorial climate

Most of Kalimantan lies south of the equator, which almost bisects the island of Borneo. The coasts are hot, up to 37° C (97° F), and humid. It can get as uncomfortable here as anywhere in the world. Things get better inland, with mean annual temperatures of 24–26° C (75-79° F). In the interior highlands, at elevations of over 700 meters (2,300 ft.), temperatures can become quite cool.

During an average year, 3,000 millimeters (120 in.) of rain pours down on the coasts, with even higher figures inland. Borneo has a monsoon climate, with dry winds from the southeast from May through September, and moisture-laden winds from the northwest arriving from October to March. The northwest winds bring the wet season, with the heaviest rains in November, December and January. July, August and September are the driest months. This is a general pattern, but there are many local variations in rainfall.

The delicate rainforest

Recently, the weather in Kalimantan has become even more unpredictable, and specialists think this may be a result of logging, which continues here at an alarming rate. Large-scale lumber operations began in Kalimantan in 1967, when some 77 percent of Kalimantan was covered by rainforest; today, the figure is less than 65 percent. 423,000 hectares (1,045,000 acres) in Kalimantan are logged each year.

A huge fire broke out in East Kalimantan in the fall of 1982, and was not extinguished until the rains fell the following May. The fire consumed an area the size of Holland. At the peak of the burning, in March-April 1983, flights were cancelled in Singapore, 1,400 kilometers (870 mi.) away because of the haze that hung over Changi Airport. Although some blamed the outbreak on the native slash-and-burn method of field preparation, many people believe it more likely that deforestation and its side effects have made the island vulnerable to fire. In fact, in 1987, there were several persistant forest fires in the same heavily logged region struck in 1982.

The rainforest is a natural "sponge," storing moisture that becomes the source of the world's rain. No one can say with certainty what the long-term effects of harvesting the world's rainforests will be, but the future does not look promising.

ALAIN COMPOST

FLORA AND FAUNA

Profusion of Vegetation, Odd Animals

Kalimantan's wildlife is as exotic as it comes. But the more unusual plants and animals—the enormous rafflesia flower, orangutans, proboscis monkeys, Argus pheasants, clouded leopards, tarsiers and others—are difficult even to glimpse in their natural habitat. The region's large nature reserves look ideal on paper, but they include almost no services for visitors. Seeing animals in the wild requires determination, organization and a willingness to spend many days in the jungle. Sometimes it seems that the only species one encounters is the common ground leech (*Haemadipsa zeylanica*), and these are not at all shy.

But even short jungle walks will give a feel for the remarkable rainforest ecosystem. Soaring trees offer support for the stout vines of lianas and creepers, and their branches are festooned with epiphytic orchids and bromeliads. The plant life is so fecund that it is difficult to recall just how fragile an environment this is. The floor of the primary rainforest is a quiet, uncrowded place, far different from the thick tangle of popular myth. Many of the forest animals spend their lives 20-50 meters (60-150 ft.) above ground in the canopy where they are difficult to see.

The rivers force a break in the forest, and here one has a much better opportunity to view Kalimantan's many species of birds. Bright little kingfishers, herons, ibises and hornbills often patrol the waterways, and can be observed from a boat. The rivers provide local fishermen with a variety of fish, including huge catfish. On the lower reaches of the Mahakam River, around the lakes district, small schools of the very unusual freshwater dolphin occasionally surface.

Super-nosed monkeys

The island's coasts are covered with almost impenetrable mangrove swamps and palm strands, an environment quite different from the forests of the interior. Here, wildlife must be observed from a small outboard canoe.

The mangrove swamps are the habitat of a most unusual species of monkey, found only in Borneo. The male proboscis monkey (*Nasalis larvatus*) sports a snozzle up to 15 centimeters (6 in.) long. This hugely disproportionate appendage serves to attract the fairer sex, which has a pert, turned-up nose of little redeeming social value. The fleshy, drooping nose strengthens its owner's vocal powers, as well as deepening, and making more resonant, the tones of his voice.

While the nose has been observed to interfere with drinking, it does prevent water from entering the nostrils while the animal swims, which—unlike most primates—the proboscis monkey does with aplomb. When frightened, or out of sheer exuberance, these monkeys fling out their arms and leap from considerable heights into water or mud.

Proboscis monkeys are herbivorous, feeding almost exclusively on the young leaves and shoots of the mangrove tree. The best times to observe them are dawn or dusk, when they move into trees nearer the water. The up to 20-kilo (45 lb.) animals have reddish backs and cream-white bellies, and their faces and buttocks are light brown. The best place to see them is on a river island near Banjarmasin (see "Visiting Kalsel," page 137), or at Tanjung Puting (see page 158).

The man of the forest

The *orang utan,* Indonesian for "man of the forest," survives—though just barely—in Sumatra and Borneo. Orangutan babies make wonderful pets, reacting very much like human children: screaming for food, whining when unhappy and showing great physical affection for their (foster) parents. Despite all laws, mother orangutans are still shot so their babies can be sold. Today, keeping an orangutan is of course illegal, and two rehabilitation centers in Central Kalimantan re-educate former pets in the ways of the wild.

A thousand years ago there were more orangutans than humans in Borneo—about a half a million. By 1960, the world's total number of orangutans had dwindled to less than a few thousand. The business of survival has become more difficult for the orangutans as large-scale logging and increased land cultivation continue to destroy most of the animals' natural habitat.

Opposite: *An adult orangutan in the Tanjung Puting rehabilitation center in Kalteng. The destruction of their habitat threatens these rare and strikingly human-like creatures.*

Orangutans are particularly sensitive to habitat encroachment. The largest fruit-eaters on earth, they require an extensive territory—about 500 hectares (1,200 acres) per adult. Because fruit trees are widely dispersed in the rainforest, orangutans cannot survive in groups, which would quickly deplete the trees. The animals supplement their staple fruit with bark, flowers, and occasionally insects and honey.

The orangutans' great weight prevents them from foraging over long distances, and most travel only some 400 meters (1,300 ft.) a day. Males live a solitary life while the females keep one or two youngsters nearby, chasing their offspring away when the children reach about four years of age. Every evening, each adult builds a temporary overnight nest, high in the trees.

The arm span of an adult orangutan can exceed two meters, which gives the animal tremendous power. Thanks to these arms, it has been estimated that an orangutan's strength is four times that of a human of similar weight. Large males can weigh over 80 kilos (175 lbs.) and sport cheek pads in a fringe around their faces.

Other jungle dwellers

While proboscis monkeys and orangutans are not commonly seen, other monkeys can be observed—or at least heard—in many jungle areas. The haunting duets of male and female gibbons enliven a trek inland or even a stay on the coast. Agile leaf monkeys perform incredible acrobatics for quiet observers. Common macaques, at home in either trees or on the ground, can be seen near the rivers where they feed on crabs, and occasionally fall prey to crocodiles.

The nocturnal, tree-dwelling slow loris peers out of eyes which in relation to its body are some 150 times the size of man's (Imagine a person with eyes the size of softballs.) The tarsier, a tiny, tree-dwelling primate, can swivel its head 180 degrees and has evolved fantastic goggle-like eyes which enhance its nightly foraging.

The pangolin (*Manis javanica*) has been described as a "miniature dinosaur in a suit of armor." This ant-eater breaks up ant nests with its strong claws and laps up its meal with its sticky tongue. To store up for a later snack, the pangolin opens its horny scales, which fill with angry ants. Later, when the mood strikes him, the pangolin ambles to a quiet stretch of water. While taking its cool bath, the animal opens its scales underwater, causing the ants to float to the surface, where they are gobbled at leisure.

Alive with birds

Armed with a pair of binoculars and Bertram E. Smythies' definitive *Birds of Borneo,* bird-watching visitors to Kalimantan will have the chance to identify some 600 species spread

ALAIN COMPOST

ing the female is taken over by another male, a most unusual trait in the animal world.

The handsomest bird on the island is undoubtedly the Argus pheasant (*Argusianus grayi*). This member of the partridge family is one of the most difficult birds to glimpse in the wild, but patient (and lucky) observers have reported on the mating behavior of the male. He constructs his own stage by flattening a circular area in the brush, and there struts his finery to attract the interest of females. The tail feathers of the Argus are covered with hundreds of shimmering "eyes"—hence its name—and are prized by the Dayaks for ceremonial costuming.

No Bornean bird is more economically important than the edible nest swiftlet (*Collocalia* sp.). The glutinous saliva this bird uses to construct its nest is the raw material for the famous Chinese soup.The gelatin is almost tasteless, and the soup requires plenty of other ingredients for flavor—but the birds' nests are considered by some to be an aphrodisiacal pick-me-up.

Obtaining the nests, which are constructed high on the walls of deep limestone caves, requires agility and entails great risk to the collector. Local entrepreneurs build rickety bamboo scaffolding, and use a long pole with a knife and torch fastened at the end to scrape off the nests. Falling is common, and almost always fatal.

A carpet of greenery

Borneo's vegetation is absolutely amazing. In a single 10-hectare plot (25 acres), 780 species of trees have been identified. To put this in perspective, consider that there are only 35 species of trees in all of England.

Borneo's vegetation falls into three principal zones or belts. The coastal fringe is characterized by swamps of mangrove, nipa and other palms, along with low-grade forest. An inland belt of gentle hills and alluvial flood plains has its greatest extension in Kalsel and Kalbar. Inland from here is the rainforest, becoming thickest in the interior's slightly higher elevations. Here the jungle blanket is dominated by the Dipterocarpacae family of trees, which form a canopy 20-50 meters (60-150 ft.) above the ground.

Fig trees rise from their own forest of stems and aerial roots. Here and there grow

over every ecological zone. Birds were very important in the beliefs of the peoples of Kalimantan—flight patterns were of crucial importance as omens of success or failure for upcoming head-hunting expeditions. Even today, in some areas a hunting trip—or a visitors' trek—can be postponed because of a bird observed flying in the "wrong" direction.

The hornbill birds are especially prominent figures in Dayak mythology, perhaps because of their habits, appearance or noisy flight, which can be detected from far away. The heavy beating of the birds' wings alternately inflates and deflates air pouches, which produces a sound remarkably like that of a chugging steam locomotive.

All nine species of hornbills are identified by the shape of the casques on their enormous beaks. In the helmeted hornbill, the usually hollow beak excrescence is solid and magnified out of all proportion. These casques have been prized for centuries by Chinese ivory carvers, and during the Ming dynasty were shaped into exquisite statues, belt buckles and snuff bottles. The birds' "ivory" cost twice as much as that from elephant tusks. Even today some Dayaks continue to carve the horns of the birds into huge, lacy earrings.

The female hornbill incubates her eggs in a hollow tree-trunk nest, which is sealed with her sticky droppings. The male feeds her through a small hole until the chicks are fledged. If her partner dies, the task of feed-

Above: *A wide-eyed tarsier, a tiny primate related to monkeys and apes.* **Opposite:** *The rafflesia, the world's largest flower, emits a fetid odor to attract the carrion flies that are its pollinating agents.*

ironwood and ebony trees. The *upah* tree produces a deadly poison. Gigantic *tapang* trees, with dazzling white, branchless trunks, shoot up to 70 meters (225 ft.) and tower over the surrounding canopy. Epiphytes, including orchids of enormous variety, decorate many trees. On the central mountains, all branches and trunks are covered with tufts of moss and long strands of hanging lichen.

Borneo also hosts 11,000 species of flowering plants, including the rafflesia (*Rafflesia arnoldii*) which produces the world's largest flower. The rafflesia is a parasite, and for most of its life lurks as a network of fine cellular "roots" inside the *Cissus* liana, a ground-trailing vine. When it bursts out of its host's body, the rafflesia is a single flower, without stem or leaves—but what a flower! The fleshy blossom can reach a meter in diameter and weigh up to 8 kilos (18 lbs.). The rafflesia is more grotesque than beautiful, and the fragrance it emits smells like rotting meat. The stench attracts hordes of carrion flies, its pollinating agents.

The plant life of Borneo's great rainforest, the world's second largest after the Amazon, provides a large variety of valuable products: *damar* resin, hardwoods,rattan and palm sugar. Borneo is also the source of a fine grade of camphor, found as a resin in the decayed center of the camphor laurel, *Dryobalanops aromatica*. Another unusual scented product is *gaharu* or aloeswood, which comes from diseased specimens of *Aquilaria malaccensis*. High-quality *gaharu* sells for several hundred dollars a kilo.

The people of Borneo have long learned to take advantage of the available ecosystem for building their homes, growing crops, hunting and gathering. The starchy trunk of the forest sago palm (*Eugeissona utilis*) provides an ample supply of carbohydrates, and a variety of fruit—breadfruit, mango, mangosteen, papaya, pineapple, and the wonderful durian—provide easy refreshment and nutrition. The Dayaks' slash-and-burn method of preparing the soil for planting rice has its critics, but as long as there are no overpopulation pressures forcing the reduction of the 8-15 year fallow period, the practice is ecologically sound.

The real danger to the rainforest ecosystem comes from farming and commercial timber operations; their influence on the area's ecological and weather patterns in recent years are an indication of their disastrous effects on the environment. The luxurious vegetation of Kalimantan rests on laterite soils poor in nutrients. When logging strips away the covering vegetation, a combination of increased bacterial reactions, sun, and rain quickly leads to the erosion of the thin, life-giving topsoil. After this stage, the forest often never returns. Only the hardy *lalang,* or imperata grass (*Imperata cylindrica*), which is too coarse even for grazing, can grow in these marginal soils.

ALAIN COMPOST

PREHISTORY

Fossil Skull, Migration and the Iron Age

Inferring from the remains of Java Man, *Homo erectus*, scientists believe that human-like beings inhabited Borneo over a million years ago. No remains have yet been found on the island. Although at first considered the earliest ancestor of humankind, Java Man—and the probable Borneo Man—has been superseded as the earliest humanoid by a skeleton called Lucy, found in the Afar badlands of Ethopia.

Long, long after *Homo erectus* hunted and gathered in Borneo, Australoids populated what is now Southeast Asia, Indonesia, the Philippines and Australia. Aboriginal peoples in Australia, New Guinea, and the Philippines share a common ancestral heritage.

Crucial evidence of the lifestyle of these ancient inhabitants of the archipelago comes from Borneo. In the late 1950s, explorations in the Niah caves of Sarawak yielded a 35,000-year-old Australoid skull, the oldest human (*Homo sapiens*) skull ever found. Ethnographer and adventurer Tom Harrisson gets the well-deserved credit for this exciting discovery, and for piecing together the puzzle of the early Bornean way of life.

The cave-dwelling Borneans of the Paleolithic period hunted, fished, and gathered edible plant life. From 40,000 to 20,000 years ago, the men brought back to their caves game such as pigs, monkeys, porcupines, deer, orangutans, bears, rhinos, squirrels, otters, badgers and weasels, and some species which are now extinct in Borneo: wild oxen, giant pangolins and the white-toothed tree shrew. Around 20,000 years ago, much better stone tools appeared, and this was perhaps when people learned to efficiently process the starch from the sago palm, a widely available staple food.

The Austronesian expansion

Whatever technologies these early people invented, history shows they were not up to resisting the expansion of Austronesians from the Asian mainland. Linguistic evidence shows that this Mongol race first arrived in Taiwan from South China around 5000 B.C., probably traveling on crude rafts. About 500 years later, one of mankind's most important innovations appeared in Taiwan: the outrigger canoe. For the people who were to populate the Indonesian archipelago, this inven-

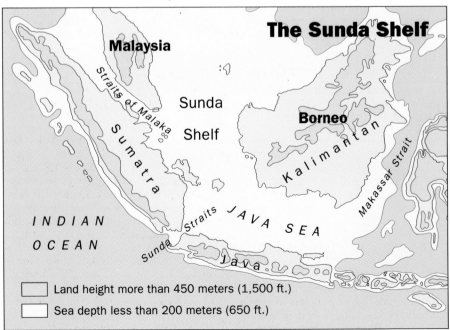

Land height more than 450 meters (1,500 ft.)

Sea depth less than 200 meters (650 ft.)

tion—which created a swift, stable craft—can be compared in usefulness to the wheel.

The language of these emigrants, Malayo-Polynesian, tells much of the story. Over several millennia, Austronesians very slowly drifted south to the Philippines, whence into Indonesia and other parts of Southeast Asia. Others crossed the vast expanse of the Pacific to populate islands as far away as Hawaii and Easter Island.

The Austronesian population expanded from the Philippines in two directions: toward the northern Moluccas, and toward Borneo. The languages of these two groups began to evolve separately, and by around 3000 B.C., two language groups were in place: western Malayo-Polynesian in western Indonesia and central Malayo-Polynesian in eastern Indonesia. Some of the Dayak languages, such as Kenyah and Kayan, can be traced back 4,000 years to their western Malayo-Polynesian roots.

The slow southward migrations of Austronesians continued, and around 1000 B.C. the language of southeast Kalimantan began breaking up into Javanese and Barito, the latter named after the great river in South Borneo. Some one thousand years later, people migrated from south Kalimantan to populate Sumatra, the Malay peninsula and much of coastal mainland Southeast Asia. The last great migration from South Kalimantan traveled the furthest. About 1,600 years ago, around the time of the fall of the Roman Empire, sailors from the Barito linguistic group, the Ma'anyan, crossed the Indian Ocean to settle in faraway Madagascar, just off the east coast of Africa.

By 3000 to 2000 B.C., the Mongol immigrants to Borneo, the Austronesians, had absorbed the aboriginal Australoids so completely that no genetic or linguistic traces remained. The newcomers brought their neolithic culture: superior tools and weapons of polished stone, pottery, dogs, pigs and, of utmost importance, the cultivation of cereals, especially rice. With food surpluses available, the division of labor and permanent settlements—what we call "civilization"—began.

The metal age

Around 400 B.C., the people of Borneo began to feel the influence of Vietnam's sophisticated Dongson culture. Metal implements—tools and weapons—radically changed lifestyles, reducing by countless man-hours the back-breaking labor of clearing fields and constructing shelters and houses. Livestock

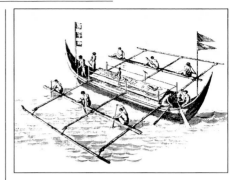

breeding and irrigated rice-growing techniques also appeared at this time. The metal age first reached the coastal Malays, who as a result gained a definite advantage over their Dayak cousins. During this bronze age, metal had to be imported because Borneo lacked copper and zinc deposits. It was only in the 6th century that the island could begin its own metal age.

The advent of technologies for smelting and forging iron, supported by local ores, yielded agricultural tools and weapons of the highest quality. Elsewhere in Southeast Asia, the blowgun did not evolve beyond the hollow bamboo shaft. But in Borneo, thanks to long iron drills, durable and strong hardwoods could be bored. A sharp metal blade fixed to the end of this strong shaft made the blowgun into a formidable weapon for both hunting and warfare.

The advent of iron agricultural tools allowed the Dayaks to evolve from sago gatherers to farmers planting taro and rice, crops that are far higher in nutrients. Metal technology reached its height in the *mandau,* or short fighting sword. These forged blades, according to experts, surpassed even Javanese metalwork in quality.

Slash-and-burn

The Austronesians introduced swidden agriculture, which is practiced by the Dayaks today. They slash out their rice fields from the forest, then burn the brush and debris producing an ash that enrichens the poor rainforest soil. Still, the *ladang* will only support one or two crop cycles, after which it must be abandoned and allowed to revert.

After 8-15 years fallow time, the field is burned again and reused. Shifting crops—rice, cassava, corn—improves the efficiency.

Above: *The Austronesians invented the outrigger, which made extended sea crossings safe. The drawing above is a kora-kora from the Moluccas.*

TRADE

Exotic Goods Bring Traders from Outside

Early references to Borneo are scant, although the Alexandria-based Greek geographer Ptolemy makes a reference in the second century A.D. that may be to Borneo. Much later, thanks to the importance of trade products, there is a large body of literature on Borneo in China.

At the beginning of the Christian era, it is likely that Indian cultural influences, including Pallawan writing and chronology, began arriving in Borneo. The first known written record from Indonesia, circa A.D. 400, was discovered among the effects of the Martapura kingdom in East Borneo. The seat of King Mulawarman's rule was at present-day Muara Kaman, at the junction of the lower Mahakam River and Kedang Kepala Rivers.

This kingdom, like others in Sumatra, Java and elsewhere in Borneo, was heavily influenced by Hindu culture and religion. Sacrificial *yupa* poles of stone, inscribed in the Indian Pallawan script, attest to King Mulawarman's participation in Brahmanic ritual and animal sacrifice. In 1895 explorers uncovered a dozen Hindu-style stone statues in the cave of Goa Kombeng, further upriver on the Kedang Kepala. Ruins and legends around the Barito River, in South Kalimantan, testify to a former Hindu-influenced culture there, and Hindu statues have also been found in West Kalimantan.

The Chinese in Borneo

Records of China's intermittent trade- and tribute-seeking policies provide the first tantalizing glimpses of Borneo based on authentic documents. By the 7th century, the China–Borneo connection was firmly established, and it does not take a great leap of faith to believe that Borneo's exports reached China and India centuries earlier.

The Chinese connection centered around trade. At times, tribute-bearing envoys from northwest Borneo traveled to China to kow-tow before the emperor, but these missions were not continuous. They depended on the local Bornean leader's perception of the advantages of cultivating the good graces of the Chinese ruler, and on the Middle Kingdom's interest in the world of the barbarians, which waxed and waned according to China's internal politics and the emperor's divinely inspired edicts.

Borneo tribute reflected these Chinese vacillations: during phases of Chinese expansionism, they were punctually adhered to; during the Celestial Empire's periodic introversions, they were not bothered with at all. Around A.D. 1200, when Chinese maritime expansion was in full swing, Borneo was known as Tanjung Pura, taking its name from a trading center located on the southwest coast. During the Ming dynasty, a Chinese colony was established on the northern part of the island.

Even as late as the first decade of the 15th century, a Bornean ruler named Maraja Kali personally traveled to the Chinese court, bearing his land's tribute. Laden in return with presents far more valuable than those he

Right: Beads, brought to Kalimantan in centuries past to trade for jungle products, are now valued heirlooms. In the old days, the large bead in the middle strand was worth an entire village, inhabitants and all. **Opposite:** Panning for gold in the upper Mahakam River. Borneo experienced several gold rushes over the years.

had brought, Kali lingered too long as an honored guest. Perhaps unable to resist the ever-tempting gastronomy, he eventually lived out his life at the Chinese capital.

By the time of Kali's death, winds of change had begun to reach Borneo. The Hindu Majapahit Empire in East Java was sufficiently organized to flex its military power in overseas adventures. In 1365 both the Kutai Kingdom on the Mahakam and Banjarmasin were briefly mentioned as dependencies in the Majapahit Empire's famous chronicle, the *Negarakertagama*. Three years later, Javanese soldiers helped to drive out Sulu marauders from Brunei. Javanese-Majapahit influence had already seeped into the Hinduized kingdoms founded in what is now Kalimantan: Berau, on the east coast, north of Kutai; Sukadana, in the west, south of Pontianak; and Banjarmasin, near the southeast shore.

Unusual exports

The trade goods which primarily interested the Chinese included luxury goods such as gold and diamonds; useful materials such as rattan and gutta-percha; food items like pepper, shark's fins, trepang and bird's nests; incense woods; and a wide variety of forest medicinals. In exchange for these valuable products, the people of Borneo received silk cloth and clothing, and a variety of porcelain and other ceramics.

Some of the ancient Chinese jars are still preserved in upriver Dayak longhouses where they function as the ultimate status symbol. The large ceramic receptacles, decorated with dragons, were (and sometimes still are) believed to hold dragon spirits. In later years, Borneo also received cloth from Gujerat in India as well as more mundane items, from Java and elsewhere, such as tobacco, guns and salt.

After the 19th century, when bulk shipping became economically feasible, rattan was probably the most important of Borneo's exports to China, where immense quantities were turned into cordage. Today, handsome, light-weight furniture absorbs much of the fine quality rattan dragged out of the jungles in the interior of the island.

Until rubber trees were introduced, gutta-percha was another of Borneo's sought-after exports. The Chinese found medicinal uses for gutta-percha but used most of the rubbery substance as caulking for their sailing ships and as a general adhesive. Gutta-percha comes from the sap of trees of the genus *Pallaquium* and *Payena*, and today this material forms the tough covering of golf balls and electrical cable, and even finds its way into dentists' torture kits.

Illipe nuts (*tengkawang*), which appear irregularly in various parts of Borneo in great numbers every two to nine years, trigger mass migrations of wild pigs, which greatly

relish the oily nuts. The people of Borneo used to squeeze the illipe for cooking oil. Exports went to England to make tallow and wax, as well as lubricating oil for steam machinery. The Spanish in Manila made candles from it. Today, illipe nuts find their way into cosmetics, including some of the higher priced brands of lipsticks.

Many of the island's exports provided the raw materials for Chinese gourmets. Shark's fins and trepang, or bêche-de-mer, were sought after as ingredients for soup. Trepang is dried sea cucumber, a lumbering, worm-like beast made edible only by the ingenious cooks of the Celestial Empire. Although these sea products were (and still are) valuable, the most exquisite food product from Borneo is undoubtedly the famous bird's nests.

Edible nest swiftlets use a sticky saliva to glue their nests to the high vertical faces of cave walls. This secretion, carefully cleaned of twigs and feathers, is the base of the famous soup. The best quality nests for consumption are fresh, and come from *Collocalia fuciphaga*. These are translucent, beige-colored secretions. Older nests, where moss and other impurities get mixed in with the goo, are inferior, as are the darker secretions of *Collocalia maxima*.

Aloeswood, also called aguila or eagle's wood, was the most expensive aromatic shipped to China. Locally called *gahuru*, this rare product remains one of the world's most highly valued spices. Small lots of the fragrant substance are exported regularly to countries throughout the Arab world, where its subtle smoke perfumes the traditional weddings and funerals of those wealthy enough to afford it.

A resin called benzoin or gum benjamin, another aromatic export, was exported for those who could not afford the expensive aloeswood. Yet another resin, *damar,* from various species of Dipterocarpaceae trees, was (and sometimes still is) burned by Borneans as a source of light.

Medicinals 'dearer than gold'

The most interesting of Borneo's exports, products such as rhinocerous horns, hornbill casques, and camphor, have long been used in traditional Chinese pharmacology. Perhaps the most exotic of all exports, however, are bezoar stones, precious nuggets touted as cure-alls, found in the gall bladders of a few species of monkeys and, occasionally in porcupines. Their rarity, and the potency attributed to them by the Chinese, led to a belief in their extraordinary magical virtues in some areas of Southeast Asia.

Still highly coveted as a medicinal ingredient, the bezoar stone is used in various ways. Its grated powder, mixed with water, alleviates chest or bowel complaints. Worn in a cloth tied around he navel, or soaked in drinking water, it is thought to possess aphrodisiacal qualities. In the past, shamans used bezoar stones to invoke the powerful Tiger Spirit in order to obtain his help in exorcising the spirit of lesser power from the body of the patient. After the advent of Islam, the bezoar stone retained its magical appeal. Some Muslims believed it to be a gift brought to humankind by Prince Gabriel, with the power to neutralize poison.

Europeans were shocked when they learned of the fabulous prices of the medical ingredients from Borneo, as they were interested strictly in more mundane items like gold, diamonds and pepper. At the end of the 16th century, camphor from Borneo was "dearer than gold" in India. Europeans in the 19th century were astonished that the Chinese would pay 50 times the going rate for camphor that was judged particularly prime. A 19th-century British historian with several decades of experience in Southeast Asia notes the "exorbitant price" of a particular variety of Bornean camphor, of which a single pound cost £4 4s 4.5p, or 78 times the price of regular camphor from Japan. To put this price into perspective, the same money would at the time purchase more than two tons of rice.

Camphor crystals were used to stimulate the heart and circulatory system, as well as for incense and embalming potions. Today, camphor is used in proprietary formulations like Tiger Balm, and that which is not up to snuff for pharmaceuticals finds its way into moth repellent, smokeless gunpowder, lacquers, cosmetics, scented soaps, industrial chemistry. Even Western medicine today recognizes the mild antiseptic and anesthetic properties of camphor.

The high price of top-quality camphor was partially due to its scarcity, as it is found only in a few older specimens of the camphor laurel (*Dryobalanops aromatica*). Another factor was that the trees were considered to be "owned" by a powerful spirit, who had to be propitiated before the camphor could be extracted. A camphor search was a complex social and spiritual event involving certain taboos, and requiring the use of ritual language and dietary restrictions.

Opposite: *This Nandi, the Hindu bull, found on the upper Mahakam, testifies to religious influence from India. Today, it is venerated by natives as well as by the Hindu Balinese working for local lumber companies.* **Right:** *A box of bezoar stones. These stones, from the gall bladder of monkeys, are worth $900-2,000 in Singapore or Hong Kong.*

The Europeans arrive

Aside from the Chinese, few outsiders had even vaguely mentioned Borneo prior to the Portuguese drive around Africa and into the Indian Ocean around the turn of the 16th century. Marco Polo probably sailed along the coast of Borneo, but there is no mention in his text. A real pioneer traveler, an Italian friar named Odoric of Pordenone, spent time in Java around 1320 and may have reached Borneo at Banjarmasin. Fra Odoric makes the first reference in Western literature to the blowgun and poisoned darts.

The age of Portuguese expansion, and its unrelenting search for spices to sell and souls to save, produced the first Western accounts of Borneo. By 1512 Malacca was under Portuguese control and the long-sought direct route to the spice islands of the Moluccas was theirs. Inquisitive officials began to write about Borneo. The most thorough of these accounts was written by Tomé Pires, stationed in Malacca from 1512-1515.

Pires states that Borneo is a group of "many islands, large and small," inhabited by a few Moors (Muslims) and many heathen. Each year, he writes, a few ships would arrive in Malacca from Borneo, carrying low assay gold and high quality camphor which were traded for beads. A few years later, another writer speaks of Borneo's diamonds as "finer than those of India."

ISLAM AND THE WEST

Sultanates and Colonial Holland

The earliest verifiable first-hand account of Borneo flows from the pen of Pigafetta, the chronicler of Magellan's expedition, which reached Brunei in July 1521. Magellan himself was killed along with several of his crew in the Philippines, and the expedition had no choice but to continue without him.

The Europeans met an impressive welcome from the sultan upon landing. The crew were received by richly attired and bejeweled attendants, who led Pigafetta and his company to the palace on elephants with silk trappings. Here was the splendid Orient of which the Europeans had dreamed during their dreary, scorching, scurvy-ridden trans-Pacific journey. One can only believe that they ate heartily, using the palace's solid gold table service, of a banquet that included "thirty or thirty-two different kinds of meat, besides fish."

Prompted by news of the Spanish-sponsored world circumnavigation, including the splendid conditions in Brunei, in 1527 the Portuguese began to sail north from their base in Malacca, via Brunei, to make their periodic runs to the Spice Islands. But it was not until 1627, when Pedro Berthelot circumnavigated the island, that the first fairly accurate map of Borneo's outline finally emerged.

Islam in Borneo

The Portuguese missionaries who had tried to proselytize around Banjarmasin in the 16th century met with no success, since Islam had already taken hold. The Christian religions found acceptance in Borneo only in areas where Muslim traders had not yet introduced their faith—a pattern that holds true for most of Indonesia. Only in the 19th century, when the interior of Dutch Borneo was opened to European exploration, did Christianity begin to find converts.

Islam reached the archipelago from India, becoming established first on Sumatra and later on Java, whence it spread along established trade routes to many of the islands.

Hinduism and Buddhism had been introduced to Kalimantan's coastal kingdoms due to the areas' centuries-long relations with Java, and when the Hindu Majapahit fell to the Muslims in the 14th century, the new faith spread to Kalimantan as well. Local rulers, who had previously assumed the Hindu title of raja, then became sultans.

The arrival of the Dutch

The Dutch first appeared in Indonesia during the last years of the 16th century. The United Provinces were at war against Spain (and by extension, Portugal, which from 1580 to 1640 was absorbed by the Hispanic crown) and the enterprising and ruthless Dutch sailed to obtain the spices for themselves. They con-

trolled the clove and nutmeg islands in the Moluccas, and sought a monopoly as well on the valuable pepper trade, including the small amounts produced in South Borneo.

The Portuguese had been unable to control Banjarmasin's pepper trade. The Dutch, even though they literally destroyed the city, were just as unsuccessful. At the turn of the 17th century, the English joined the fray, and the British East India Company tried to trade at Banjarmasin. Holland quickly expelled the interlopers—the Dutch wanted a monopoly, and if they couldn't get it, they were at least going to keep out all other European powers.

Holland's failure in south Borneo was at least partially due to Chinese competition: not only did the Chinese merchants offer much better prices and more useful trade goods for the region's pepper, diamonds and gold, but they bought large quantities of high-profit items such as camphor, trepang, shark's fins and bird's nests.

By the middle of the 17th century, the Dutch became aware that their monopoly on Moluccan spices was worthless unless they held Makassar—now Ujung Pandang— where spices were being diverted. Exploiting existing rivalries and applying ruthless military force, Holland finally forced Makassar to accept the Dutch as her sole trade partner.

The internecine fighting which Holland encouraged in the south Celebes (now Sulawesi) resulted in some of the nobility losing their positions and a surplus of experienced soldiers. Many royal dynasties, such as those of Kutai in East Kalimantan, and Johore and Selangor in Malaysia, were either taken over by or united with these Bugis and Wajo immigrants from the Celebes.

The Bugis in Borneo

In 1785, an army of 3,000 Celebes warriors invaded the Banjarmasin sultanate. The sultan turned to the Dutch, who gladly came to his aid. With their superior weapons, the Europeans quickly won the battles. Then, as the price of its assistance, Holland installed a weak puppet-ruler on the Banjarmasin throne. The new sultan gave the Dutch suzerainty of not only his own domain, but also most of the east coast of Borneo, an area over which he had only the most tenuous legal claim and no effective control.

By this time, the Sultanate of Kutai Kartanegara had been firmly established at Tenggarong on the shores of the great Mahakam River, just inland from the Makassar Strait. In the 4th century A.D., this Malay kingdom had produced the earliest written records ever found in Indonesia. The kingdom was mentioned briefly 10 centuries later in a 1365 Javanese manuscript and, not located on any major trade route, Kutai was lost to history once more.

Then Arung Singkang La Ma'dukelleng, a top noble of the Bugis royal family of Wajo, conquered Kutai and Pasir in 1726. He made himself Sultan of Kutai, then returned to his homeland to fight in local wars and led an unsuccessful action against the Dutch. His descendents mixed with the established royalty of Kutai. Around 1730, the Bugis founded their own town, Samarinda, now the capital of the province of Kaltim. The whole east coast of Borneo moved into the Bugis' orbit.

A colonial scramble

During the Napoleonic Wars, the Dutch East Indies fell briefly under French, then British authority. When England allowed Holland to return to her East Indies possessions, the Dutch realized that control over Java and a few strategic areas would no longer be sufficient to keep other European powers out of the archipelago.

Abdul Rahman, an enterprising Arab adventurer, founded Pontianak in the 1770s with the help of the Dutch, and the new city quickly became a thorn in the side of the Sultan of Sambas. The sultan, who had traditionally been the ultimate power in the region, had grown used to extracting exor-

bitant fees from the European traders who called in his domain. Pontianak offered them another port of entry, and allowed them to avoid the sultan's taxes.

Deprived of an important source of income, the sultan turned to piracy. A British military expedition under a certain Captain Brown was sent to Sambas in 1812 to punish the sultan, but the landing force was ignominiously defeated. The next year, a better organized British military party trounced Sambas in a half-hour battle.

Opposite: *The Sultan of Kutai, Mohammad Suleiman Khalifat. From the* Illustrated London News, *June 19, 1880.* **Above:** *A portrait of the sultan in glazed tile at the palace in Tenggarong.*

When Holland returned to her former base of power in the Indies, she was slow to reassert herself in Borneo, having learned that the economic benefits of investment in the unruly island were scant. In 1817, however, the Dutch signed a contract with the Sultan of Banjarmasin, who needed help in his not-too-legitimate claims to his throne. In return for Dutch protection, the sultan ceded his claims to east, south and central Borneo, retaining only a core area in what is now Kalsel. In the agreement, Holland also stipulated that it would have the right to choose the sultan's successor, a clause which led to a vicious and costly war with the independent minded Banjarese in 1859.

Holland takes action

In 1818 the Dutch sent an expedition to show the flag in West Borneo. They arrived in the nick of time, putting down an unforeseen rebellion against Holland's ally, the Sultan of Pontianak. The force also stopped a large-scale pirate raid directed against Pontianak, headed by the Sultan of Sambas.

Increased commercial competition from British merchants from Singapore— established by Sir Stamford Raffles after the Indies were returned to Holland—for trade with Chinese gold miners led Holland to try to establish her sovereignty in West Kalimantan. However, the great Javanese Rebellion of 1825-30, led by Prince Diponegoro, absorbed all available Dutch resources and manpower for several years. Holland's plans for a stronger presence in the region were thus stalemated for a time.

Later, two events would prod Holland into taking assertive measures in Borneo. In the 1830s, a British gentleman adventurer was given a part of what is now Sarawak in return for aiding the Sultan of Brunei in putting down a rebellion by his subjects. James Brooke, the legendary "White Raja" and inspiration for novelist Joseph Conrad, began asserting his authority from Kuching, just north of Sambas. Too close for comfort for the Dutch.

In 1842, after China's defeat in the infamous Opium Wars, her ports were forced open to international commerce. The west coast of Borneo was obviously an ideal base from which to exercise control over the China–Singapore–India sea trade. The British crown was thinking seriously about a foothold in Borneo, encouraged by James Brooke who called several times on the Royal Navy to wipe out nests of pirates. The pirates had been preying, quite effectively, on both European and native shipping.

The Borneo gold rush

During the 18th century, the discovery of gold deposits on Borneo led to mass migrations of Hakka Chinese to the area south of James Brooke's "rajadom." By the time all-

out exploitation of the gold deposits had begun, the Chinese population in Borneo was estimated to be around 200,000. Yearly output from the gold fields reached 100,000 ounces of pure gold.

No one except the Dutch had paid much attention to western Borneo since 1622. In that year, Sultan Agung from Java sent his fleet, massacred the British traders there, burned the Dutch warehouse and brought back the local queen, 800 attendants, and a hoard of diamonds—including a 367-carat monster the size of an orange. Up to the time of their abandonment in the 19th century, the diamond fields of Borneo produced enough of the valuable gems to create the Amsterdam diamond-cutting trade. Even after the fields themselves fell into disuse, gold profits—and Raja Brooke's uncomfortable proximity—convinced the Dutch to assert their control over West Borneo.

Holland did have some "legal" basis for her claims to the area. At the close of the 17th century, the ruler of the Landak region was at war with the neighboring sultanate of Sukadana. He appealed for assistance to Bantam, a Javanese kingdom already under Dutch control. Holland supported Landak's plea, and destroyed Sukadana by organizing a combined Dutch-Bantam-Landak force. Henceforth, in recognizing Bantamese authority, the Landaks were forced to accept Dutch suzerainty.

As though there were not enough problems to keep harried Dutch officials on their toes, a newspaper article from Singapore stung them into scrambling to show flag and force in East Borneo.

Trouble in East Borneo

In 1844, the Honorable Erskine Murray, a Scot, led a two-brig task force to Kutai. While the sultan was initially well disposed toward the adventurer, Murray was impatient and played his hand too quickly, asking to set up a permanent British residence. Was he trying to be the next James Brooke? Whatever the reasons, fighting broke out between the sultan's forces—supported by his Bugis allies—and the British party. One ship escaped, but only after three Europeans, including Murray, lost their lives.

When the news of the skirmish reached Singapore, the Dutch seized their opportunity. A small naval force was sent to Kutai, and the sultan, fearing reprisal from the Europeans, accepted Dutch "protection." From now on, it would be "Dutch" Borneo, and Holland would do its best to keep the other Western powers out of the region.

Opposite: *Sintang, on the west coast of Borneo. The building flying a flag is the assistant resident's house, and at right is the Dutch fort. Lithograph by J. C. Rappard, 1888.* **Below:** *"Up the Sambas River" by P. Lauters, 1843.*

EXPLORATION

Epic Treks Open Borneo's Interior

The ferocity of Borneo's inland Dayaks and the rough and uncharted terrain made the island one of the toughest places in the world to explore. Even in the early 19th century, the interior was completely unknown to the West, and in 1825 a Dutch official named George Müller led a party to the Kapuas basin.

Müller signed a treaty with the sultan of Kutai and, his work with the sultan finished, headed up the Mahakam river and crossed the mountains to the Kapuas basin. There his party was ambushed, and wiped out by Dayaks acting on the sultan's orders. Müller himself lost his head to a Dayak *mandau*. Perhaps the sultan had second thoughts about recognizing Dutch sovereignty. The treaty was never ratified by Batavia, which kept mum on the massacre. Decades later, a mountain range in central Borneo was named for the betrayed Dutchman.

Three years after Müller's death, an English trader named John Dalton spent an exciting 15 months in the Kutai area. We owe to him one of the first accounts of the inland Dayaks. A series in *The Singapore Chronicle* reveals an incomplete but tantalizing glimpse of the Dayak way of life: a war party returning with 700 heads; poisoned blowgun darts which kill in four minutes; locally forged blades capable of cutting through a musket barrel in one sweep; and the *palang,* a metal pin permanently inserted through the glans of the penis to stimulate the opposite sex.

The first explorations

It wasn't until 1843 that the Governor General in Batavia reluctantly consented to allow more thorough exploration of Borneo. This also required that regional administrators be allowed to support the explorations through small scale military interference in local affairs. Holland's manpower and financial resources were limited, and their priorities were Java and Sumatra. The 1843 administrative rules opened the doors for missionaries and explorers, and in an effort to recoup some of its expenses, the government ordered that the land explored be tested for useful mineral deposits.

A German geologist named Von Gaffron covered the first great recorded trek. In 1846 his party went from Kota Waringin, on the south coast, to Pontianak, in the west. In 1848, Dutch Borneo was divided into two districts: the West, with its capital at Pontianak, and the East and South territory, which was governed from Banjarmasin. But the opening to the interior from Sintang allowed another geologist, C.A.L.M. Schwaner, to travel further inland on the Kapuas, whence he headed south to cross the mountain range which now bears his name.

Carl Bock, a Danish naturalist, traversed part of the island in 1879. Persuading the sultan of Kutai to accompany him, Bock traveled up the Mahakam River, then crossed over to the Barito watershed and reached the coast at Banjarmasin. At the time, according to his account, the Kutai sultanate was the largest and most important of Borneo's semi-independent states, controlling nearly one-fifth of the island.

The sultan's revenues came from a monopoly on salt, and from taxing the region's commerce. In the 1880s, salt prices upriver were 16 times those in Samarinda (in some places this was still true 90 years later), forcing many Dayaks to make the arduous journey to Sarawak to obtain the vital condiment at a reasonable price. Although in the late 19th century the sultan lived in Tenggarong, even then Samarinda, with 10,000 people, was more important.

During the 1890s, the geologist G.A.F. Molengraaf explored the Kapuas basin extensively before crossing the mountains—using a different route from Schwaner's—and following another river system to the south coast. Molengraaf had been frustrated in his attempt to cross from the Kapuas to the Mahakam River due to hostilities left over from the Banjarmasin War.

Head-hunters' summit

In 1894, a most unusual peace gathering was convened under Dutch auspices at Tumbang Anoi, far in the interior, upstream on the Kahayan River. At the summit, the Dayak chiefs agreed to stop head-hunting and cease

Opposite: *"Crossing the River Benangan" a lithograph by Danish explorer Carl Bock. Bock crossed part of the island of Borneo in 1879.*

hostilities. This agreement allowed doctor-explorer A. W. Nieuwenhuis to cross from the Kapuas watershed to the Mahakam—Pontianak to Samarinda—becoming the first European to travel across Borneo from west to east. The epic journey took the party of more than 100 men some 15 months, and opened the heart of Borneo to the Dutch.

At the headwaters of the Mahakam, the warriors asked for Dutch protection, fearfully remembering a well-organized 1885 raid by the Batang Lupar Iban from Sarawak. Nieuwenhuis saw that the relations of the Dayaks with the sultanate downriver on the Mahakam were marred by stolen goods, exploitation by Kutai traders, imprisonment and heavy-handed attempts at proselytization.

In keeping with the general Dutch policy of the time, aimed at slowing the spread of Islam, Nieuwenhuis assured the Dayaks, who loved pork and their local rice wine, that there was no valid reason to become Muslims. His word was reinforced by the establishment of a Dutch military post at Long Iram. In 1908 the sultan of Kutai ceded his claim to the upper Mahakam in return for a yearly compensation paid by Holland.

The missionaries arrive

Prior to the mid-19th century, European contact with Borneo had been largely restricted to the coasts. These areas were predominantly Muslim, and thus resistant to Christian proselytization. As a result, Western missionaries who wanted fresh souls to save had to travel inland to find them. German Protestants were the first to take advantage of the permits, making their way into what is now Kalsel, and from there moving on to south-central Kalimantan.

The Banjarmasin War of 1859, which resulted in the deaths of several missionaries and their families, put a brake on Christianization of this area. Elsewhere, missionaries had to wait until there was some exploration and contact with the inland Dayaks before they could get on with their job. Mission stations were eventually established along the Kapuas and the Mahakam Rivers, near government posts and well inland from the areas of Islamic influence.

Unlike Sarawak, where under Raja Brooke Dayak traditions (with perhaps the exception of head-hunting) were admired and missionaries forbidden to travel inland, Christian proselytizing was encouraged in Dutch Borneo. Holland sought to end head-hunting by punishing offenders with hard labor prison terms, a strategy which had little effect on the seasoned warriors. The Dutch used every means to sever the Dayaks from their pagan traditions, including the destruction of "trophy" collections whenever they found them. In spite of these efforts some head-hunting continued into the early decades of this century.

RECENT HISTORY

World War II and Indonesian Independence

In 1940, just before the Japanese swept through Asia, Dutch Borneo had a total population of about 2.4 million, and the British protectorates on the island, about 800,000. Out of 7,800 Europeans on the island, 7,000 lived in the Dutch section, concentrated on the oil-rich east coast. Most lived in Balikpapan, a bustling little town of 30,000, with the rest in Samarinda and Tarakan, where the oil was so pure that no refining was needed—it could be pumped directly into the crankcase of an engine.

The British and Dutch sections of Borneo had evolved under markedly different circumstances. In the words of ethnographer and adventurer Tom Harrisson:

"Little could be more different than the Brooke and the Dutch approaches to the inland peoples. The Brookes did what they could … to leave their inland people undisturbed by outside influences. Mohammedan and Christian missionaries, traders, self-seeking Chinese or Europeans, legislators, policemen, magistrates and above all lawyers, were excluded altogether from the interior. The people were encouraged to keep their own ways of life, provided only that they kept the peace."

Compared to Sarawak, the equivalent remote inland territories across the border in Dutch Borneo were far more, and far "better" administered (before 1945). There were embryo educational services, crude medical facilities, even iron-wire bridges over rivers and chasms, undreamed of in Sarawak. Administrative officers probed far inland. The Dutch put a lot of effort into organizing Borneo, but organizing it *for* the Dutch.

By comparison, Sarawak was almost anarchic. This disorganization worked almost entirely in favour of the resident people and to the great disadvantage of the few Britons who casually ran the country.

The Dutch, unlike the Brookes on the west side of the border, encouraged the missionaries. This was a logical stage of their planned "development" of the country for economic purposes, and was, they thought, to their and the Borneans' ultimate advantage. They wished to Westernize the inland people, and left it to the missionaries to do the spade work. Dutch rule was based not on affection or respect, but discipline. Calvinism

was markedly unsuitable to the ways of life on Borneo, and the fierce monsoons and rugged terrain imposed sufficient discipline for any people.

World War II

In East Borneo, the Japanese quickly took over the essential oil-producing centers of Balikpapan and Tarakan. The Europeans who did not surrender made their way inland to Long Nawang, which in peace time had been the only major Dutch administrative center anywhere near the center of the island. Long Nawang offered them the security of a regular Dutch camp. Or so they thought.

Tom Harrisson describes the ensuing tragedy:

"Eventually, there were quite a lot of English and Dutch subjects, plus some American missionaries and others at Long Nawang. Evidently they felt very safe there. ... [T]hey underestimated Japanese capacity for vigorous travel and jungle sense. The Japanese sent up a warning that if they did not surrender voluntarily and come down, as by now all Europeans except one [holed up elsewhere] had done, the Japs would take action. Some months later some Kenyahs from the Mahakam side came dashing in to say that the Japanese were only a couple of days away, in strength. The Dutch officer in command of the post militarily, did not believe this. The Kenyahs were put in the beastly little lock-up (four cells) which the Dutch kept for interior purposes. Three days later, these cells were occupied by the wretched wives of such Europeans and Americans who had gathered here *en pair.* The men were all dead."

Harrisson himself parachuted into the Kelabit highlands and had organized the Dayaks into as efficient guerilla fighting force by the time the United States dropped its atomic bombs on Japan. One crucial ingredient in winning Dayak support was Harrison's "ten-bob-a-knob" campaign to collect Japanese heads.

Some Dutch beat a hasty retreat to the Upper Mahakam, as well as to Long Nawang. Captured by Japanese troops, they were herded together and, after digging their own graves, were beheaded by their captors. History did not record the (former) head-hunting Dayaks' reactions, but two Dutchmen who escaped were taken in by the Penihing Dayak chief, Luhat. Others lost their heads in the Müller Mountains to Dayak *mandaus.* Their heads, along with their wives, were

taken to the Japanese at Putussibau.

The Allied invasion of three strategic spots in Borneo—Brunei, Tarakan and Balikpapan—was spearheaded by Australian troops. The ensuing loss of life was unnecessary as the main thrust towards Japan, well on its way, had bypassed Borneo and the Japanese there presented no threat. But MacArthur had committed himself to use the 1st Australian Corps somewhere.

Balikpapan was being considered as a base for the invasion of Java, but the Joint Chiefs of Staff squelched the idea. Balikpapan, with seven piers, a big oil refinery and two airfields, was the scene of some of Borneo's fiercest fighting. While the fighting was still in progress, MacArthur, accompanied by two Aussie generals, landed on the beach for publicity photographs. Once resistance was mopped up, Borneo, along with the rest of Indonesia, returned temporarily to the once more over-confident Dutch.

Independence

The country was not about to resubmit meekly to its former colonial master. Thanks to some tough fighting, mostly in Java, and some diplomatic maneuvers, Indonesia declared independence in 1945, and won its freedom from the Dutch four years later.

Though Kalimantan saw little military action during the revolution against Holland, many of the later raids in the "confrontation" with Malaysia took place here. Military men on both sides realized that Sukarno was only trying to gain internal political capital with the confrontation, so no major battles were fought. Dayaks from either side of the border took advantage of the opportunity to gather a few heads to show their valor.

Opposite: *The Indonesian national flag, born in the independence struggle, is proudly carried by students in East Kalimantan.* **Above:** *Oilworkers on one of East Kalimantan's modern rigs.*

THE DAYAKS

The Inland Peoples of Kalimantan

The inland tribes of Borneo—generically called Dayaks—fascinated the island's early explorers, and continue to interest today's travelers and tourists. Their huge stilted longhouses, striking and beautiful art, and their head-hunting captivated European adventurers and early ethnographers. That the Dayaks were considered quite handsome physically—and were at times promiscuous—added an element of titillation to an already "exotic" subject.

A world of spirits

All Dayak religions were concerned with attracting good spirits and chasing away evil ones. For most groups, head-hunting was an essential component of this spirit manipulation. Once a head was chopped off and brought back to the longhouse, its spirit was cajoled or forced to help the captors. To

ensure that the spirit would readjust to its fate, the skull was honored and treated with offerings of food, drink and tobacco.

Dayak artwork, aesthetically equal to the best produced in Africa or Melanesia, also served to control the world of spirits. These ethereal entities—either permanent deities or the spirits of human beings—decided on matters of sickness and health, the quality and quantity of harvests, and success in head-hunting. The latter, of course, leading to added spirit-power. Quite simply, spirits controlled everything that really mattered.

Both the Dutch and the British effectively confined Islam to the coastal areas, and to the mid-reaches of the great Mahakam and Kapuas Rivers, to where it had spread in pre-colonial times. But with the advent of Christianity and the eventually enforceable ban on chopping off heads, Dayak religion and art lost their foundations. However, even today, under Western clothes and a superficial layer of Christianity, many of the traditional ways remain.

The Dayaks still prepare their fields using the ancient but serviceable slash-and-burn method; they still comb the jungle for game and forest products; they don traditional garb at times of celebration, if not everyday; and in some areas they still live in longhouses. In all the Dayak areas a generalized belief in the world of spirits is very much alive.

The Kaharingan religion, a traditional faith, has even—with a few modifications—received government approval as part of the catch-all category of "Bali-Hinduism." The followers of Kaharingan, which includes elaborate funerary practices, live in central and northern Kalteng, as well as adjacent areas in Kaltim and Kalbar. (See "Kaharingan Faith," page 152.) In general, the further one travels from the coast, the more evident is the traditional way of life: shamans curing disease, body decoration, rituals, longhouses and, of course, the spirits. Nonetheless, U.S.-based evangelical faiths have made inroads into even the most isolated areas, to the detriment of traditional customs.

Head-hunting and warfare

No Dayak custom upset Borneo's colonial

Opposite: *An orangutan skull today substitutes for a human one in this Kenyah* mamat *ceremony.*
Left: *A Bahau Dayak woman near Long Iram in East Kalimantan is dressed in her traditional finery, including a hat studded with honey bear claws. She is a dancer in a rice-planting ritual.*

Dayak Groups of Kalimantan

Malay groups
Iban groups
Ngaju and Barito River groups
Land Dayak and Western groups
Kayan and Kenyah groups
Nomadic groups
Central-Northern groups

Bernard Sellato 1990

masters—Dutch and British alike—more than head-hunting. It was considered the most "uncivilized" trait of the "savages." Even the White Rajas Brooke, otherwise enamored of Dayak culture and tradition, ended head-hunting on their territory. Some sources suggest, however, that the Brookes occasionally sanctioned massive head-gathering raids when it suited the British rajas' political or military purposes.

When criticizing the Dayak practice, sanctimonious Western moralists tended to forget their own barbaric wars, conducted in the service of religious hubris, to avenge often dubious points of honor, to acquire territory, or to satisfy a ruler's arrogance.

A freshly severed head was a crucial unit of spiritual power, and brought a fresh transfusion of magical energy to the village. Such heads could ensure a good crop, ward off disease, and generally bring success to a village. Heads were required in rituals of all kinds, including marriage, dedication of longhouses, the completion of woodcarvings and funerals.

Head-hunting also provided an arena for able young men to demonstrate their personal prowess, impressing both lissome young women and their peers. Success in head-hunting qualified a warrior to wear special tattoos and decoration, such as, in some areas, clouded leopard fang ear plugs. Thus the raids provided the crucible wherein the talents of future village chiefs and strategy makers were forged.

It mattered not at all whose head became the trophy, whether it came from an able rival warrior or a boy. Returning from a raid with one's own head securely attached was a feat in itself, and nobody bothered to ask the origin of the trophy.

A head-hunting raid was usually a well organized affair, with dozens—if not hundreds—of warriors led by a supreme commander with years of experience in the art of war. These war parties at times contained a thousand head-thirsty men, but smaller groups were usually more effective and were preferred. The logistics of a small foray were simpler, and the important element of secrecy was easier to maintain with a small group. Although not unknown, particularly among the tough Iban, a freelance head-hunter was rare. A major raid was generally a social event, with an entire village, or even several allied villages, participating in the expedition.

Weapons and combat

The head-hunting weapon par excellence was the *mandau*, a machete-like sword fashioned of excellent local ore. The weapon originated with the Kayan, but was readily adopted all across the island. Different Dayak groups have different styles of *mandau*, but all had the same deadly efficiency. The *mandau* handle was fashioned of deer antler, sometimes elaborately carved and decorated with tufts of human hair.

For defense, the warrior relied on a narrow body shield, carved of relatively soft, open-grained wood, sometimes bound with rattan to prevent splitting. The shield was designed not just to ward off blows, but became something of an strategic weapon as well. The warrior would try to catch his opponent's *mandau* thrust just right, so the sword became stuck. Then he would quickly cast aside the shield, and neatly decapitate his weaponless opponent.

The rattan war caps, leopard skin ponchos and other decorative war gear did not provide much physical resistance to the *mandau's* steel. But this "armor," decorated with magic motifs, tufts of hair, teeth and claws, served to strike fear in the opponent, hopefully eroding his courage enough to tip the balance of power in one's own favor.

Attack on a longhouse

Before an expedition could be launched, the omens, particularly the flight patterns of certain birds, were carefully scrutinized. If the signs were favorable, the war canoes were eased into the river. These canoes, carved from a single trunk, reached 30 meters (100 ft.) or more. Each could carry 60-70 eager warriors, and their strong backs urged the craft forward with remarkable speed.

The war party tied up its canoes a couple of hours' walk from the target village, to prevent detection. A few scouts were sent out to make sure conditions were right; the favorite time for an attack was just before dawn.

If word had leaked out of the upcoming attack, the planned victims would have gone on the offensive, booby-trapping the river and stationing warriors for an ambush. Trees in strategic locations were chopped almost all the way through, waiting for a few strategically timed *mandau* strokes to send them crashing down on the river—and the hapless raiders. At this point, the opponents, now on

Opposite: *Dayak war dancers. In the old days these men, Kenyah from Datah Bilang in the Mahakam basin, would have been their village's most experienced and capable head-hunters.*

the offensive, would rain poisoned blowgun darts down on the capsized expedition.

Even if the attack was a surprise, every village was in a state of constant readiness for defense. The longhouses were built near rivers, and were perched on a forest of ironwood posts sometimes 3-6 meters (10-20 ft.) off the ground. The ladders were always drawn up at night, and an arsenal of weapons kept at strategic positions in the longhouse.

At dawn the raiders would strike, setting fire to the sleeping longhouse and picking off the fleeing villagers as they sought to escape to the river or jungle. Ideally, the longhouse was burnt to the ground, and the village decimated. But situations were rarely ideal. At the first sign of an attack, the longhouse was electrified into action, grabbing ironwood spears, rocks, and quivers of poisoned blowgun darts which were sent in volleys down on the attackers. A siege was not a common strategy, and in a very short time the outcome of the attack would have been decided, with either the defenders fleeing for their heads, or the attackers retreating at a fast clip through the jungle.

A successful raid brought a number of fringe benefits, including captive women and children, who stocked harems or became slaves, and loot—ancient beads, brass gongs and, the most prized of all, ancient Chinese dragon jars. The warriors returned as heros, and the whole village celebrated their achievement. Beautiful young girls would snatch up the heads and use the grisly trophies as props in a wild and erotic burlesque.

The skulls, after being used in a special ritual lasting several days, insured the village's prosperity—for a while. Although all Dayak groups were head-hunters, there were numerous local variations. The Kenyah put particular emphasis on captives; the Kayan, on the other hand, required great numbers of skulls for the funerary rites of their chiefs.

The Iban were the most feared—they took heads merely for the sport of it. When in the late 19th century the Sarawak government allowed native warriors to practice their traditional ways—"a legitimate outlet for their pugnacity"—the only problem Raja Brooke faced was a surplus of volunteers.

A diverse group

The name "Dayak" is derived from the words meaning "inland" or "upriver" peoples. In the past, though this is not true today, it implied "backward." But the people gathered under the name "Dayak" are members of a culturally and linguistically diverse set of tribes, much like the Indians of the Americas.

Many anthropologists have stumbled in their attempts to classify the various Dayaks into neat categories. The variations in languages, art styles, customs and history are too great. Even the broad "inland tribes of Borneo" has important exceptions. Much of

The Punan had a healthy fear of their fellow Borneans—the Dayaks and Malays enslaved them or just cut off their heads—and were thus not highly sociable. Early travelers report Punan leaving their jungle products near Dayak villages, and then picking up the items left in trade (salt, tobacco, metal) when the place was deserted. The forest skills of the Punan are legendary, and some imaginative 19th century accounts claimed that they had tails, lived in trees, and could smell men from several kilometers away.

Some Punan came out of the forest a few generations ago and settled in permanent villages along the upper reaches of rivers, and others were assimilated into various Dayak groups. The rest settled down in response to government incentives, and pressure, in the last decade. Although they are no longer truly nomadic, the Punan still roam their former hunting grounds, collecting jungle products such as rattan, resins, camphor crystals and aloeswood, as well as the occasional bezoar stone. They still weave fine rattan baskets and mats.

The wild sago palm (*Eugeissona utilis*) was the key to Punan survival. After crushing and filtering, the trunk of this tree yields some 4 kilos (9 lbs.) of almost pure starch. The caloric yield from one trunk is enough to last an active adult one week. Since most Punan moved around in bands of 25 to 50 persons, the sago tree requirements for each group ranged from 1,300 to 2,600 per year.

The Punan territory covered the mountainous area of central Borneo, the headwaters of all the island's major river systems. The inland Dayak groups, and then the Malays on the coastal regions, encircled the Punan. The advent of trade—especially with the Chinese, who greatly desired the forest products the Punan could provide—and the introduction of metal technology led to changes in the Punan lifestyle.

Although wild pigs were the Punan's preferred prey, rhinos, monkeys, birds and just about anything else that walked, crawled, or flew in the forest was fair game for the Punan hunter. The blowgun, which could deliver a 25-centimeter (10 in.) poisoned dart with great accuracy over an amazing 100 meters (330 ft.), was the preferred Punan weapon.

the confusion stems from a long history of large- and small-scale migrations within Borneo, a result of population pressures, warfare and communications. Groups sometimes adopted the language, rituals and other customs of their neighbors, then brought this mixture of tongues and traditions with them when they moved on. Although warfare no longer exists, villages still shift location frequently in search of easier access to outside goods, markets and jobs.

With the above in mind, Kalimantan's Dayaks can be said to fall into several very broad geographical/cultural complexes: The nomadic Punan of the forested interior; the groups of northeastern Kalimantan; the Lun Dayeh and Lun Bawang of north Kaltim; the Kayan and the Kenyah of the Kaltim highlands and the Mahakam basin; the Barito River groups; the "Land Dayaks" of Kalbar; the Iban, though most of these live in Sarawak; and the "Malays," or Islamized Dayaks.

The nomadic Punan

In the past, hunting-gathering nomads, generally called Punan, wandered from temporary site to temporary site deep in the most remote jungles of Borneo. Bands of Punan—also called, variously, Penan, Bukat, Bukit, Bekatan and Ot—wandered the rainforest in splendid isolation, and with complete self-sufficiency. Today, almost none maintains the ancient lifestyle.

Above: *A Bahau Dayak dancer displays the business end of his* mandau. **Opposite:** *The Bornean blowpipe, or* sumpitan, *is the best in the world. A solid piece of ironwood with a spearhead fixed to the end, it is a very versatile weapon.*

The introduction of metal technology to the island brought two basic improvements to the Punan blowgun, transforming it into the world's best in its category. A "state-of-the-art" blowgun is a tough ironwood rod 2-3 meters long, with a hole bored through its length using a metal bit. To the end of the weapon is fastened a sharp "bayonet" of metal—the Bornean wild boar is a fierce beast when cornered or wounded, and can weigh 200 kilos (450 lbs.).

Honey bears are another excellent argument in favor of improved hunting technology in Kalimantan—mother bears have been known to attack without provocation, and their size and ferocity make them a menace.

In the rest of the world where the weapons are in use, blowguns are made by splitting bamboo or wood, carving a channel inside, and then binding the two halves together. Nothing approaches the physical strength of the Borneo blowgun. With the introduction of metal and domesticated dogs, the balance of power shifted dramatically to the side of the Punan, who no longer had to rely exclusively on the effects of the poison from the darts.

While hunting still entails the risk of a mauling by a wild boar or honey bear, the combination of well-trained dogs and the spear-tipped blowgun took some of the danger out of bringing home the bacon in the forests of Kalimantan. There are even accounts of Punan maidens participating in pig hunts, but we do not recommend the sport for casual Westerners.

While the process of settlement had begun before the colonial governments arrived in central Borneo, it accelerated during the first decades of this century. Governments, both colonial or nationalist, have a low level of tolerance for free spirits. Facing both the carrot and the stick, the Punan groups today have all built huts in permanent locations. Still, many continue to take long treks in their beloved forest, bringing home the still-valuable products and, one imagines, refreshing their spirits.

The northeastern groups

Although the Dusun and Plains Murut are the chief groups inhabiting Sabah, this culture group is represented in Kalimantan only by the Tidung and Bulungan of the lower river basins of northeastern Kalimantan. Their languages are related to those spoken in the Philippines, and they are rice farmers. They have adopted Islam through the influence of the small coastal sultanates that were vassal to the sultan of Kutai to the south.

Lun Dayeh and Lun Bawang

The Lun Dayeh and Lun Bawang of northeastern Kalimantan are related to the Kelabit of Sarawak and the Hill Murut of Sabah. In the south of their lands they merge with the Kayan-Kenyah group. They practice swidden

(slash-and-burn) agriculture, but also some local irrigation agriculture in natural swamps.

These two groups are what is left, after the Kayan takeover of the region, of a once large and widespread set of tribes with a rich megalithic tradition featuring stone seats and other structures, and monumental funeral art. They probably adopted rice cultivation from the Kayan, prior to which it was likely that the Lun Dayeh and Lun Bawang grew tubers and harvested sago. Their society is vaguely stratified, also probably a borrowing from the Kayan, and they distinguish only informally between the rich and poor.

Kayan

The Kayan are found chiefly in the central highlands of Kaltim, although there are a few Kayan villages along the upper Kapuas River. Their homeland is the Apokayan, but their traditional history still has them coming from somewhere overseas. One of the most successful Dayak groups, in the 18th and 19th centuries they spread from the Apokayan to Sarawak, the Mahakam Basin and the Kapuas. These now scattered groups maintain a homogeneous language and set of customs.

Kayan society was strictly stratified into feudal classes: *maren,* the top aristocrats; *hipuy,* the nobles; *panyin,* the commoners; and *dipen,* the slaves. Each class had its rights and obligations which were defined down to minutiae. The aristocrats monopolized power in the political, economic and religious spheres, but were also required to protect their subjects. Slaves—captured in raids— were indispensable to these societies. Although each nuclear family worked its own plot, the rice was stored in the longhouse's communal granaries.

The beautiful hardwood longhouses of the Kayan reflect their social structure: the best central apartment was reserved for the chief, and his quarters were flanked by those of the nobles. The slaves lived at the edges of the longhouses, the areas most at risk from a surprise head-hunting raid.

Although today's national governments have greatly curtailed the power and privileges of the aristocracy, this class still commands a great deal of respect. Among these groups, members of the traditional aristocratic families hold whatever local political positions are allowed by the government, and they are consulted in all important matters by their fellow villagers. It is not unusual even today for the aristocrats to receive free labor for their fields, "gifts" of firewood, choice pieces of game, and general assistance whenever it is required. The traditions of the Kayan have spread over the northern half of Borneo, including rice cultivation, woodcarving, the *mandau* , and the social structure.

Kenyah

The Kenyah are an odd set of groups of various origins, and they speak languages that are not always mutually intelligible. Some were originally forest nomads who settled under Kayan patronage. They gradually replaced the Kayan in the Apokayan, and some later migrated into Sarawak and the Mahakam River basin. Like the Kayan, the Kenyah are now rice cultivators, with a stratified society. Their villages are generally large, with many longhouses sometimes containing a total of more than 2,000 people. The Kenyah are famous for their woodcarving, which is distinct and florid, and their music, dance and colorful costume. (See "The Apokayan," page 83, and "Dayaks of the Mahakam," page 100.)

Barito River group

This is the largest group of Kalimantan's Dayaks; their lands cover the southern half of the island. The powerful Ngaju live in Kalteng; the Ot Danum straddle the Schwaner Mountains; the Siang and Murung in the upper Barito; and the Tunjung, Benuaq, and Bentian, in the middle Mahakam.

The languages spoken by these groups fall into three families, although cultural similarities are strong. They all follow sophisticated death rituals which include the sacrificing of water buffalo. In some areas there is a secondary funeral wherein the bones or ashes are placed in special mausoleums. Many among these people follow the Kaharingan Faith, a government-sanctioned traditional religion (See "Kaharingan Faith," page 152.)

In the Melawi area, the Tebidah, Kebahan, and Limbai practice the death rituals, while they have adopted Malay dialects. Although some of the Barito groups display a social structure seemingly inspired by the Muslim sultanates, most live in scattered villages consisting of a single longhouse. (See "Central Kalimantan," page 149.)

Opposite: *A Tunjung Dayak shaman, near Long Iram, examines the liver of a pig. The animal was sacrificed to honor the deceased relative of the man with the cigarette, who shows obvious interest in the outcome of the proceedings.*

'Land Dayaks'

These people, so-called "Land Dayaks," live in the northwestern part of Kalimantan and in adjacent regions in Sarawak. They arrived in northern Kalbar from the southwest in the 18th century. They form a language group of their own, but some, for example the Selako, speak a Malay dialect. The Land Dayaks formerly lived in longhouses, and their villages feature a special round meeting house, restricted to men, where skull trophies were once on display.

Land Dayak society is only loosely stratified, and distinguishes roughly between rich and poor. These Dayaks are best known for the large carved wooden figures which are used in their funeral feasts. (See "West Kalimantan," page 167.)

Iban

The Iban moved from what is now West Kalimantan into Sarawak, where they now form a huge group—350,000. There are only about 7,000 living in Kalimantan, in the lakes region of the Kapuas River in Kalbar. Related groups live in the same area, such as the Mualang, Seberuang, Desa and Kantuq. All these languages are related to Malay.

The Iban live in communal longhouses and practice shifting, slash-and-burn rice cultivation, and they tend to prefer fresh *ladang* sites in primary forest. Their societies are more or less egalitarian, with none of the strict stratification of, say, the Kayan.

The Iban are the most notorious of Dayaks, due to their excessive enthusiasm for head-hunting, and they were greatly feared by all other groups. They launched expeditions both on land and sea—under the appellation "Sea Dayaks," they were the region's most feared pirates in the 19th century. (See "West Kalimantan," page 167.)

Malays

Of Borneo's total population of 12 million, only about one-fourth are classified as Dayaks—the rest are Malays. Ninety percent of the so-called Malays, all of the Muslim faith, are Islamized Dayaks. Whatever indigenous Australoids (similar to Papuans) lived in Borneo, they have disappeared, except for a few ancient bones in the Niah caves of Sarawak. All of Indonesia's current population comes from a slow, centuries-long migration of Mongol peoples, called, confusingly, Austronesians. (See "Prehistory," page 24.)

The Malays live along the coasts and on the middle courses of most of Kalimantan's major rivers. Their conversion to Islam began in the 15th century, when Muslim sultanates replaced the earlier Indianized kingdoms such as Kutai and Banjarmasin. The process of conversion then moved upriver, and is still going on to some extent.

— with assistance from Bernard Sellato

LONGHOUSES

Traditional Communal Dwellings

While head-hunting shocked European concepts of warfare, communal living in longhouses offended the prevailing notions of morality: such collective living, they feared, led inevitably to promiscuous sexuality.

This was in fact not the case, and in some longhouses, thin walls between apartments and creaking floorboards put a premium on discretion in nighttime sexual encounters. Each Dayak group had its own rules of sexual conduct, although these were generally more relaxed than those of the Victorians.

Longhouses could reach a kilometer in length, and sheltered anywhere from a few families to a village of several hundred. First and foremost, the dwellings, raised on posts, provided a measure of protection against attack. In addition, the communal dwellings provided a framework for continuous, informal contacts and harmonious social relations.

Although each family could retreat to its private apartment, all but the most private activities took place on the communal porch— a wide, roofed space that ran the length of the longhouse. This is where the children played, where people of all ages socialized, where the women wove baskets and sewed beads, where the ceremonies took place, and where important meetings of all kinds where held. In fact, these events were usually going on all at the same time.

Sometimes called *betang* or *lamin,* the longhouse was the usual dwelling of most, but not all, of the Dayak groups. The Ngaju and related groups lived in large homes (*umah hai*) which sheltered extended families, but not unrelated folks, as did the true longhouses.

A clue to social structure

Where longhouses did exist, the architecture and form construction reflected the group's underlying social structure. Iban longhouses, for example, gave the impression of not being very carefully constructed, and were not par-

ticularly solid. But the Iban were migratory, periodically picking up and moving to virgin lands where, if the work of clearing was harder, the higher yield from fresh fields justified the extra labor.

The Iban longhouse was not "owned" communally. Each contiguous apartment was built by the family that lived in it, of whatever materials the family felt like using. Often, Iban longhouses were not raised very high, and rested on slender support posts. Light wood, which did not require much work to cut and shape, and bamboo, bark and leaves were used extensively in the construction.

No self-respecting Kenyah or Kayan would have stepped foot in such a flimsy structure. Their longhouses were built to last for generations. Massive ironwood pillars raised them several meters off the ground. Ironwood required a tremendous amount of labor to cut and shape, but it is impervious to rot and insects. Heavy timber went into walls and floors, and the pieces were joined with exacting care. The skill of talented Kenyah and Kayan craftsmen of generations ago is still visible today in the old longhouses: ironwood floorboards, some over 60 centimeters (2 ft.) wide and 9 meters (30 ft.) long, fit side by side with nary a crack between. The surface of the wood, polished smooth by generations of bare feet, has a beautiful patina.

The roofs of these longhouses were covered with ironwood shingles, strong enough to ward off the rainy season's tremendous torrents. Long ironwood trunks, with notches for steps, served as the longhouse's staircases. These ladders were often topped by a distorted face meant to scare off evil spirits who might attempt to sneak into the longhouse.

The craftsmanship and solid materials used in Kenyah and Kayan longhouses reflected a stable, sedentary society. The arrangement of the interior displayed its stratifications. The long verandah running the length of the longhouse was communal space, but the apartments in the back served as a constant reminder of the status differences among nobles, commoners and slaves. The central apartment, reserved for the aristocrat in charge, was the most spacious, and sometimes had a higher roof. This "penthouse" was flanked by the nobles' rooms. The headman and the nobles could decorate

Opposite: *A longhouse near Tumbang Kurik, a village far inland on the Kahayan River. The Ot Danum Dayak post carvings at the entrance are designed to scare off evil influences.*

their apartments with certain special motifs, further setting them off from the others. On either side of these were the rooms of common families and finally, at the very ends of the longhouse—the place most vulnerable to enemy attack—the slave quarters.

Longhouses today

After Indonesian's independence, the new government went about the complex task of nation-building and creating a unified Indonesian identity. There was a tendency to impose Javanese values on the other islands of the archipelago. Longhouses shocked Javanese morality and ideas of hygiene.

Although abandoning the longhouses was never a declared government policy, single-family dwellings were definitely favored by the Javanese administrators of Kalimantan. The means employed to encourage Dayaks to move from longhouses to "normal" homes varied widely, depending on local circumstances and the personal tolerance of the local administrators.

Within the past two decades, however, the government has become more sensitive to—even proud of—the cultural diversity of Indonesia's many and varied citizens. It has seen the psychological and political benefits of this approach, as well as the possible economic benefits brought by tourists who are interesting in visiting traditional cultures. As a result, there is no longer any pressure on Kalimantan's Dayaks to abandon their longhouses. On the contrary, they are encouraged to stay in them. The provincial government of Kaltim has even used development funds to completely rebuild a longhouse at Mancong (near Tanjung Isuy and Lake Jempang) with an eye on its potential value in attracting tourists. The first general manager of the Benakutai Hotel in Balikpapan also lobbied successfully for Dutch funds to help finance this project.

Partially as a result of former government attitudes, when the Kenyah Dayaks left the Apokayan in large numbers in the 1960s and 1970s, these emigrants did not build longhouses at their new village sites. However, rather than abandon the concept altogether, they built large meeting halls, quite acceptable to officialdom at the time. Although no one lives in these buildings, they are painted and decorated in the colorful Kenyah style and quite worth a visit.

In the Apokayan itself, many families still live in longhouses, but others prefer individual family homes. Also, the design of some of the longhouses in the Apokayan has evolved from the traditional style. These have few apartments, and they are just barely raised above the ground. There is still a long covered meeting hall in front, and it is decorated with long, hallucinatory paintings and statues—but these include such modern touches as figures wearing shorts and wristwatches.

DAYAK ART

Powerful and Florid Art Styles

At its best, traditional Dayak art equals the finest of Melanesia and Africa, generally considered the source of the world's best traditional art. Powerful, expressive Dayak woodcarvings and other art forms—cloth, beadwork—have universal appeal. Styles and motifs varied from group to group, and not all Dayaks had a strong artistic tradition.

Unfortunately, fine-quality Dayak art is, for all practical purposes, a thing of the past. Dealers have to travel to the most remote areas to find old carvings, some worth a small fortune in Europe or the United States, and production of really artistic new pieces is just about nil. The traditional religion, which gave inspiration to Dayak artists, has been replaced by Christianity or Islam. Although copies of original works are available—some made in Java and Bali—they lack the feeling of their prototypes. The sad fact is that the best place to see authentic Bornean art is in the museums of Europe.

One can still come across some examples of Dayak art in the inland villages, and seeing these pieces in their proper setting is an experience no museum environment can hope to duplicate. Elaborate funerary structures dot villages along the middle and upper parts of some rivers in Kalteng and the Melawi basin to the north.

In the Apokayan, Kenyah longhouses, rice barns, and the more recently constructed meeting halls are decorated with the group's distinctive baroque style of carving. Most of the places where traditional art can still be found are off the beaten path, and require time and effort to reach.

Motifs and styles

Experts, analyzing Bornean art, trace the source of Dayak motifs to the Asian mainland, particularly China and Vietnam. Art styles from the Dongson civilization—at its height, 300 B.C. to 100 B.C.—spread through much of the archipelago. The Dongson-inspired motifs in Borneo include the spiral and the repetition of various curved lines. Instead of humans or animals standing alone, these figures appeared in a tangle of varied and repeating geometric forms. In other parts of Indonesia, hour-glass–shaped, cast bronze drums from Dongson have been found, but no traces of these have yet been discovered in Borneo.

The late Chou period in China—400 B.C. to 200 B.C.—left more noticeable marks on Dayak art, though few traces of Chou influence exist elsewhere in the archipelago. Chou art styles are said to be visible in the Dayaks' fantastical animals, and in wild compositions that blend a variety of asymmetrical designs into a harmonious whole. Late Chou influences can most clearly be seen on Borneo's masks and shields which, according to one art historian, display decorative work that is of a form unique in Indonesia. *Pua,* a fine woven cloth produced by the Iban, is also Chou-influenced, and its motifs are unique among the many types of cloth produced in the archipelago.

Hindu influences came later to Borneo—about 2,000 years ago—and reached the island after passing through Java. Dragon and tiger motifs (there are no tigers on Borneo) remain as the most important contribution of Hindu art. The dragon remains an essential art form, even in the Islamized Malay cultures of Borneo.

Because of the many internal migrations of Dayaks in Borneo, and the groups' cultural flexibility, it is difficult to attach a particular set of motifs and styles to a particular Dayak group with any degree of confidence. This is particularly the case with the Kenyah and Kayan groups, which show considerable cultural similarities, including art forms. Because the spirits and supernatural world of many of the Dayak groups spring from the same basic pantheon, the art of one group was easily adopted by, and combined with, that of another.

Bahau, Kenyah and Kayan art often features the *asoq*—a stylized motif that is a kind of dragon-dog. This composite animal, considered a protective beast, has links to a distant mythological ancestor with animal traits that are greatly admired. The incorporation of fantastic zoomorphic attributes into ancestral representations is common to many Dayak groups.

In Dayak art, frightening animals generally function to scare away both evil spirits and human enemies. Kenyah, Kayan and Bahau war shields were often decorated with large, hypnotic eyes and mouths studded with fangs. These same designs appear on masks and graves, created by the craftsmen of these three tribes as well as of others. (Many motifs, especially the human figure, were reserved for aristocrats.)

Art and Dayak religion

Although there are notable differences in the various Dayak groups' religious beliefs, the common environment of jungle and rivers, along with rice-based agriculture, seems to have led to similar Dayak "faiths." Spirits crowd the Dayak supernatural world. These powerful beings—some beneficial, some harmful—are manipulated through rituals, offerings and various artistic expressions.

The Dayaks held a vague, generalized concept of a Supreme Being, the Creator, but

no special importance was attached to this particular spirit: he had done his job, and that was that. There are no known representations of this deity. Emphasis on the Dayak Creator came only with the advent of Christianity, which in the process of conversion, sought out points of similarity with the local religions.

Most Dayak art was, and to a large extent remains, intimately associated with religion and social hierarchy. Funerary structures are the most obvious extant examples. These

include raised coffins and carved poles to which the animals—formerly, slaves—are tied before being sacrificed in the ritual. Among the Ngaju, the Ot Danum and other groups, the coffins—really ossuaries or mausoleums—were (some still are) adorned with elaborate carvings. People of wealth and status, the aristocrats, received the most elaborate funerals, and special motifs were reserved for their coffins.

The aristocrats were more powerful than other men on earth, and similarly their spirits were more powerful in the afterworld. But among certain groups, all of the deceased required a "secondary burial," an additional ritual treatment of the remains to send the soul on its way.

The human body was believed to house two souls. One stayed with the corpse until the flesh decomposed. The other remained in the area of the village until the rituals were performed that would help send the soul on its dangerous journey to the Land of the Dead. This afterworld was a heavenly abode often associated with unusual mountains. This concept is generally adhered to, with

Opposite: *Though practical, a baby carrier's chief purpose is to offer spiritual protection to the child.* **Above, left:** *A newly carved baby carrier.* **Above, right:** *A detail from a particularly fine baby carrier. Note the colonial-era coins, the leopard and bear claws, and the valuable beads.*

numerous local variations.

In preparation for the secondary ritual, the body is buried in an urn or coffin with a hole in the bottom so that the fluids will drain. It is then stored in a home or shelter for a few months until the process of decomposition has taken place and until a propitious time is reached.

Then the bones are exhumed from their container, cleaned, and placed in an ossuary or mausoleum, in the context of a huge ceremony that, for a noble, may last for weeks and involve the slaughter of a dozen water buffalo and a hundred pigs.

Funerary art

Among the Ngaju, and other Dayak groups that were influenced by their culture, the long, complex rituals of the secondary burial required elaborate carvings.

The mausoleum, called a *sandung,* is an intricately carved "house" that rests on one to five pillars, the whole structure standing about 2 meters high. The bones of the deceased are placed in a compartment in this carving. The *sandung* was covered with carvings, including the hornbill bird, symbolizing the upper world, and a dragon/snake, standing for the lower world.

At the climax of the ceremony, the priest enacts the reunion of the deceased with his spirit, and at this moment a water buffalo tied to a *sepunduq*—the sacrificial post—is speared to death by the relatives of the deceased. Pigs are also sacrificed. In earlier times, a slave would have been used rather than the animals. The *sepunduq* were often the finest examples of the woodcarver's art, and depicted demons with fangs, huge protruding tongues, and long noses.

The highest, most complex carving associated with Ngaju funerary ritual is the *sengkaran,* a 6-meter (20 ft.) pole that supports a carved hornbill bird flying over a forest of spears, which are stuck like a fan into the back of a dragon. The dragon rests on an heirloom Chinese jar. This carving represents a cosmos, or a tree of life.

Particular to Ngaju culture are the ships-of-the-dead, small model sailing ships manned by a crew of benevolent spirits, and designed to help a soul on its way to the afterworld. Today, these soul ships are constructed out of gutta-percha for sale to tourists.

The cultural diffusion of many of these Ngaju funerary rituals into a large area of central Borneo began before the arrival of the Europeans. The recently named and officially recognized Kaharingan faith of the Ngaju also has been at least partially assimilated by several Dayak groups in East and West Kalimantan. This religion incorporates a secondary funeral called *tiwah* which requires much of the artwork mentioned above. (See "Kaharingan Faith," page 152.)

The Kenyah, Kayan and Kajang groups,

north of the Ngaju sphere of influence, also built most elaborate tomb huts for their aristocratic families. Called *salong,* these structures were raised high off the ground on massive posts and decorated with carvings and paintings of birds, dragons and humans. Although most members of these three groups are now Christian, recent graves are still decorated in the traditional style with curved strips of wood. The crowning sculpture of the *salongs* can be a stylized hornbill or fish, although some sculptors have added

modern touches to this element: One grave is topped by an airplane; another, the grave of a lumberjack, is topped by a chainsaw. (See photograph page 92.)

Other art forms

Longhouses, especially those of the Kenyah, Kayan and related groups, are works of art on a large scale. These ironwood structures, sheltering a whole village under one roof, are perched on a forest of stilts, two or more meters off the ground. Painted and carved decorations cover stairs, doors, outside walls and roofs of longhouses: a gentle giant's doll house where baroque imagination ran wild. (See "Longhouses" page 48.)

Tall poles topped by a carved figure were formerly widespread in many parts of Borneo. Placed at village entrances, in front of longhouses or at burial sites, the sculptures were designed to frighten away evil spirits. The Kenyah, who migrated from the Apokayan area in the past two decades, have put these poles to novel use. The carved poles in front of some of the Kenyah meeting halls—which have replaced the longhouses—have been fitted with a rope and pulley arrangement, which is used to hoist the Indonesian flag on important occasions. Perhaps, in the minds of the older Kenyah, the flagpoles' frightening carvings still serve to keep evil spirits at bay.

At key points in the cycle of rice grow-ing—planting and harvest—a dance using grotesque *hudoq* masks is performed to keep maleficent spirits from taking over the "soul" of the rice. An alternate interpretation is that the masked dancers are representations of benevolent ancestors, and the dance attracts their prototypes who then keep the evil spirits from destroying the rice. The *hudoq* masks are oversized compositions in wood, with huge noses and round, bulging eyes. *Hudoq* masks are still used by the Kenyah, Kayan, Kajang, Bahau and Modang groups.

Agricultural implements were adorned with carvings, either to ward off evil or to attract the supernatural protection necessary for plentiful harvests. Even utilitarian items were decorated with special designs or carvings that made reference to the supernatural: textiles, baskets, mats, blowguns, hats, stools, wooden dishes and various containers.

Baby carriers were (and are) especially important, because the tender young souls inside—just like the rice shoots—were particularly vulnerable to nefarious influences. Carved or beaded designs served to ward off evil, as did the claws and fangs of powerful wild animals such as bears and the clouded leopard. Ancient beads, handed down for generations, were especially powerful charms for protecting children.

Warfare required all the protective powers available. The flight patterns of certain birds were the best omens, but art also contributed to successful raids. War shields were carved and painted on the outside with patterns designed to concentrate bad luck on

Opposite: *This interior of a Kenyah longhouse at Nawang Baru in the Apokayan shows the Kenyah love of baroque styles of painting and sculpture.*
Above, left: *Detail from a tapestry woven by Umaq Suling Dayak women at Long Pahangai. The asoq, or dragon-dog motif is visible.* **Above, right:** *A Kenyah grave marker in the Apokayan marks the burial place of a prominent member of the village.*

the enemy, while occasional artwork on the inside of the shield bestowed beneficial powers onto the user.

The *mandau,* a short sword fashioned from local ores, ranks among the greatest achievements of Dayak art and technology. Their blades, worked by specialists, were often inlaid and fretted. Not only were they beautiful, but the forged steel blades were strong. The *mandau* handle, usually made of deerhorn, was carved into elaborate, flowing designs. The finest *mandaus* were made by the Kayan and Bahau groups.

Dayak art today

High-quality art is no longer produced in Borneo. Art dealers have recently begun paying good prices for Dayak art, which has had a positive influence on the artistic tradition, but this can not immediately counteract the stifling effect brought about by years of Islam and Christianity. Only the Kaharingan religion, recently "approved," offers hope that new productions will eventually be able to communicate the feeling of the best old pieces. At the moment, the carvings used to accompany Kaharingan rituals are fairly crude copies of older works.

There is also hope for renewed creativity in some of the Roman Catholic areas, where the church has been encouraging traditional art. Ironically, some of the best contemporary Dayak art adorns Catholic churches deep in the heart of Borneo. Protestant enclaves, where traditional art is usually frowned upon, are aesthetically impoverished by comparison.

Among the approximately three million Dayaks in Borneo today, the Kenyah, Kayan, Bahau and Modang groups have retained their traditional art style to the greatest degree. The retention of a class of aristocrats within these groups offers a partial explanation for this continuing tradition. While the nobles have lost most of the prerogatives of their former status, they still generally command a great deal of respect. Many remain economically well off, at least in comparison to their fellow tribesmen, and they occasionally commission art works.

Some of the best places to see traditional art are in villages of transmigrant Kenyahs: Long Segar and Long Noran on the Kedang Kepala River, Data Bilang on the Mahakam, and several others. In these areas, which are not that difficult to reach, one can see exuberant Kenyah art. The few Kenyah remaining in the Apokayan also produce new art

according to the traditional forms, which can be seen in the recently built meeting hall at Long Nawang Baru.

At Long Ampung, the longhouse cum meeting hall is topped by traditional designs as well as a few contemporary figures: a hunter stalking his prey with a rifle, and a hilarious, suspiciously non-Dayak–looking man in a baseball cap, throwing up his hands in amazement or horror.

Although beaded baby carriers, forged *mandaus,* woven baskets, and large hats topped with colorful beaded designs are all still painstakingly made in the Apokayan, for the most part utilitarian objects are either brought in from the outside or fashioned at home with little if any decoration.

In spite of Christianity's considerable inroads into local culture, belief in the ancient spirit cosmos has not entirely disappeared. However, the imposed layer of religion has effectively quenched the feeling that was present in old Dayak art. The ancient motifs are sometimes still used, but the pieces tend to be lifeless.

There are a few exceptions to this, particularly some of the baby carriers still made by the Kenyah and Bahau. But few and far in between are the recent creations that are anything more than just relatively uninspired copies of old objects.

If recently produced art pieces seldom approach the ancient ones in quality, there is at least a growing market in items designed for tourists. Every souvenir shop stocks *mandaus,* and in shops throughout Kaltim, miniature shields, *mandaus* and blowguns come packaged as a set in a frame under glass. Even local residents buy these mini-sets for home decoration.

The tourist market

In Kaltim, some shop owners or their employees travel to the interior to purchase art objects and commission specific pieces for sale on the coast. Several stores purchase painted shields, carvings and masks made by Dayaks or others who have settled in Samarinda. Since Kaltim receives the bulk of the tourists to Kalimantan, the souvenir and antique stores here are the most active. In the other provinces, the choice is more restricted. ships-of-the-dead, made from gutta-percha and complete with a crew of spirits, are ubiquitous in Kalsel, Kalbar and Kalteng. These ships can also be purchased at the Sarinah department stores in Jakarta. All the ships are made in a few Ngaju villages on the lower Kahayan River.

Genuine antique Dayak pieces are few, but all the shops display plenty of fakes. Some are good enough to fool even experts. Some of the copies are carved by Dayaks, while others are produced in Java and Bali for sale either locally or to be shipped to Borneo. Some of these fakes are exact replicas of ancient art, copied from photographs and left outside to weather for a couple of years until the proper patina is achieved. Others are polished and rubbed in strategic places so that they appear to have been used for generations.

Genuine old pieces rarely find their way on the market. A dealer might be able to find an object for sale in a remote village, but there are few old ones left, and these are charged with spiritual power. No matter how tempting the offer, many villages are understandably reluctant to part with these. Occasionally a village or individual, badly in need of cash, brings a carving or other art piece to town for sale. Sadly, the price paid is often ridiculously low.

Foreigners who travel to remote villages in search of antiques almost always return disappointed. Even newly made items such as baby carriers are difficult to purchase, as they were made for a specific purpose and substitutes are not readily available. An inquiry is often greeted with an astronomical price, just to discourage further bargaining. Of course, if the owner happens at that time to be strapped for cash, the situation could be quite different.

The lakeside village of Tanjung Isuy is a special case. Here, the tourist trade has fostered the continued production of traditional weavings made from local plant fibers, an art form otherwise almost extinct. Because of the availability of modern clothing, this cloth is found nowhere else in Borneo except the Iban areas in Malaysian Borneo. Tanjung Isuy is the most visited Dayak village in Kalimantan. Within relatively easy reach of Samarinda, this village is easy to get to, and guarantees a traditional, if perhaps uninspired, show. (See "The Lower Mahakam," page 104.)

Any hope for a revival of Dayak art lies in the marketplace. At the moment, most visi-

tors purchase inexpensive items as souvenirs, and there is little incentive for craftsmen to spend painstaking months producing fine items, except in areas where the traditional rituals are still strong. But if Dayaks with artistic talent are encouraged by greater economic reward, Bornean art could perhaps be rescued from its current slide towards cheap commercial oblivion.

— *with assistance from Bernard Sellato*

Opposite: *A talented young Aoheng carver fashions a baby carrier for the tourist market.*
Above: *This crucifix at a Protestant church is set among some roughly painted Kenyah motifs. This is an exception in Kalimantan, as it is the Catholic areas where traditional art is usually encouraged.*

BODY DECORATION

Tattoos, Earrings and Penis Pins

Although many Western observers have commented on the natural beauty of Borneo's people, the Dayaks themselves have seen fit to improve on nature in a number of ways. Traditionally, Dayak men and women pierced and distended their ears to display bright hoop earrings and covered their bodies with elaborate tattoos. Dayak men inserted the famous *palang,* or penis pin, to increase the capabilities of the male member.

Although this is uncommon today, in the past the process of stretching the earlobes of Dayak women began when they were young. The girls' ears were pierced, and a pair of large hoop earrings inserted. Rings were added periodically until by the time the girl had become a woman, her distended lobes could display as many as 100 bright hoops.

These bangles, which could reach a half kilogram in each ear, were considered to accentuated the woman's beauty—a small discomfort to win the attentions of a lover equipped with a *palang.* According to an early 20th century ethnographer who visited Borneo, if an earlobe broke, and could no longer hold earrings, it was a mark of shame and was hidden by the woman with a cloth headwrap or by growing out her hair.

Men also wore an assortment of ear-decorations, either in stretched lobes or in holes pierced through the upper part of the ear. Large, lacy carvings from the casque of the hornbill bird were inserted, as were—for successful head-hunters—the claws and fangs of leopards and bears. Facial hair was (and still is) considered unseemly, even unmanly, and Dayak men pluck their beards and sometimes even their eyebrows.

Both men and women, especially of the aristocracy, were extensively tattooed. Some tattoos served as protection against disease, others commemorated success in warfare or other forms of personal prowess. These designs were elaborate, and candidates could spend 600 hours under the painful needle. The patterns were tapped out using a needle fixed in a wooden handle, the tip of the needle dipped in damar and soot.

Among some groups, accomplished headhunters were permitted a tattoo on the throat, most painful but very attractive to the fairer sex.

Necklaces and beads, often the older the

more valuable, added status. One account, written some 60 years ago, mentions a necklace of Venetian beads belonging to the sultan of Kutai as being worth "an entire Dayak kingdom." The most valuable beads, called in some places *lukit segala,* were round and black with delicate white and orange markings. (See photo page 26.) Merchants tried to foist new copies of these beads on the Dayaks, but they had a sharp eye for fakes.

A famous marital aid

The *palang* was, and to a certain extent remains, the male body decoration par excellence. First, the driest clinical description: "the Kenyah, a few Kayan and Katingans mutilate the membrum viril by transpiercing the glans and the urethrae, and a piece of brass wire is inserted."

Got that? Redmond O'Hanlon, in his lively *Into the Heart of Borneo,* asks his guide about the famous device: "When you twenty five, when you no good no more. When you too old. When your wife she feeds up with you. Then you go the river very early in the mornings and sit in it until your spears is small. The tattoo man he comes and pushes a nail through your spear, round and round. And then you put a pin there, a pin from the outboard motor. Sometimes you get a big spots, very painful, a boil. And then you die."

This practice of male enhancement was mentioned in the early 1830s by John Dalton, a merchant-traveler in Kaltim. He observed that gold, silver, copper and bamboo pins were used, depending on the Dayak's wealth. Followed chiefly by the Kenyah of Dutch Borneo, the practice spread to other areas of the island. According to Tom Harrisson, in 1944 the *palang* was still a relatively new technology in Sarawak.

Harrisson, who attested from first-hand experience to the *palang*'s efficiency, became the foremost expert on the subject. He dug up an uncensored manuscript by Pigafetta, Magellan's chronicler, written in 1521: "I often asked many, both young and old, to see their penis because I could not believe it…. They say that their women want it this way and if they did otherwise would not copulate with them. When the men wish to copulate with their women, they never insert it the usual way, but very slowly begin to put it inside…. When it is inside it takes the usual position and thus stays inside until it becomes soft, because otherwise they can not pull it out. These people use this because they are of a weak nature."

Harrisson, who hints that he had the operation himself, elaborates further: "The basic operation simply [!] consists of driving a hole through the distal end of the penis; sometimes, for the determined, two holes at right angles. In this hole, a small tube of bone, bamboo or other material can be kept, so that the hole does not grow over and close.

"When the device is put into use, the owner adds whatever he prefers to elaborate and accentuate its intention. A lively range of objects can so be employed—from pigs' bristles and bamboo shavings to pieces of metal, seeds, beads and broken glass. The effect, of course, is to enlarge the diameter of the male organ inside the female."

One cannot but mark the contrast between this operation, which though dangerous is submitted to voluntarily to give pleasure to women, and the forced clitorectomy and infibulation (sewing up the vagina) which are unfortunately practiced in other parts of the world.

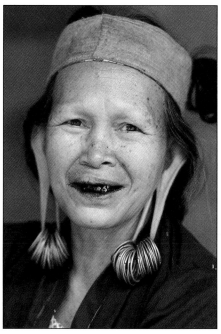

Opposite: *Tattoos were formerly strictly controlled, with certain motifs reserved for aristocracy or to reward head-hunting success. Very few young Dayaks, such as this Penihing living in the interior of Kalbar, still wear tattoos.*
Right: *Some older women still wear heavy rings in their distended lobes. The teeth of this woman, from the Apokayan, are stained with betel.*

TREK ACROSS BORNEO

Into the Heart of Kalimantan

As I pulled the third leech of the day from my groin, the inevitable question popped up again: was this worth it? Earlier in the day, squeezing out of my boots, I disturbed an even dozen leeches from their meal. Some had already gorged themselves, others were in the process of sucking their fill, with a few late-comers just starting to wiggle their way to an unoccupied spot.

We continued our trek over slippery rocks, stumbling over roots, crossing raging, waist-high rivers. As we waded yet another stream, we heard a chugging sound, like an old locomotive building up a head of steam. Then two magnificent rhinoceros hornbill birds swooped over us, huge beaks topped by bright red daubs. We watched them fly off into a majestic tree, its gargantuan trunk soaring straight up over 30 meters before the first branches broke. The question, still kicking around in my head, was answered: Yes, it was worth it.

Trekking across Kalimantan is neither a hair-raising adventure nor an easy stroll. The trail we were on normally takes the Dayaks about two to three days to cover. It took us a week. A chap who tried it recently broke a leg and had to be carried by his porters on a makeshift litter. His trek took more than three weeks.

Then there was the matter of this name-sake of mine. Major George Müller of the Dutch colonial army had crossed these mountains back in 1826, and they now bear his name. Although he was the first European to make this journey, he never completed it. Reaching the other side of the mountains, he was ambushed by a party of Dayaks, who were not then as friendly as the Dayaks of today. He had been double-crossed by the Sultan of Kutai. (See "Exploration," page 34.)

The trek I planned would take us across the central mountains of Borneo, the Müller Range, and we would walk from the Mahakam River watershed to that of the Kapuas. Our group included six Dayak porter-guides and four palefaces: an Australian, a Frenchman, a Mexican and myself. I was of course writing this book about Kalimantan, but I also had in mind to regain some of the mental and physical fiber of my younger days.

Some basic mistakes

Not keen on organizing an elaborate expedition, I kept things simple. No tents, because each evening the Dayaks would build an overnight shelter called a *pondok*. As for rations, only rice would be essential, because we were following the courses of rivers, and would be able to find plenty of fresh fish. Or so I thought.

In fact, my failure to bring a variety of food was the worst mistake I made. Each day we ate our monotonous meals in silence and post-dinner conversations often touched on succulent dishes we dreamed about. Phil yearned for a thick steak and Foster's Lager. For Irma-Maria, it was fresh seafood and beer. Jean-Claude craved croissants, butter, cheese and wine. I wanted all of the above—in triple portions.

Another mistake was the sheet of plastic I had purchased to seal the roof of our nightly *pondok*. When I showed it to our porters, they laughed: way too small, and way too flimsy. Fortunately, one of them owned a large, tough orange tarpaulin, lightweight and the right size. *Pondoks* with leaf roofs, or those with a plastic too small or too thin have a decided tendency to leak; we slept soundly under many a downpour, blessing the orange tarp every night.

From Samarinda, we flew 350 kilometers (220 mi.) inland—past the rapids—to Data Dawai. From there we traveled upriver by canoe to the last important village on the Mahakam. There we hired our porter-guides, six eager young men, each as tough as nails. They had all crossed the mountains several times before, and patiently explained that we should forget our silly paper with all the lines on it: They knew the way.

The guides explained that our route would follow a tributary of the Mahakam, then cross the mountains, and finally end on the Bungan River, which flows into the Kapuas. The path would be a well-traveled one. Indeed, on the first day of our walk, we passed a group of a dozen Dayaks, who were

Opposite: *Trekking in Kalimantan means slogging through rivers and across slippery logs.*

on their way to settle on the other side of the Müller mountains.

One old grandmother, too weak to make the trek on her own, was being carried the entire way in a basket on the back of a powerful young man. He seemed in good spirits, and completely unfazed by the burden. The bill for his services for the two-week hike was $100. Later, we thought wistfully of that basket and that strong back.

Daily regimen

Most days we walked for five hours, not counting periodic rests. Each day's jaunt ended early to give the Dayaks sufficient time to perform camp chores. As soon as the location of the overnight spot was decided, our porters quickly split into several efficient work teams.

While the *pondok* was being set up, two or three were fishing, a fire was lit and two kilos of rice set to cook. While our campsite and dinner was being prepared, we sat down exhausted, despite not carrying any loads, and considered our leech-laden boots. Our porters, fresh as daisies, bustled about.

By the time the coffee was brewed we had extracted ourselves from our boots, flicked or pulled out our leeches, and bathed in the river. The Dayaks would bring each of us a plate of rice with a small tangle of noodles and a couple of pieces of fish. Healthful, but too boring after a couple of days.

On the trail, the scenery revealed itself in infinite shades of green, a monochromatic patchwork. Only seldom did a red flower appear, and when it did it stood out in stark contrast to the rich green, immediately catching and holding our eyes. The only other splashes of color were the regiments of bright mushrooms, standing at attention in well-ordered rows on rotting trunks.

Some of the best scenery was to be found along the river banks that we followed, sometimes sloshing through the shallower sections. Trees curved overhead, occasionally touching those growing from the other bank. In places, the water was calm and muddy; elsewhere it gurgled over rocks and pebbles, and was crystal clear.

Crossing the divide

After two days of walking we crossed a low ridge in the Müller Mountains and reached the western watershed of Borneo. We stopped for a rest amidst a strange set of offerings to the spirits. A bewildering variety of clothing had been hung on the branches here or stuck on reeds.

Our guides explained that this was the place where the spirits of the Mahakam and the spirits of the Kapuas met. Anyone passing through here should leave an offering to make certain that no supernatural problems would follow. Our guides made some joking references to superstitions, but I noticed that

they discreetly added a couple of T-shirts to the spirits' wardrobe before we moved on.

We followed a creek down over a steep, slippery set of rocks and cascades. At the bottom of the mountain, the little tributary emptied into the Bungan River. Since the elevation dropped much more rapidly here than it had risen on the other side of the mountains, the water broke into rapids and waterfalls. Huge boulders created swirling whirlpools.

Continuing on, we occasionally encountered strange geological formations. These

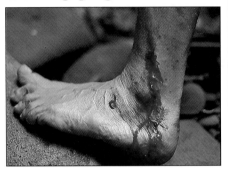

were vertical-sided outcroppings, with such steep sides that large areas were bare—even the resourceful local creepers could not find a roothold. The formations contrasted sharply with the usual sloping, green hills. One of these strange buttes was a mysterious gnarled mass of dark, deeply eroded granite. Our guides told us that there were burial caves on the far side of this formation. It was not hard to imagine these mountains as the haunt of spirits.

The vegetation, rivers and mountains were impressive, but we were disappointed by the lack of wildlife. Other than the close-up view of two magnificent hornbills, we caught only the most fleeting glimpses of a couple of wild pigs, gibbons and an unidentified, large, weasel-like creature. One thin snake and a couple of lizards completed the scant fauna on display. The king cobra, native to these parts, was the one animal we were happy to have missed.

If there were no cobras to enliven our trip, however, there were plenty of leeches, and the ever-present and always irritating ants, to keep us on our toes.

Jungle skills

We found plenty of opportunities to test our sense of balance, and we acquired confidence as the days rolled by. The straightforward uphill stretches, where one needs only maintain forward momentum and grab a tree or

root once in a while when the going gets steep, were the easiest. Downhill, the hiking was somewhat more difficult, and a walking stick proved an essential crutch. Level ground would probably be the easiest, but I don't remember crossing any.

At all times we had to be alert to lianas and roots concealed under leaves, especially when we were tired and not lifting our feet high enough. Another hazard was the thin, thorny streamers which caught on our clothing or skin. These were unnoticed at first, but after a couple steps the thorns dug in and brought forward motion to a screeching halt. Our guides had an appropriate name for these—*tunggu sebentar,* "wait a second."

The long, slippery logs that served as bridges over stretches of deep mud or chest-high rivers required a tricky balancing act to cross. Each log had to be carefully evaluated before attempting the crossing: Could the walking stick reach down far enough to offer support? What is the degree of curve of the log? How slippery is its surface? And ultimately, Is it worth risking an ignominious, ego-shattering fall or worse, a twisted ankle or broken bones? Sometimes the better part of valor required slogging through mud or receiving a good soaking.

As much as three-quarters of the walk was along the shallows at the side of rivers, or in ankle-deep creeks. And there were numberless river crossings, with the water, particularly towards the end of the trip, often waist-high. Crossing the rivers, with their strong current and slippery footing, was always flirting with disaster: one slip and you could be swept into the nearest set of rapids.

Lost in the middle of Borneo

Although at first we found the tropical jungle to be magnificent, after five days' walk we had had our fill of scenery. At this point in the trek my mind began to wander back to accounts I had read by the early explorers of the island, who described the tedium brought on by marching through seemingly interminable stretches of these beautiful, silent and motionless forests.

On the morning of the sixth day, our guides announced that by mid-afternoon we should reach the first village on the western side of the mountains. We set out early and with extra energy. By 5 p.m. we all knew something was wrong. We pushed on for another couple of hours or so, hoping to find the right trail, but finally darkness forced us to make camp. We were lost.

Our guides' apologies were not very gracefully accepted, particularly as our campsite was crawling with leeches and it had started to rain before we had a chance to set up the *pondok*. Also, we noticed that our rice supply was running out. And our feet were raw from days of walking in wet boots. Morale was very low.

But the next morning things looked better. Two of our guides had set out at the first light and found the path. Nevertheless, we faced the steep hill with a notable lack of enthusiasm. But as soon as we reached the other side, we saw some overgrown gardens—a village could not be far away. Never have I seen Dayak houses that looked more inviting than those that appeared around that curve in the Bungan River.

The joys of civilization

We settled in the home of one of our guides' relatives, and had a smooth floor to sit or sleep on and a solid roof overhead. All the little things we usually take for granted suddenly seemed like luxuries.

A large kettle appeared from the kitchen. We watched anxiously as a thick, brownish liquid was poured steaming into an assortment of cups and glasses. What could it be? Sampling the brew, we couldn't believe it: indescribably delicious hot chocolate. The advantages of a settled, quiet life never seemed so clear.

Although the difficult part of the trip was over, a personal quest remained for me. I wanted to visit the site where my "namesake" had been separated from his head, at the third set of rapids on the Bungan, above the Kapuas River. We rented a large outboard-powered canoe for the 10-hour journey downstream to the town of Putussibau.

The fateful rapids

Major Müller met his demise at the very first set of rapids we came to. When we reached the site, our boatman made us get out and walk along the sides while he powered our craft through the rapids. It was too dangerous to remain in the boat: The canoe could easily overturn with a false move. We made our way as best we could along the steep sides of a huge rock, the slipperiest one we had yet encountered. The white water thundered by below, reminding us that any slip would be our last. This was indeed a perfect place for an ambush.

I wondered what Major Müller's last thoughts were. Did he have children? Did he think of all the geographical knowledge which would be lost with him? The accounts of his death are thin on detail—just the location, and the means, a Dayak *mandau*.

As we safely finished our rock-crossing and settled in the canoe again, I reflected on how insignificant our journey had been. I thought of the explorers of the last century, men who had set out for months at a time into the interior of Borneo, without the slightest idea of what to expect from either the people or the geography.

Opposite, left: *Leeches feasted on the author's foot before meeting their maker between a rock and a hard place.* **Opposite, right:** *An elderly Dayak woman, too frail to walk, hired a carrier for the two-week journey across the mountains.*
Right: *Our party rests briefly before soldiering on through the mud and tangle of Borneo's interior.*

PART II

Introducing The East Coast

Thanks to the enormous stockpiles of oil, gas, timber and coal found here, East Kalimantan—Kaltim—is Indonesia's richest province. In the coastal cities of Samarinda, the provincial capital, and Balikpapan, a bustling oil town, the visitor can find excellent accommodations, Western-style food, and well-developed communications. Kaltim covers a staggering 211,440 square kilometers (81,637 sq. mi.). To put this in perspective, the province, which straddles the equator, could hold England and Scotland both, and have room left over. Some 1.9 million people live here, mainly on the coast.

Two hopping towns

Samarinda, the capital of the province, sits astride the Mahakam River, some 45 kilometers (28 mi.) from the sea, and is the key to inland communications and commerce. The city proudly inaugurated its first—and now indispensable—bridge in 1986. The outskirts of Samarinda are the headquarters of Kaltim's flourishing timber industry.

Balikpapan, a town built on oil, relies on efficiency and a "go-go" economy. Shops are well stocked with consumer goods. The airport under expansion is 7 kilometers (4 mi.) out of town, and hosts an endless stream of passenger jets, helicopters, and various smaller airplanes. The city's finest hotel is the splendid $25 million Benakutai Hotel, which impresses even the most finicky businessmen and travelers with it's polite, English-speaking staff, full facilities, impressive decor and gourmet restaurants.

History of Kaltim

During the rise of the powerful Hindu Majapahit Empire in East Java in the 13th century, several smaller Javanese kingdoms were destroyed or driven off the island. Refugees from one of these, called Singasari, are believed to have fled to the east coast of Borneo, founding the kingdom of Kertanegara in 1300. From 1300 to 1960, when the last sultan gave his remaining powers to the government in Jakarta, Kertanegara saw 20 rulers.

Rivalries soon developed between the trade-oriented Kertanegara kingdom and the existing Mulawarman kingdom, which was centered upstream on the Mahakam. A royal marriage between the two kingdoms kept the peace for a couple of centuries. Eventually, competition became too keen, and the two kingdoms fought: the Mulawarman army was defeated and its nobility wiped out.

By the early 1600s, Kertanegara had firmly embraced Islam, and after the defeat of the Mulawarman the new religion began to spread inland. It was perhaps also around this time that Kertanegara became known as Kutai, from the Chinese traders' *ko-tai*, meaning "faraway place" or "great country."

The *kabupaten*

There are four *kabupaten,* or provinces, in Kaltim. The largest and most populous of these is Kutai, which has as its capital the old capital of the sultanate, Tenggarong. South of Kutai is the *kabupaten* of Pasir; its capital is Tanah Grogot.

North of Kutai is the *kabupaten* of Berau with its capital at Tanjung Redeb. Blessed with several offshore islands which offer excellent beaches and snorkeling, Berau is also the home of some Bajau Sea Gyp-sies who have now settled down. Tanjung Selor, the capital of the Bulungan *kabupaten,* is near the coast, across the Kayan River from the old sultanate and palace of Tanjung Palas.

Tarakan, an island just off the north coast of Bulungan, is an important oil-producing center. The island of Penyu near Tarakan has one of the world's largest methanol plants.

Overleaf: *The fuel processed at the liquid natural gas plant at Bontang is shipped to Japan to generate electricity.* **Opposite:** *The docks of Balikpapan from the air. By Luca Invernizzi Tettoni.*

BALIKPAPAN, SAMARINDA

Kalimantan's Bustling East Coast Cities

The province of East Kalimantan exports a cool $4 billion a year, over half of which comes from oil, some 40 percent from natural gas and its byproducts (methanol, fertilizers) and about 6 percent from timber, mainly plywood. Gold, coal, huge river shrimp, cloves, copra, and a variety of agricultural products are also exported.

The coastal cities of Balikpapan and Samarinda serve as the communications and business centers of the province.

Balikpapan

Balikpapan is an oil town—big, modern and relatively expensive. There is not much here of interest to the visitor except for a hillside overview of the Pertamina Oil Complex. Balikpapan has much more nightlife than anywhere else in Kalimantan, and better restaurants and accommodations, especially

the five-star Benakutai Hotel. This city is also the best place in all of Kalimantan for transportation to and communications with the rest of Indonesia and the world.

The modernization of Balikpapan is all a product of oil money, the backbone of the area economy. In fact, when world oil prices took a nose-dive in the '80s, the city went into a slump. When oil prices rose, the economy started picking up again, and the airport has recently been expanded and the harbor has been improved.

This city of some 370,000 inhabitants retains its pre-World War II ground plan. The big refinery is next to the deep-water harbor, then comes the town proper, then the modern housing developments, covering the hills at the back of the bay, for the foreign and Indonesian oil industry employees.

The Hotel Benakutai has provided a focus in recent years for an area that has become a "downtown" of sorts, with banks, travel agencies, hotels, shops, restaurants and a market concentrated nearby. Tourism is picking up, and there is hope that it will make the local economy less dependent on world oil prices.

The people of Balikpapan are used to foreign faces, although most working expats ride around in cars. Walking tourists still attract a bit of attention. If you are in Balikpapan with a half a day to kill, check out some of the art shops and the nice view from the hillside.

LUCA INVERNIZZI TETTONI

Samarinda

The capital of Kaltim, Samarinda, is the point of departure for all river travel inland on the Mahakam river and its tributaries, as well as for flights to the interior—to the upper Mahakam and to the Apokayan region.

There are plenty of hotels in various price ranges, as well as restaurants. Samarinda is a busy place with lots of traffic, art shops for bargain hunting, and a sports complex with a swimming pool and tennis courts. This is not a bad place to spend a day or two while you organize your trip inland, or to decompress on the way out.

Samarinda was founded by Buginese warrior-merchants who migrated from South Sulawesi at the beginning of the 18th century. Today, it has grown to a city of some 290,000 and serves as both the government and commercial center of the province.

The Mahakam River, which is here almost half a mile wide and as much as 90 meters (300 ft.) deep, splits the town in half. Downstream, the river opens into a wide delta before reaching the Strait of Makassar, some 40 kilometers (25 mi.) away.

Recently a bridge has been built across the Mahakam, joining the two halves of Samarinda. This bridge stops ocean-going freighters, which call frequently at Samarinda, but coal barges still slip under the bridge to transfer their loads from upstream to ships for export. The Mahakam River in front of Samarinda is a busy highway filled with ships of all sizes and types, as well as huge log rafts heading to the nearby mills.

Beginning in the 1970s, the Samarinda economy experienced a boom in "green gold," the timber industry. There are mills both upriver and downriver from the city. Indonesia recently forbade the export of whole logs, and business at the mills has boomed, producing sawn lumber and plywood for the rest of Indonesia as well as the United States, Hong Kong and Japan.

Visiting Samarinda

Today, Samarinda is still a town full of pot-holed streets, with lots of small stores and businesses. The airport is small, and practically in town—flight paths run right over the main street. A large complex of modern shops, restaurants and food stalls, the Citra Niaga, has just been built. This spread is located just off Jalan Niaga Timur. Another modern, well-lit shopping center and restaurant complex, the Mesrah Indah, lies on Jalan

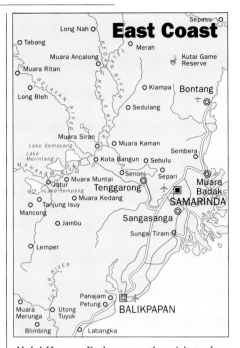

Abdul Hassan. Both are worth a visit to shop or have a cheap and tasty Indonesian meal.

A short distance upstream from downtown Samarinda is the governor's office, which dominates the riverfront. To get there, grab a colt minibus on Jalan Gajah Mada. Get off when you see some elaborate Dayak carvings off to one side, and a statue of a heroic Dayak warrior in front. About 15 kilometers (9 mi.) from town on the road to Muara Badak and Bontang is a landscaped park called the Rindana. The park, with its fruit trees and flowers, is a relief from the bustle and traffic of the city.

The Senyur Permai (also called Sumber Mas) on Jalan Diponegoro, is Samarinda's brand-new sports complex. The large swimming pool here is virtually empty during business and school hours, and the complex also offers badminton and tennis courts. Two of the tennis courts are covered, and one of them has an artificial turf surface.

If you have a few hours to kill in Samarinda, charter a boat from the dock near the taxi terminal and explore the river. You will have a great view of the town, and see huge ocean-going ships, Bugis schooners, log rafts, and smaller vessels transporting all manner of produce and goods.

Opposite: *The Benakutai Hotel, the only five-star hotel in Kalimantan, is a modern landmark in the bustling city of Balikpapan.*

Coast Cities Practicalities

City code for Balikpapan 0542; city code for Samarinda 0541; all prices in US$ unless otherwise noted.

Balikpapan

Most tours to Kalimantan originating abroad or in Jakarta include a night in Balikpapan, usually at the Benakutai Hotel, before proceeding inland. Independent travelers try to make the air connection from Balikpapan to Samarinda or head straight from the airport to the bus or taxi station for the 115-km. ride to Samarinda.

When you arrive at Sepinggan Airport, porters dressed in yellow overalls vie for your luggage. Tip them Rp 500-1,000, depending on the weight and number of bags. Just outside the baggage claim area, purchase a taxi ticket, $2.80, good for any destination in Balikpapan, 7 km. up the coast from the airport. The taxis are lined up just outside the terminal doors.

ACCOMMODATIONS

Balikpapan has plenty of hotels—at last count, 22, with 1,397 rooms. All foreigners who can afford it stay at the Benakutai Hotel. There are cheaper ones but you get what you pay for, no bargains. There is often a 21% surcharge.

Benakutai. Jalan Antasari, P.O. Box 200, Tel: 23522, Telex: 37102 BEAUTX IA, Fax: (0542) 23893, Reservations hotline: 218113, or through Beaufort International. 187 rooms in this international-class hotel, the only high-rise landmark in town, with a helipad on the roof. All and more than one would expect from a five-star hotel, the only one in Kalimantan. Airline bookings, business conference rooms, barber shop and beauty parlor, telex/fax/cable facilities, car hire, delicatessen, florist, health club, house doctor, large swimming pool etc. Beautifully designed and executed, with friendly, attentive staff. Rates range from $60 for a single to $200 for the Governor's Suite. All prices subject to 21% tax and service charge. Group discounts available.

Bahtera. Jl. A. Yani 2, Tel. 22603, 22563, 22604. Good location on the main road running parallel to the seafront. 52 clean, AC rooms with TV with video. The cheaper rooms have ladle baths. Barber shop and massage parlor—rubdowns are $7.50 per hour. Dining room open from 5:00 a.m. to 9:00 p.m. when it becomes a disco. The cover charge is higher for women than men, as elsewhere in Balikpapan. No cover for hotel guests. $20-$30, cash discount possible.

Mirama. Jl. Sutoyo 16, Tel. 22960 or 22961.

Good downtown location, 43 rooms. Restaurant, barber shop, drug store, cheap stall-type restaurants close by. Some rooms are small and without windows. $20-$30 plus 21%.

Balikpapan. Jl. Garuda, Tel. 21490. A short walk away from the main road following the coast. 33 rooms, all large and clean. All AC, color TV, icebox, conference room, dining room, night club (8:00 p.m. to 2:00 a.m.), fitness center, sauna, barber shop, massage available. $21-$27 plus 21%.

Pirsa. Jl. Sepinggan Bypass, Tel. 23048 or 22981. About 2 km from the airport. 45 rooms, all AC, attached bath, sit-down toilets. The better rooms have TV and icebox. Restaurant, massage ($6/hour), barber shop. The Tiga Kuda, said to be the hottest disco in town, produces loud music from 9:00 p.m. to 2:00 a.m.. Cover charge: $1.80 for men, $2.50 for women—remember that this is an oil town with lots of single men drawing good salaries. $20-$28.

Blue Sky. Jl. Suprapto, Tel. 22268 or 22267. Near the Pertamina complex on Balikpapan Bay. 70 rooms. Completing a renovation program which will inevitably result in higher prices. Spacious rooms with AC and TV. Dining room, conference room for up to 500. Sauna, fitness center, billiards. $15 on up.

Budiman. Jl. Antasari, near the Benakutai, Tel. 22583. 30 rooms, all AC, good location, good value. $13.

Sederhana. Jl. A. Yani 7, Tel. 22564. Actually two hotels by the same name, next to each other. The old one, with 15 rooms, outside baths and fan-cooled rooms charges $6 while the new one, with 20 rooms costs $14-$16. The higher-priced rooms have AC and TV. Lots of shops across the street.

Tirta Plaza. Jl. Panjaitan 55, Tel. 22132. 30 rooms. Not too well located on the main street running through town. A not-too-clean pool available to guests. Cafeteria. All rooms have attached toilets. Some AC, some fan, some w/icebox. $5-$9; detached bungalows, $13.

The next two hotels are low cost flophouses, not recommended unless you are in dire financial straits. Both are close to the minibus station where frequent transport is available to the inter-city bus station (to Banjarmasin or Samarinda) located just out of town.

Aida. Jl. Panjaitan 50, Tel. 21106. 35 rooms. The cheaper rooms share toilet facilities: ladle baths and squat toilets. Cafeteria. $3-$6.

Mama. Jl. Panjaitan, just past the Aida, Tel. 22104. With 12 rooms. No AC or fan, all out-of-room toilets. $3.

LOCAL TRANSPORTATION

Minibuses running on all major streets cost 15¢. The numbers on the sides mark the different routes. Just tell the driver where you want to go. If you change to another route, it's another 15¢. The taxis found outside the Benakutai and the other bigger hotels can take you just about anywhere in town for $3 one-way. AC taxis can be hired for $2.75/hour, non-AC ones for $2.50—both have a two-hour minimum. After some bargaining, you can get one of these taxis to take you all the way to Samarinda for perhaps $18-$20.

DINING

Balikpapan can boast of a delicious variety of restaurants, from the Hotel Benakutai's superb Tenggarong Grill to food hawkers who offer some dirt-cheap delights (don't look when they wash the dishes). There are lots of excellent Chinese restaurants, as well as plentiful seafood.

Benakutai Hotel. (See "Accommodations.") Three restaurants to choose from. The **Tenggarong Grill** serves international cuisine such as smoked salmon and lobster salad ($3.50), flamed lobster soup, steak or lobster ($12), duck, prawns, pork dishes ($6-$10). The **Sampan** specializes in Chinese cooking with a good menu including crab, chicken, shrimp, fish and lots of other dishes: $1.50 to $6 per dish. On the ground floor, the popular coffee shop serves a full range of Western and Indonesian food, all reasonably priced.

Atomic. Jl. Antasari, close to the Benakutai, open 10:00 a.m. to 2:00 p.m., and 4:00 p.m. to 10:00 p.m. Lots of Chinese-style variety in each of the following basics: crab, prawn, frog, chicken, pork, beef, pigeon and fish, all running in the $2.50-to-$3.50 range. Typical noodle and rice plates, $1.50-$3.00.

Hap Koen. Jl. A. Yani 19 RT 36, open from 11:00 a.m. to 3:00 p.m. and 5:00 p.m. to 10:00 p.m. Basically the same as the Atomic, not as conveniently located but fairly close to the sea. Shark fin or bird nest soup with various ingredients $2-$4. In general prices are the same or a bit lower than the Atomic.

New Shangrila. Jl. Gunung Sari Hilir (same as Jl. Sutoyo), Tel. 23124 or 22129. A 15-minute walk from the Benakutai, this is claimed by some to be the best local Chinese restaurant in town. Proof: you might have to wait for a table if you arrive between 7:30 and 9:00 p.m. Open from 10:00 a.m. to 3:00 p.m., and 5:00 to 10:00 p.m. Basically the same menu as the two above Chinese restaurants, plus "masakan special" hot plate—vegetables with pigeon eggs and either chicken, shrimp, beef or squid. *Kangkong asap,* a steamed vegetable with either chicken, shrimp or beef. Trepang (sea cucumber) also available. Shanghai-style or Cantonese chicken or duck. The prices are very reasonable.

Bondy. Jl. Sutoyo, near the Benakutai. The front is an ice-cream and pastry parlor while in the back a partially open-air restaurant specializes in *ikan bakar,* grilled fish, mostly of the *ikan mas* or carp type, swimming around in sev-eral tanks. You pay by the size, $3-$6. Other kinds of fish available, along with seafood including lobster. Local and imported steaks $3-$10. Lots of ice cream and pastry, $1 to $1.50. Nice place, tends to get crowded at peak hours in the evening.

Ikan Bakar Dalle. Jl. K. S. Tubun RT4 No. 32, just out of the downtown area on the way to the airport. Specializes in grilled fish. Prices depend on fish size and species.

Salero Minang. Jl. Gajah Madah 13, next to the hotel of the same name, opposite the bank BNI '46. Typical padang-style, lots of dishes on your table, pay only for what you eat.

Benua Patra. Jl. Yos Sudarso, past the hospital complex. A circular restaurant overlooking the sea from its second floor location: best view in town, with oil platforms at the horizon. Open 12:00 m to 2:00 p.m., and 7:00 p.m. to 10:00 p.m. Owned by Pertamina Oil, but open to the public. European, Korean, Japanese and Chinese food. Table d'hôte $10, set menu $15. Average meal $10-$20.

Barunawati. Jl. Yos Sudarso 127, just outside the harbor entrance. Excellent *sate*—try the *sate kambing* (goat) at 20¢ per brochette. Next door, the **Sari Bundo** serves an inexpensive padang-style menu.

BANKS AND MONEY CHANGING

The **Bank Dagang Negara,** across the street from the Benakutai, will change travelers' checks in a mind-boggling variety of currencies. Cash from many countries is also accepted, but bills must be in mint condition—as everywhere. Best rates here.

Balikpapan

Bank BNI '46. Jl. Gajah Madah. Accepts US$ travelers' checks from American Express, Citibank, Bank of America, Thomas Cook. The bank will change U.S., Singapore, and Australian dollars.
Bank Bumi Daya. Next to the BNI '46. Takes US$ travelers' checks from American Express, Barclays, Citicorp and Thomas Cook. Aus.$ from ANZ and Commonwealth, ¥ from Fuji Bank and £ from Barclays and Thomas Cook. Also U.S., Australian, Singapore and HK dollars, and Dutch guilders.

Bank hours: all open from 8:00 a.m. to 12:30 p.m., Monday through Thursday, with some closing at 11:30 a.m. on Friday and Saturday. Afternoon hours from 1:30 p.m. to 2:30 p.m. with the Bank Dagang Negara staying open (for money exchange only) until 4:00 p.m. All the banks are concentrated near the Benakutai Hotel on Jl. Antasari or nearby Jl. Gajah Madah.

NIGHTLIFE

Mostly at the hotels: the Bahtera, the Balikpapan and the Pirsa (see "Accommodations"). Many foreigners prefer the El Dorado (on Jl. Garuda, near the Balikpapan Hotel). Stay away from the "disco" by the harbor as fights are frequent there. Remember, this is an oil town, full of randy men with money to burn.

SHOPPING AND SOUVENIRS

There is a fair selection of contemporary Dayak crafts, reasonably priced. You can also—with luck—find good traditional carvings, cost closely following age and quality (some fakes). Chinese ceramics and ancient beads are available over a wide price range.

Blowguns (*sumpit*) are among the most common souvenirs purchased by visitors. Including a quiver with darts, they cost $30 to $60, depending on the patina and how well-made they are. (These are a hassle to carry home). Authentic baby carriers with quality beadwork run $200 to $1,200, according to the type and number of old beads, leopard fangs, bear claws and old coins complement the decorations. Carriers made for sale, with decent carvings but no beadwork or other frills, will set you back some $80 to $100. A decent Dayak *mandau* or short sword costs $150 and up, depending on the decorations. Model Dayak supercanoes full of figures cost $50 to $150 (these are much cheaper in Kalsel and Kalteng, or even at the Sarinah stores in Jakarta). A mini-set of Dayak weapons, nicely framed under glass (a most popular souvenir) sells for $25. Traditional cloth woven from vegetable fibers costs some $20. There is a lot more, including fine rattan baskets, but remember that you have to lug it all home.
Kalimantan Art Shop. Jl. Gunung Sari Hilir (also called Jl. Sutoyo) next to the Shangrila Restaurant. What you see out front gives a good idea as to the range, but if you are really interested in the best available (expensive) pieces, see the owner, Eddy Amran, and ask him to show you what he keeps in the back. Good range of Chinese ceramics, old and new Dayak carvings, craft items, beads. Eddy goes to the hinterland to buy his wares directly from the Dayaks or they bring goodies right to his shop. Open from 8:30 a.m. to 10:00 p.m. Bargaining expected here, as elsewhere.
Susilah Art Shop. Jl. Supropto 7, open 8:00 a.m. to 12:00 p.m. and 2:00 p.m. to 6:00 p.m. Mostly new things, some ceramics. Their main shop is at the Benakutai Hotel where the best pieces are kept, reasonably priced.
Martapura Art Shop. Next to the Susilah, Jl. Suprapto 40. Mostly new crafts, a bigger store with more of a selection than the Susilah (but not as good as at the Susilah at the Benakutai Hotel).

Many craft pieces can be purchased at the **Pasar Inpres** on Jalan Suprapto, quite a bit cheaper than at the art shops—if your bargaining skills are up to the challenge.

AGENCY TOURS

Several agencies provide group tours to the interior of Kaltim, emphasizing Dayak culture, often setting up traditional dances. Travel is almost exclusively on river boats which offer an occasional opportunity to see wildlife, mostly birds, but sometimes freshwater dolphins and monkeys, including the unusual proboscis. These tours start out in Balikpapan, and visitors board boats where the highway from Balikpapan reaches the Mahakam River. (For details on river tours, see "Mahakam Practicalities," page 126.)

In general, **Tomaco** tours are shorter, but more comfortable, while the other three agencies go further afield, especially **Musi Holidays**.

Aside from river tours, **Natrabu** offers a fishing package which includes a traditional boat and reef snorkeling. Minimum of four in the group, $369 per person. Musi Holidays offers group tours to Japanese and Australian soldiers who want to visit their former combat zones around Balikpapan, along with a trip to Tenggarong and the Mulawarman Museum. The same agency occasionally runs 10-day trekking tours to the remote Apokayan region, accessible only by airplane. Groups must be between 5 and 10 and the price is $575 per person.
Candra Wirapati Tours. Jl. Antasari 5, Balikpapan, Tel: 21762.
Musi Holiday Travel Service. Head office in Jakarta: Jl. Cikini Raya, Jakarta 10330, Tel: 322709 and 335509. P.O. Box 4259. In Balikpapan, at Jl. Dondang 5A (near the Benakutai) Tel: 22502.
Natrabu. Head office, Jl. Agus Salim 29A, Jakarta 3105939; in Balikpapan, on Jl. Sutoyo, Klandasan, near the Benakutai.
Tomaco Tours. In Jakarta, Jl. Thamrin 9, Tel:

347453; in Balikpapan, at the Hotel Benakutai, Tel: 21747.

AREA TRANSPORTATION

Bouraq. Jl. P. Antasari 4, Tel: 23117, 23114. Also at the Hotel Benakutai, Tel: 21107 and 21087. Twice daily to Banjarmasin ($26), three times daily to Jakarta ($115), twice daily to Manado ($120), twice daily to Palu ($32), three times daily to Samarinda ($19), three times daily to Surabaya ($56), twice daily to Tarakan ($43), once daily to Yogyakarta ($64), and once daily to Ujung Pandang ($58).

Garuda. Jl. Antasari 21, Tel: 21768, 22300, 22301. Four daily flights to Jakarta ($87); three flights weekly to Banjarmasin ($31); once daily to Palangkaraya ($35); three times weekly to Pontianak ($64)—this flight continues to Singapore for an extra $111; once daily to Surabaya ($61); once daily to Ujung Pandang ($67).

Merpati. Jl. A. Yani 29, Tel: 22380 and 24452. Four to five times daily to Samarinda, $18; twice weekly to Brunei ($160, depending on number of passengers); once daily to Surabaya ($58); once daily to Ujung Pandang ($60); once daily to Banjarmasin ($30); once daily to Jakarta ($66); and once daily to Tarakan ($45). Merpati also has flights to Berau, Data Dawai, Long Ampung and Tanjung Selor, all via Samarinda. (See below under "Samarinda.") Twice a week, there are also flights to Darwin, Australia, via Ujung Padang and Kupang.

All the above flight schedules and prices are subject to change.

Samarinda

There is a good range of hotels in town, from not quite international standards to real cheap lodgings only for the down-and-out. The proprietors of the real cheap places might be reluctant to accept foreigners, because the reporting of non-Indonesian guests can be a hassle. You get what you pay for. The cheapest hotels don't even have fans, and all the bathrooms are outside—squat-toilet and ladle-bath. The least expensive rooms in the medium-priced hotels are of this kind also. In the $6-to-$10 range, you usually get an attached bathroom, perhaps even AC. Check out the room, especially the toilet, before you settle in.

Mesra. Jl. Pahlawan 1, Tel: 21011. Best hotel in town, with 56 rooms, all with AC and color TV. Good restaurant, pool and golf. Located away from downtown but taxis available. $15-$26 S; $25-$38 D.

Swarga Indah. Jl. Sudirman 11, Tel: 22066. Downtown location, opposite the Pasar Pagi ("Morning Market"). Multi-story building with 69 rooms. Restaurant, TV, and AC. A bit gloomy, and the service in the bar and restaurant is slow. $10-$21 S; $13-$24 D.

Andhika. Jl. Agus Salim 36, Tel: 22358. 10-15 minute walk from downtown. 50 rooms, most rooms AC, with TV. Friendly staff, good restaurant. Mosque just across the street with usual loudspeakers awakens the faithful, and light-sleeping infidels. $4.50-$15 S, $6-$18 D.

Rahmad Abadi. Jl. Serindit, close to the airport with 26 rooms, all rooms fan-cooled w/attached ladle bath and squat toilet. Restaurant only serves goat or chicken *sate* at 30¢ per brochette. $4-$8 S; $10-$15 D.

Nian. Jl. Rajawali 176, Tel: 22422. A good ways from downtown, with 12 rooms, some with AC. $8-$12.

Sukarni. Jl. Panglima Batur 154, Tel: 21134. Located downtown with 35 rooms. Not too keen on having foreign guests. $4-$11 S; $8-$12 D.

Rahayu. Jl. Abdul Hassan 17, Tel: 22622. Close to downtown with 20 rooms. $3-$8 S; $6-$9 D.

Bone. Jl. Juanda 70, Tel: 22240. Near the bus-taxi terminal for Muara Badak and Bontang, with 42 rooms. $6-$7.50 S; $7.50-$9 D.

Siar. Jl. Khalid 35, no phone. Close to downtown with 35 rooms, all toilets outside rooms. $2-$3 S; $4 D.

DINING

A good variety of restaurants, all reasonably priced. Lots of bargain meals at food stalls. Not easy to find Western-type food, but try the Mesra Hotel's restaurant if you can't face another Indonesian or Chinese meal. The restaurants below are usually open from 10:30 a.m. to 3:00 p.m., and 5:00 p.m. to 10:00 p.m.

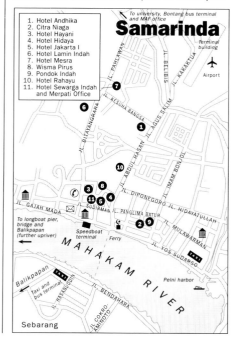

1. Hotel Andhika
2. Citra Niaga
3. Hotel Hayani
4. Hotel Hidaya
5. Hotel Jakarta I
6. Hotel Lamin Indah
7. Hotel Mesra
8. Wisma Pirus
9. Pondok Indah
10. Hotel Rahayu
11. Hotel Sewarga Indah and Merpati Office

Samarinda

Haur Gading. Jl. Sulawesi 4, specializes in grilled fish and shrimp. You pay according to weight, about $2-$3. *Nasi goreng* at $1.50. Popular place at night.

Lezat. Jl. Mulawarman. Excellent Chinese restaurant. Various soups and lots of different dishes of frog, crab, chicken, pork, squid, fish, beef, oysters and shrimp, all about $4.50. Open from 10:00 a.m. to 11:00 p.m.

Sari Wangi. Jl. Niaga Utara. Chinese place, menu less varied than at the Lezat. Fish, crab, cuttlefish $3-$3.50 each, pork and beef dishes at $2.50-$3, simple rice and noodle dishes $1.50-$2. Open 10:00 a.m. to 2:30 p.m., and 5:00 p.m. to 10:30 p.m.

Ayam Panggang Banjar. Jl. Diponegoro. Set meal of vegetables, plenty of rice and a piece of fried chicken: $1.50. Clean, Muslim-type.

Semarang. Jl. Gajah Mada. Soups and simple Indonesian dishes, $1.

Sudut Indah. Jl. Awong Long. Chinese dishes of chicken, shrimp, beef, fish, squid, crab and frog $2.75-$4. Steaks $3-$4. Indonesian dishes $1-$1.50. The AC here is welcome on a hot day.

Lembur Kuring. Jl. Bhayangkara. Roasted fish $2-$2.50, grilled shrimp $1.50-$2, chicken $1, *sate,* squid $2-$2.75. Open 12:00-3:00 p.m. and 6:00-$11:00 p.m.

Prambanan. Jl. Agus Salim. Grilled chicken $1, fish $1-$2, grilled shrimp $1-$1.50, chicken *sate,* 10 brochettes for $1.25. Beer available. Small place, clean. Fresh vegetables.

Borobudur. Jl. Agus Salim. Grilled fish, $1.50, roast chicken $1, and simple Indonesian dishes. Clean bathroom.

Mirasa. Jl. Agus Salim. Roast chicken, 50¢ to $1, and other basic Indonesian dishes. Beer available.

Gumarang. Jl. Veteran. Padang-style, $1.25-$2.50. Beer extra.

Soto Madura. Jl. Sulawesi. Excellent beef soup, rice for $1, tea included.

LOCAL TRANSPORTATION

Lots of public "taxis," i.e. minibuses, run all over town on set routes. These vehicles are called "colt." Fare is 12¢ to anywhere on the route.

Sedan taxis are found outside the better hotels and charge $1.25-$3.00 to in-town locations. They can be rented for $3 per hour, with a 2-hour minimum. Chartering colts is half this price, also with the 2-hour minimum.

SHOPPING AND SOUVENIRS

There are quite a few art shops in Samarinda selling contemporary Dayak craftworks and sculptures, as well as antique Chinese porcelain, bead necklaces and ceramic water jars. But genuine, high-quality art is very difficult to find and is priced accordingly when available: $500 and up. Lots of high-quality recent carvings such as baby carriers and spirit figures

from $50 to $200, spear-tipped blowguns at $10-$25, rattan-strip baskets $5-$25.

Most of the art shops are concentrated on Jalan Martadinata, the upriver extension of Jl. Gajah Mada. Try the **King of Dayak** store for a wide selection and the **Putra Borneo,** almost next door. Closer to downtown, the **Dewi Art Shop** is on Jl. Awang Long 21. Bargaining is expected everywhere. Ask the age of the piece, which Dayak group produced it, and its use. It is helpful to be able to speak some Indonesian both for bargaining and to find out what you are buying.

TOURISM OFFICE

Tourism Office. ("Kantor Pariwisata"). Jl. Ade Irma Suryani 1, just off Jl. Kesuma Bangsa, Tel: 21669, 22641. They are very helpful. Ask to see Pak Budiarjo.

AGENCY TOURS

Ayus Wisata is by far the best travel agency and the only one with "houseboats" set up for foreigners. Other agencies (including those in Jakarta and Balikpapan) rent Ayus' boats or an ordinary one which they spruce up with whatever is at hand for tourists. Ayus also has the most varied programs and the experience to back them up. They need advance notice to set up some of their tours.

All the agencies can set up tours for individuals or groups. Prices vary widely depending on the degree of comfort and food required, as well as the programs and number of days (see also "Mahakam Practicalities," page 126). You can also travel by regular riverboat with an English-speaking guide. We recommend that you go see the people at Ayus for helpful tips. If you can afford it, hire one of Ayus' boats for yourself and take along your friends. The Ayus I and the Ayus IV, each set up for six to nine passengers, rent for $50 a day. The Ayus II, for 14 passengers, goes for $60 a day. The largest, the Ayus III, sleeps and feeds 16 people for $90 per day. If a reserved tour has space, you can hop aboard for $12 a day.

Ayus Wisata. Jl. Agus Salim 138, Tel: 22026 or 22644, telex 38117 AYUSSRI IA.

Angkasa Express. Jl. Abu Hassan, Tel: 22098

Mansub Anindya. Jl. Sudirman, Tel: 22624

Paradisa Indah. Jl. Abu Hassan, Tel: 21750

Cisma Tour. Jl. Imam Bonjol, Tel: 21572

AREA TRANSPORTATION

Land and river

The ferry landing, past the bridge, is the departure dock for all the boats headed upstream from Samarinda, either on the Mahakam or its tributaries (to the dock from downtown, 15¢ by colt). The crowded terminal for these taxis is located just off Jl. Gajah Mada, near the Pasar Pagi ("Morning Market"). The terminal for buses and collective taxis to Balikpapan is a couple of blocks from the dock for large boats. Colts to Balikpapan charge $1, buses $1.10. In collective sedan taxis, it's $4.50 per passenger to your destination, or $3 to the taxi terminal in Balikpapan. The taxi terminal to Muara Badak and Bontang is away from the center (see map).

At the time of this writing, only 4-wheel-drive vehicles could make it all the way to Bontang overland, charging $8 per head. Prices will come down as soon as the paving of this road is completed, scheduled for 1991 if funds are available and God is willing. Prior to that, it is much easier to take a boat to Bontang. Regular boats charge $2 and take about 10 hours; faster boats make the trip in 6 hours, charging $4; speedboat charter (4 to 6 passengers) costs $175. The dock for the Muara Badak/Bontang departures is close to the Pasar Pagi.

Tenggarong, 45 km from Samarinda, can be reached either by river or land. Regular boats, taking 3 hours, charge 30¢. Chartered speedboats, one hour each way, cost about $30 for the round trip, and carry 4 to 6 passengers. By land, it's one hour by colt for 50¢, or by sedan, $4.50 per head.

The most common way to travel inland, as most natives do, is on ordinary passenger boats leaving from the ferry landing on the outskirts of Samarinda. Speedboats for four to six passengers can be chartered from the Sapulidi Company, on the river side of Gajah Mada street, opposite the Bank Rakyat.

(For boat fares upriver, see "Mahakam Practicalities," page 126.)

Air Travel

Merpati flies several times a day to Balikpapan ($18), and to three places on the coast to the north: Tarakan (daily, $46), Tanjung Selor (three times a week, $55), and Berau (daily, $49). Merpati also runs two flights into the remote interior: Data Dawai, past the worst rapids on the Mahakam (twice a week, $38), and Long Ampung, in the practically inaccessible (except by plane or days of walking) Apokayan region (twice a week, $38). There are often delays and cancellations on these interior flights and at times too many passengers for the available space. **Merpati.** Jl. Imam Bonjol 4, Tel: 23928. Reserve your flight as soon as possible.

You could also try to catch a ride on a MAF (Missionary Aviation Fellowship) flight in small Cessnas heading to really inaccessible places. No fixed schedules here and it is strictly on a seat-available basis. **MAF.** Jl. Ruhui Rahayu, Tel: 23628.

Kutai Game Reserve

With several days and a firm sense of purpose, you could try to see some wildlife at the Kutai Reserve, located to the north of Samarinda via

Bontang. If the road is not washed out, inexpensive public transportation will reach Bontang when paving is completed. Otherwise, it's by boat, which runs daily. There are hotels in Botang in which to overnight. (See "Northeast Practicalities," page 78.)

Upon arrival in Bontang, which is also the site of a huge liquified natural gas plant, head for the Nature Reserve Office, known under its Indonesian abbreviation of PHPA. You must report to this office before traveling to the park. The staff, who speak some English and are unusually helpful, will arrange a schedule to fit your time and budget. This includes boat rental and a stay in the park of any number of days.

This office will contact their field units by radio, advising them of your time of arrival. The PPA has several guard-posts in the reserve where you can sleep and (likely) purchase simple Indonesian food. The first PHPA post, Teluk Kaba, is on the coast, some 15 km from Bontang. The other posts are strung out along the Sengata River, past the village of Sengata and its Pertamina complex. The village has shops for the purchase of food and other essentials—but no film. The main PHPA unit is just up the river from Sengata village.

Facilities at the PHPA posts are most rudimentary at the moment but there has been talk of improvements. Plans are also afoot to build a road through part of the reserve, or to go around it, to reach Sangkulirang to the north from where a good dirt road has been completed to Muara Wahau in the interior.

From Samarinda by boat, it's about 5 hours and $5; by road, less than $2. Pelita (an airline belonging to Pertamina, the national oil company) occasionally flies paying passengers on a space-available basis from Balikpapan to Bontang, $40 one-way. They have several flights a day except on Sunday. At Bontang, there are accommodations in various price ranges, including the Kutai Indah ($9-$28), and even cheaper digs, down to $3 a night.

Inside the reserve, daily charges run as follows: accommodation, $2.50; each meal, $1.50 (noodles, rice and fish are typical); and guide (one guide is required for each 3 visitors), $5. It is a good idea to bring your own bedding and at least some food unless you are completely used to Indonesian fare.

The price of boat rentals varies tremendously, depending on the type of vessel and time required. A safe, motorized canoe will cost $15 to $25 for a 2-5 hour trip, while the same journey in a sleek speedboat could run $200 or more. And there are lots of intermediate craft to choose from.

BERAU

Rarely Visited Region Near Tanjung Redeb

The Berau district's 22,500 square kilometers (86,900 sq. mi.) cover the drainage basins of the Kelai and Segan Rivers, which unite to form the Berau River close to the coast. The district also includes a narrow strip of land to the south, as well as a handful of tiny off-shore islands.

There has been no tourism in this area of Kaltim, but this is the only place in Kalimantan with good beaches. There are no facilities yet for diving, but government divers have given positive reports to the reefs around the offshore islands. This small chain of islands is inhabited by Bajau. In the past, the Bajau were nomads, wandering the islands in their boats and trading sea products—shells, trepang, shark's fins, and sea turtle eggs—for rice and other essential land products.

Hook-shaped Maratua Island is the largest of the offshore island group, and forms a beautiful bay where locals used to dive for pearls. Kakaban Island has a freshwater lake, and a large variety of birds nest here. On Derawan and Samama Islands, there are many species of sea birds and turtle spawning grounds. Plans are afoot to build accommodations for visitors on Derawan Island, but for now it's homestay if you get there. To reach these islands, you first take a boat from Tanjung Redeb to Tanjung Batu on the coast (at least twice a week, $4.50). From Tanjung Batu, boats frequently leave for the various islands.

Dayaks of Berau

Scattered groups of Punan, some still following animist beliefs, live furthest inland, along the Kelai and Segah rivers and their tributaries. In the 1960s, two Kenyah groups from the Apokayan moved to this region. One group settled at Tepian Buah on the Segan River, the other at Merasa on the Kelai.

At these villages there is a fair amount of traditional carving and painting, but people no longer live in longhouses. Unless you get lucky and find a boat headed upstream, you have to charter a twin-engine outboard to reach these Kenyah villages. The trip upstream could take about 2-3 hours, and although the price is negotiable, count on $150-$350 for the round trip.

If you travel to Merasa, stop at Tumbit Dayak village on the way, home to a group of Segai Dayaks. They perform a masked rice-cycle ritual, and are unashamed of the traditional ways. Some still live in longhouses.

The Basap Dayaks, who live near the coast, can be reached from the small port town of Talisayan by motorcycle. (Incidentally, there is a motorcycle path all the way south to Sangkulirang on the Karangan River.) Some of these Dayaks have adopted the Muslim faith, but all keep some of their ancient traditions. You might find "gifts" along the river, such as chickens, rice, eggs, fruit and baskets. These are goods set out for barter, and if you take anything, leave something else of equal value, such as cigarettes, batteries, clothing, or some other city goods.

Tanjung Redeb

The town of Tanjung Redeb nestles in the spit of land between the Kelai and Segan Rivers, right at the point at which they join to form the Berau River, about 60 kilometers (40 mi.) from the sea. A part of the urban area spills over to the far side of the Segan River to form the village of Gunung Tabur, the seat of a now-defunct sultanate. Another nearby village, Sambaliung, is located on the other side of the Kelai River, the center of another old sultanate.

The shops in town are run by ethnic Chinese and Bugis, the latter group making up some 20 percent of the town's population. Most of the people are Muslims, but there is a Chinese cemetery on a hillside just off the road to the airport and a Chinese temple in town, near the Tanjung Hotel.

The Berau district takes its name from an ancient kingdom. After a civil war in 1770, the lands were split into four minor sultanates: Bulungan, Gunung Tabur, Sambaliung and Tidung. Both the powerful sultan of Sulu and his counterpart in Banjarmasin claimed this coast, but the Dutch prevailed, thanks to their control of south Borneo.

Tanjung Redeb is not particularly interesting, so take a boat across the Segan River (20¢ each way) to visit the palace of Gunung Tabur. The current building, which serves as

Opposite: *The Berau River at Tanjung Redeb.*

a museum, is an exact copy of the old palace. The original was a victim of Japanese bombs. The museum has artifacts from the palace: old European furniture, ceramics, brassware, and clothing.

There is also a very special cannon, believed to be endowed with supernatural powers. Said to have been made by the gods, the cannon was found lying in the jungle when the founder of the kingdom went for a stroll. The last sultan died in 1951, and some of his descendents live nearby.

The palace of another local sultan, Mohammed Aminuddin, was located just across the Kelai River at Sambaliung. His heirs have sold most of the furniture and furnishings, but they preserve some decaying *lontar* leaves in which the names of the royal line are recorded in Bugis script. There are also two sacred cannon, each covered with a yellow cloth, which can also heal the sick and bring luck. In fact, these are said to be stronger than the cannon at Gunung Tabur, since no Japanese bombs ever struck the Sambaliung palace.

The Dutch in Berau

In 1881 the colony of British North Borneo was created, encompassing the northern tip of the island. The southern border of this territory was vaguely defined, and reached down the east coast towards Kutai's newly found wealth. To prevent possible encroach-ments on "Dutch" territory, Holland set up a small military post at Tawau. The garrison also helped reduce slave trading and piracy, which had been rampant in the area. To consolidate the coastal administration, a controller was posted at Berau and Bulungan, and another looked after Pasir and the islands of Pulau Laut.

After some initial difficulties, the coastal border between Dutch and British territories was ratified in 1891. As no explorations had yet been made to the interior, it was only in 1912 that a joint survey team drew the inland part of the frontier.

Joseph Conrad

Captain-writer Joseph Conrad visited Borneo in 1887-1888. Sailing out of Singapore on the *S.S. Vidar*, Conrad called at Berau where he met Charles Olmeijer, the "model" for Kaspar Almayer of his first two novels: *Almayer's Folly* and *An Outcast of the Islands*. Several other Conrad novels were also partially set in Borneo: *Rescue, The Lagoon, Karain* and *Because of Dollars*. One of his masterpieces, *Lord Jim*, was inspired by the exploits of the "White Raja," James Brooke of Sarawak, but the setting of the latter part of the novel was probably based on his stay at Tanjung Redeb. Busy with trade and responsible for his ship, Conrad never stayed ashore for long and we unfortunately have little factual descriptions of Borneo from him.

BULUNGAN

Tarakan and Up the Bahau River

The huge Bulungan district includes the oil-producing island of Tarakan as well as the nearby island of Nunukan; the inland area around Long Bawan, near the border with Sarawak and Sabah; the sub-district of Long Punjungan on the Bahau River; and isolated regions in the interior including the Datu Dian area situated on the uppermost reaches of the Kayan River.

Tarakan

Tarakan, an oil-producing center on an island off northeast Kaltim, is the communications center of the northern part of the province. The town of 50,000 stretches along Tarakan Island's west coast.

If you are stuck on Tarakan, take a look at the fish market at Pasar Lingkas, spread on the pier. As befits an oil town, Tarakan has its share of money changers, bars, dance halls, movie houses, restaurants and accommodations ranging from quite good air-conditioned modern rooms to dirt-cheap *losmen*.

While oil production has lost some of its former importance, the town maintains its importance as the trading and distribution center for northern Kaltim. The booming timber industry also gives an indirect boost to Tarakan's economy.

Because of its oil fields, Tarakan was taken by Japanese forces during World War II. MacArthur sought to drive them out so he could use the airfield to support his efforts to recapture the Philippines. After a murderous pounding by Allied bombers, Australian soldiers stormed ashore. The fanatical 2,500-strong Japanese garrison put up one hell of a fight, and the casualties were shocking. All, as it was to turn out, for nothing. The landing strip was so heavily cratered by the bombing that it was declared useless.

Tanjung Selor

Tarakan is the most important town in the Bulungan district, but the political and administrative capital is Tanjung Selor, on the lower Kayan River. This was the seat of the Bulungan sultanate, with its rival, Tidung, on the other side of the river. Both the powerful sultan of Sulu in the southern Philippines and the sultan of Banjarmasin claimed this area, but the Dutch eventually squelched the conflicting claims with a colonial outpost.

Nothing is left of the old palaces—one withered away and the other was looted and burned by the Communists in 1964.

Up the Bahau River

Pak Samuel Moming keeps a well-stocked store in Long Bia and runs regular longboat trips up the Kayan and Bahau Rivers to Long Punjungan. If the water is high enough, his longboats travel as far as Long Lango, 5 hours from Long Punjungan up the Bahau River. He buys rattan from the inland Dayaks and is familiar with the upriver towns.

A river taxi runs daily to Long Bia from Tanjung Selor, and the trip takes 6 hours. Along this stretch you can see the lumber operations that are beginning to contribute to the local economy. One cubic meter of raw ebony wood goes for $320 on the coast, and with a small amount of processing, its value overseas soars to $10,000. Three villages along this stretch—Long Belua, Mara Satu and Antutan—are decorated with new, but traditional, carvings and painted rice barns and meeting halls.

From Long Bia onward, you should ride one of Pak Moming's weekly, wide-beamed longboats. These 12-meter craft are powered by three 40 HP outboards. The scenery along this river is beautiful, and the flat banks alternate with hillsides carpeted in green.

Upriver traffic does not follow the Kayan, because of the hairy rapids, but turns onto the Bahau about 4 hours out of Long Bia. From here to Long Punjungan, travel time varies widely. If the river is high, the 9 sets of rapids disappear, and the triple-engined craft powers upriver in about 5-7 hours. Otherwise, it's two days, and all the cargo is unloaded for each pass through the rapids.

It is thrilling to watch Pak Laing, who usually heads the upriver journeys, as he cranks all three engines up to full power and makes a headlong run against the rapids, weaving around rocks and foaming water, trying desperately to find a spot where there is enough water for the screaming propellers to bite. All too often, even his valiant efforts are not enough, and all able-bodied passengers help haul the boat over the rocks. Some of these rapids carry such colorful local names as "Don't Try," "Deadman" and "Stranded."

Between the rapids, the Bahau River can be mirror-smooth, reflecting a relentless equatorial sun. This is not the place to get a tan. Even fully clothed, bare hands and feet can quickly blister. Because the river here is almost uninhabited, wild animals abound:

barking deer, wild pigs, large monitor lizards and swarms of fruit bats. These creatures show themselves at their peril, however, as the boatman usually carries a rifle. This occasionally brings fresh meat to the typical rations of rice and fish.

Long Punjungan

The village is a welcome sight after the usual two days and one night from Long Bia. Long Punjungan, the "capital" of a sub-district by the same name, is a riverside town of some 400 inhabitants. The houses are built on stilts and the town is swarming with dogs which, if they prove incapable of hunting, end up in the pot themselves. The district includes 18 villages, about 3,000 people total, mostly Kenyah Dayaks although there are about 300 recently settled Punan. The schoolteachers at the Punan villages have trouble keeping the children in school, as they prefer to follow their parents into the jungle for weeks at a time, collecting camphor, *gaharu* wood and other jungle products. The Punan have not yet adjusted to settled ways, and epidemics of disease have periodically struck.

Pak Moming owns a store here, and he can provide room and board for travelers. Pak Ifung, a Dayak from the Data Dian area, runs the store and doubles as a government official. He doesn't speak English, but can arrange boats further upriver if the water is high enough.

Visiting a Punan village

There are several trips you can make out of Long Punjungan, with help from Pak Ifung. To reach the largest of the Punan villages, Long Lamei, a metropolis of 140 people, first take a riverboat to Long Apan Baru (downstream from Long Punjungan), then hike for a tough 10 hours, which takes one or two days. Hire a guide and bring your own food. At Long Lamei, you can stay with the schoolteacher, who will probably be overjoyed to have the company.

Long Alango, if the longboat cannot make it, takes two or three days in a small craft. If the people here are not too busy with their fields, they can perform a traditional dance. Although there are no set prices—as there are no tourists—you could offer to pay perhaps $50. Also, some local alcohol or "whiskey" (bottled in Java, $2) from the store could help out.

Opposite: *Loading one of Pak Moming's triple-engined longboats for the ride up the Bahau River.*

Northeast Practicalities

Overland transportation is scarce north of Samarinda. There is a 136-km. (84-mi.) road to Bontang, the liquified natural gas center, but the road goes no further, although there are plans to extend it to the coastal town of Sangkulirang. An all-weather dirt road already heads inland from Sangkulirang to Muara Wahau on the Kedang Kepala River, a tributary of the Mahakam.

A lumber road runs from Muara Wahau to Tanjung Redeb, but this thoroughfare is not recommended for any vehicles except trail motorcycles with good tires and spare fuel, plus a driver who has the ability to construct a raft to cross the rivers. Ditto for the road between Tanjung Redeb and Tanjung Selor.

Air travel is good between Balikpapan and Samarinda and the larger towns to the north. Sea travel may take long, crowded hours, with delays likely. The exception to this is the Pelni passenger boat which calls regularly at Tarakan every two weeks on its scheduled run from Java to Sulawesi.

Passenger boats run frequently in this region out of Tarakan. Riverboats travel inland various distances, usually to the last village before the rapids. Beyond that, it's by outboard powered *longbot* or canoe. Mission Aviation Fellowship (MAF) has many flights, some scheduled, to inland strips from its base in Tarakan.

Berau

GETTING THERE

From Balikpapan to Samarinda, Bouraq and Merpati have several flights a day, $24. Both Bouraq and Merpati fly daily from Samarinda to Tanjung Redeb ($47). Merpati's Twin Otters are slightly larger craft than Bouraq's Britten-Norman Trilanders.

The ride to town from the airport, 10 km. (6 mi.) costs $1.20 in a minibus. Merpati is on Jl. Pemuda, Bouraq is on Jl. Antasari.

Although there are frequent cargo ships from Samarinda to Tanjung Redeb, there is only one passenger ship a week, 36 hrs. ($20). There are two or three passengers ships a week from Tarakan, 10 hrs. ($10). An average of 4 cargo boats a month arrive here from Surabaya, Java, and you might be able to catch an inexpensive ride on one of these ships.

LOCAL TRANSPORTATION

Around-town transport is by *becak,* about (15¢)

to any destination. Same price to cross either river. An hour or two's river ride, including waiting time while you visit the two "palaces," costs $2 after some bargaining.

ACCOMMODATIONS

A new hotel, to be called **Citra Indah**, is under construction. It is planned to have 35 rooms, of which 15 or more will be AC, the only ones in town to have this luxury. Planned price: $20 w/AC; $9 w/o AC. A restaurant is also planned, to serve Indonesian and Chinese meals and cold beer.

Herlina. Jl. Kartini. 25 rooms Currently the best hotel in town, quiet unless there is a Muslim wedding reception here. Indonesian meals available. Showy wedding paraphernalia are on permanent display. $9 w/attached toilet/bath and meals; $6 w/shared toilet. Deduct $3 if you eat out.

Kartika. Jl. Antasari. 15 rooms Across from the Citra Indah hotel. All shared facilities. $3.50 w/meals; $2 w/o meals.

Berlian. Jl. Antasari. 10 rooms Meals 90¢. $3.25 w/attached toilet/bath; $1.50 w/shared facilities.

Tanjung. Jl. Niaga. 12 rooms Best restaurant in town is downstairs, serving Chinese and Indonesian meals ($1-$3). Shared toilets. $3, including breakfast.

Rahayu. Jl. Antasari. 14 rooms No meals, but there are *warungs* across the street. $3 w/attached toilet; $2 w/shared toilet.

Wisata. Jl. Maulana. 15 rooms Meals $3/day. $3 w/attached toilet; $2 w/shared toilet.

Nirwana. Jl. Aminuddia. 17 rooms. $3 w/breakfast.

Rahmat. Jl. Panglima Batur. 9 rms, more under construction. Shared facilities. $3 w/meals; $1.50 w/o meals.

Sederhana. Jl. Pelabuhan. 13 rooms Meals can be ordered ($1.25) and all rooms have shared toilet. $2.

Other areas

Bontang, the access point for the Kutai Game Reserve, has 11 hotels including the nice **Kutai Indah**, $9-$22 S; $20-$28 D. The other lodgings are considerably cheaper, meant for local LNG workers.

The Pasir district has 8 *losmen*, all in Tanah Grogot.

Malinau has 4 *losmen*, Nunukan has 8, all $2-$5/night.

DINING

While most of Tanjung Redeb's hotels provide meals, you can still eat out for variety's sake. Try the restaurant at the **Tanjung**, or the **Warung Syukur** on Jl. Durian, across from the movie house. Indonesian meals, $1.75, large bottle of beer, $1.40.

Tarakan

City code for Tarakan, 551.

From Balikpapan, Bouraq flies twice a day and Merpati once a day to Tarakan ($55). Both Bouraq and Merpati fly daily from Samarinda to Tarakan ($33).

ACCOMMODATIONS

Tarakan Plaza. Jl. Yos Sudarso, Tel: 2187, Telex: 38316. 50 rms. Restaurant, bar, all airconditioned rooms. Best in town by far. $30; $45 for VIP room. **Bahtera**. Jl. Sulawesi, Tel: 21821. 34 rms. All AC. Favored by Malaysians and Filipinos in the timber industry. This and the Oriental are on the edge of town next to a girlie bar, a short walk from the end of the taxi route and just beyond the Catholic church. $12; $17 VIP room. **Oriental**. Jl. Sulawesi, Tel: 21348. 7 AC rms. $11. There are half a dozen inexpensive hotels ($4-7 w/fan-cooled rms.) next to each other on Jl. Sudirman, a short way from Jl. Yos Sudarso. On Jl. Yos Sudarso, the somewhat seedy **Taufiq** charges $3 for a bare room. Slightly better is the nearby **Indah**, $4-6.

DINING

The best restaurant in town is at the Tarakan Plaza Hotel, but for inexpensive Chinese food and seafood ($2-4), try the **Cahaya**, Jl. Sudirman, opposite the *losmen* Jakarta. There are plenty of grilled fish joints and *warung*s serving simple Indonesian meals, very cheap.

The Nirwana complex, on Jl. Yos Sudarso towards the airport, has an outdoor restaurant, bar, disco and a gang of pretty bar girls. Nothing much happens here before 10 p.m. and the place closes at 2 am.

BANKS AND MONEY-CHANGING

There are lots of money-changers in town and the major banks handle foreign currency—bills must be perfect—and travelers' checks.

REGIONAL TRANSPORTATION

From Tarakan, Merpati flies 4 times a week to Nunukan Island ($27), and 3 times a week to Long Bawang ($36). Bouraq flies 3 times a week to Tawau in Sabah, East Malaysia ($36), but you cannot take this flight if you are traveling on a 2-month tourist visa.

Missionary Aviation Fellowship (MAF) flies its 4-passenger Cessnas to various inland destinations: Malinau, 3 times a week ($18); Long Bawan, 3 times a week ($36); Long Nawang in the Apokayan, 2 times a week, ($60); Data Dian, two times a week ($55); Tanjung Selor, 2 times a week ($8). These flights are on a space-available basis, and mission business takes priority. You can also charter a MAF plane for $95/hr, it's about one hour to Long Bawan, but if there is nothing for the plane to pick up there, you pay for the return as well.

Bouraq. Jl. Yos Sudarso 133, Tel: 21248, 21987.
Merpati. Jl. Yos Sudarso 10, Tel: 21911, 21908.
MAF. Jl. Jend. Sudirman, in the Tax Building (Kantor Pajak), Tel: 21181. You can also call the chief pilot at home, even from outside the country, to make arrangements. Call at least three weeks in advance, Tel. 21994.

By boat

Once or twice a day to Tanjung Selor, 3-4 hrs, $2.50; every other day to Malinau, 10-12 hrs, $5; twice weekly to Berau, 12 hrs, $9.50; daily to Bunyu Island, 2.5 hrs, $2.50.

Bulungan

ACCOMMODATIONS

Gracias. Right off the dock. Best of the lot. 14 rooms. AC rooms $9, fan-cooled, $5.
Hotel Asooy. Across the street from the Gracias. 10 rooms. Pak Samuel Moming's place (see "Transportation" below). $5 w/attached bath, $2.50 w/shared bath.
Bahagia. Next to the Gracias. 12 rooms, $3-4 w/shared bath.
Bulungan Hotel. Opposite a mosque. 12 rooms. $2-4.
Wisata Hotel. On the main street, opposite the fish market. 8 rooms, $1.30 w/shared bath.
Bulungan Indah. At the end of the riverside road, near the vegetable market. 8 rooms. $1.30 w/shared bath.

Upriver, at both Long Bia and Long Punjungan, Pak Moming charges $3 for a room and excellent meals.

DINING

The Gracias. Chinese and Indonesian meals $1-3, and beer (over ice) for $1/can.
Cempaka Warung. In front of the Asooy, part of the dock area. Indonesian meals, 50¢-$1.20.

River transportation

See Pak Moming at the Hotel Asooy for upriver travel. Tanjung Selor to Long Bia, 6-8 hrs (daily, $6); Long Bia to Long Punjungan (weekly, $18)—charter, with room for up to 10 people w/gear, $300; Long Punjungan to Long Alango (monthly, $5)—charter, $30-60; Long Punjungan to Long Gelat, 6 hrs. (charter, $90 rt); Long Bia to Naha Kamang, the limit of longboat travel on the Kayan River, 10 hrs. (charter, $150 rt).

GUIDES

Darius Naming (one of Pak Moming's sons) is an fine guide and speaks English. If he is available, $6/day. Other guides and porters can also be hired, $3/day. Stock up at Pak Moming's stores before your trip, his goods are the cheapest in Long Bia.

PART III

Introducing
The Apokayan

The Apokayan region of Kalimantan is the area around the headwaters of the Kayan River, near the border with Sarawak. This area, together with the upper Mahakam, is the home of some of Kalimantan's most traditional Dayaks, and the recent ease of access to the Apokayan makes it perhaps the best place in all of Kalimantan to see the Dayak way of life.

Because fierce rapids cut the Apokayan off from the rest of the Kayan River, there has been no commercial logging in the region, and the ecology here remains in balance. Bird watchers can rent a canoe, motor a short way up a tributary, and from there paddle quietly to "paradise." Wild pigs, birds and deer (including the unique muntjak or barking deer) can be seen just from the footpaths that connect villages.

A great exodus

The population of the Apokayan region has shrunk drastically in the past three decades. In the 28 years between 1954 and 1982, the the area lost 25,000 people, and only about 5,300 remain today. A shortage of arable land reasonably close to the villages, and the high cost of even basic commodities—which had to be hauled laboriously upstream and portaged around the rapids—led the Dayaks to pack up and move. Today, the villages of the Apokayan vary between 40 and 800 inhabitants, far fewer than in the past.

One of the first groups to leave were about 1,800 people from the area of Long Betaoh who trekked for three days across the mountains to settle in Long Musang in Sarawak. Others stayed in Indonesian Borneo and built new villages on the mid-Mahakam and its tributaries. The main areas chosen for resettlement are: the villages of Ritan Baru, Bila Talang and Tanjung Manis around Tabang; Miau Baru village near Muara Wahau; the villages of Long Segar, Long Noran and Gemar Baru near Muara Ancalong;

and the villages of Rukun Damai, Batu Majang and Data Bilang, which are near Long Bagun.

The migrations were led by the nobles and involved entire longhouses, sometimes several of them, often a total of 800 Kenyah Dayaks at one go. The routes and final settling places, in areas of scant or no existing population, were carefully scouted. It usually took one year—and up to three years—to reach the sites of the new homes, with rice planted and harvested along the way.

For those remaining in the Apokayan, the situation began to improve in the early 1970s, when the people built several airstrips and the skilled pilots of the Missionary Aviation Fellowship (MAF) began regular flights to the region. (The first airplane ever to land in the region was piloted by missionary George Fiske, who landed his hydroplane here in 1940.) Even with the missionary flights, however, the price of goods flown in was still prohibitive for all but government officials and the wealthy few, as were passenger fares.

Only in 1986, when a longer airstrip was completed at Long Ampung, and Merpati began government-subsidized flights with Twin Otters, did the cost of passage and goods become affordable. Cargo on Merpati was only 20 percent of what MAF charges, and passenger fares some 30 percent.

Now that there is plenty of land, regular air service, and government-built schools, the exodus from the Apokayan seems to have ended. Still, the remote region faces some problems. Teachers, as well as doctors and medicine, are still either in very short supply or are nonexistent. Some government money is beginning to find its way into the area, giving the economy a boost through local

Overleaf: A Kenyah dancer wearing a headdress of hornbill and pheasant feathers. **Opposite:** A Dayak woman poses with her prized rooster in Long Betaoh, a remote village in the Apokayan.

staffing of government offices and building "roads"—actually wide footpaths. The subsidized Merpati flights could well become the decisive factor in the government's aim to prevent further depopulation of its border with Sarawak.

The Apokayan today

The region is made up of two administrative districts or *kecamatan:* Kayan Hulu ("upstream") and Kayan Hilir ("downstream"). Kayan Hulu has a population of 4,500; Hilir just 800. The population of Kayan Hulu is all Kenyah, while three-quarters of the people of Kayan Hilir are Kayan. About 75 percent of the Dayaks of the Apokayan are Protestant, the rest Catholic. The beginnings of the

Catholic missionary effort in 1967 coincided with the official end of the animist religion, although a widespread belief in spirits and some of the old practices remain.

The land here is some of the best in East Kalimantan, and dry (unirrigated) rice agriculture often produces a surplus. But rice is quite vulnerable to drought or early rains, and the changeable weather can ruin a year's rice crop. There is no starvation, however, as resistant tuber crops such as yams and manioc or sago trees from the jungle keep bellies full until the next rice crop.

Some cash enters the region from the sale of jungle products: damar resin (up to 10 tons a year); the fragrant aloeswood, *gaharu* (some six tons a year of various qualities);

and gold (some three kilos a year). The region's abundant rattan is little exploited at the moment because of difficulties in hauling it out of the highlands, but it represents a promising source of income for the future.

Many parts of the Apokayan lack cash-producing exports, and the people there have a hard time buying essentials such as soap, cooking oil or gasoline for outboards. All these materials still cost much more here than in the coastal cities. The main cash income in the Apokayan comes from jobs in Sarawak. A few years ago there were 300 to 400 men working in Sarawak—some single, some with families—from Kayan Hulu alone.

Impassible rapids

The Kayan River is passable through the highlands, but it becomes a swift and dangerous rapids before meandering past the town of Tanjung Selor and finally emptying into the Strait of Makassar. Brem-Brem, or Giram Ambun—"The Rapids of Spray"—stretch 33 kilometers (20 mi.), and no one has ever made it alive through the foaming, roaring waters. In the 1930s a run was attempted by eight experienced Dayaks, some of the most experienced river runners in Borneo. They all drowned in the attempt.

The rapids sever the Apokayan from river trade with the district capital of Tanjung Selor as well as Long Bia, the last upriver settlement where goods can be bought cheaply, because it is the last point to which the Kayan River is still navigable.

During colonial times, a two-meter-wide path was cut around Giram Ambun in order to bring in supplies. In the 1920s and '30s, Dutch colonial government boats and crews were stationed on either side of the rapids to ensure a smooth flow of supplies. Porters and paddlers shuttled up to 12 one-ton boatloads at a time from the beginning of the rapids to Long Nawang. Everyone was well paid, and subsidized merchandise flowed into the Apokayan. After World War II and Indonesian independence, the path around the rapids was no longer kept up, and has today become almost impassable.

History of the Apokayan

According to a consensus of Kenyah elders in Long Nawang, their ancestors originally migrated to the Apokayan from the Belaga River area of Sarawak. They left their downriver settlement because of widespread Iban

Above: *Husking rice in front of the longhouse.*

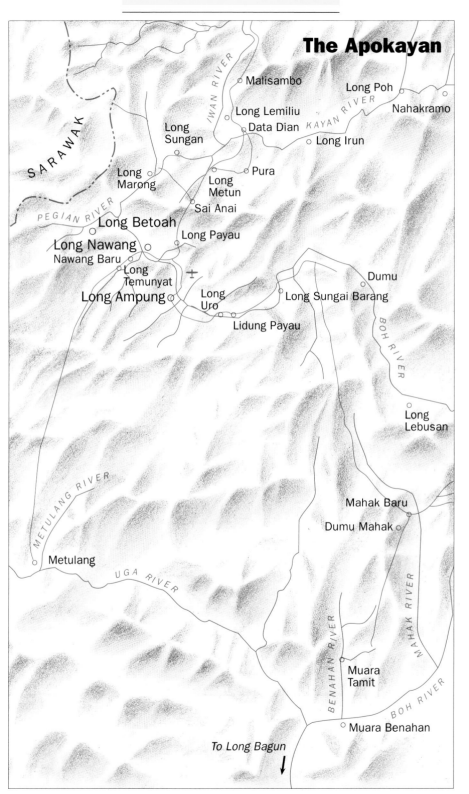

The Apokayan

head-hunting raids. This migration took place three generations before the first Dutch visit to the region in 1901. Scattered groups of Kayan already had already made their home there—indeed, "Apokayan" means "The High Plateau of the Kayan River." Wars were fought between the immigrant Kenyahs and the Kayan, although on a small scale, and eventually the more numerous and better-organized Kenyah dominated the area.

Ethnographic accounts tell a slightly different story, and state that up until the 18th century, downriver Kenyah settled among the Kayan in the Bahau River area to the north of the Apokayan. Here they were partially "civilized" by the more sophisticated and less warlike Kayan. Following the Kayan diaspora of the latter half of the 18th century, the Kenyah then eased their way south into the Apokayan.

Social hierarchy is still important in the Apokayan, although not nearly as much as it was before Indonesia's independence. The members of the former aristocracy still command respect, and in some cases free labor for their fields, and they tend to be the village leaders. Today, marriages between classes are frequent, especially since the bride price has virtually disappeared.

In the past, the Apokayan was self-sufficient in all essentials except salt. There was trade in a few valuable, high-priced goods, such as beads, Chinese ceramics and gongs,

for which the Kenyah traded jungle products—aloeswood, bezoar stones, rhino horns and camphor. Salt was brought to the Apokayan from either the coastal regions or the Kelabit highlands, now located in Sarawak.

The Apokayan fell within the vague inland claims of the sultan of Bulungan, who resided at Tanjung Selor. However, the sultan's control effectively stopped at the rapids separating the lowlands from the highlands.

The Dutch and Christianity

In 1901 the first Dutchman, an official of the colonial government, trekked and canoed into the Apokayan from the Mahakam basin. At the time, the administrators of the Netherlands Indies were anxious to squelch the supposed territorial ambitions of Raja Brooke and the spread of British influence from Sarawak, sometimes spearheaded by Iban head-hunters who may have operated with Raja Brooke's unofficial approval.

In 1907, the Dutch established a temporary post at Long Nawang, the strategic center of the Apokayan, and by 1911 had stationed a permanent military garrison there. The troops were partially a response to accu-

Above: *Dayak villagers planting a hillside* ladang *in the Apokayan.* **Opposite:** *A still-smoldering* ladang, *which has been cut and burned in preparation to planting rice. The ash from the burnt brush enriches the thin soil.*

sations by the Sarawak government that "Dutch" Kenyahs were conducting raids into British territory. To simplify administration, the Dutch made the chief of Long Nawang the leader of all the Apokayan and held him responsible for ending head-hunting there.

In 1924, an international conference was held in Kapit, Sarawak. Seated at the table were representatives of the Dutch government, Sarawak authorities, Kenyah chiefs, Iban representatives and emissaries from other Dayak groups. A formal peace hammered out here between the traditionally warring groups was accepted by the Dayaks, and organized head-hunting raids ended. Although scattered incidences of freelance head-hunting remained, by the 1930s, these had ended as well.

Missionaries began their work of Christianizing the Apokayan in 1921. Five Dutch officers were permanently stationed at Long Nawang, together with about 70 colonial army soldiers from Ambon, Manado and Java. In 1929, the U.S.-based Christian and Missionary Alliance supported missionary George Fiske and his family—first in Tarakan, then in Tanjung Selor. Fiske was a particularly zealous Protestant, and his work bore fruit. As Christianity took hold in the region, the irreconcilable differences between the new religion and the traditional beliefs resulted in trauma, as villages split and some of their members moved away.

In 1947, a nominal Christian belonging to the Lepo Jalan group, had a dream. The goddess Bungan Malan appeared and demanded a simplified version of the traditional religion, with none of the onerous obligations of the old faith, and herself as the Supreme Deity. The only offerings required would be eggs.

The dream led to the Bungan Cult, which also advocated simplifying the hierarchical social structure. The Bungan Cult did not enjoy much success in the Apokayan. Some visiting Kenyah and Kayan aristocrats from Sarawak were attracted to the new belief, however, and took the teachings home with them. From there it eventually enjoyed considerable diffusion, with some followers maintaining the cult to the present.

The Japanese invasion

When the Japanese invaded Borneo in 1942, groups of Dutch, both civilians and soldiers, made their way from the coast to Long Nawang. All told, about 150 Europeans gathered there, believing themselves safely hidden. But the Japanese eventually sent soldiers there, and the Europeans were executed. (See "Recent History," page 36.)

During a brief military confrontation with Malaysia in the 1960s, about 100 Indonesian soldiers were stationed in Long Nawang. After the confrontation ended, most of the soldiers went home, leaving only a small contingent to hold down the fort.

VISITING THE APOKAYAN

The Art and Longhouses of the Kenyah

The group of elderly Kenyah women, their enormous earlobes weighed down with dozens of heavy brass rings, edged closer, talking excitedly among themselves. When Irene, my art trader-dealer friend, pulled out her string of beads, their usual reserve vanished. She had just played her conversational trump card, a string of 84 rare trade beads.

The women fondled the old beads with a mixture of respect and admiration. Each bead had a name of its own, either male or female, and there were hundreds of names for the trade beads that came to Borneo from Europe, Africa, China and India. Here in the Apokayan, trade beads formerly were an essential element of the bride price for aristocrats. Sometimes a single bead could be worth "a whole village," or at least a longhouse with its hundred or so inhabitants. (See photograph on page 26.)

Today, most of the beads have disappeared from the Apokayan. Traders snapped them up, knowing full well their ludicrous value to a special breed of fanatic—the bead collector. Still, a few valuable old beads remain as heirlooms, strung as necklaces or decorating baby carriers.

Although there are few valuable ancient beads left in the Apokayan, the region remains one of the most traditional in Kalimantan. Many of the Kenyah here still live in longhouses, although some of these sport imaginative new decorations mixed in with the ancient motifs. The aristocratic class here retains a large measure of the respect and power from the old days.

Long Ampung

A pair of communal rice barns perched on stilts brightened our passage, their planked sides painted with a fanciful sun sprouting a profusion of curved tendrils. The residence of the chief, which doubles as a community meeting hall, is fronted by a wide, open-sided room. The back wall of this room is covered with a long mural in which the traditional is mixed with the modern—in one scene a hunter, wearing shorts, bags a wild pig with his blowgun. Tacked to the wall on one side are prints of Jesus and Indonesian political figures, keeping a watchful eye on the room.

The roof of the meeting hall was alive with wooden animals and figures. The centerpiece

is the torso of a mustachioed foreigner wearing a baseball cap. He has thrown up his hands, and wears a loony, startled expression. The hall is protected by a tall wooden pole, topped by a warrior brandishing his sword, standing in front. This *belawang* is a holdover from the Kenyah's head-hunting past.

Food and dance

Dinner that evening was rice with tasty pieces of deer meat and wild boar, accompanied by hot sauce. A heap of pineapple

chunks provided dessert. After we had sated our appetites, we had the pleasure of being treated to a surprise show.

The first act was a group dance by girls dressed in an assortment of traditional and Western clothes. Following this, individuals got up and mime-danced solo. The women executed delicate, fluttering bird dances, and the men, resplendent in leopard skins, beaded headdresses and decorated shields, wielded their Dayak *mandaus* in a dance of wild, mimed combat.

Young men provided musical accompaniment on two outsized string instruments called *sape,* and male and female voices harmonized from across opposite sides of the meeting hall porch between dance numbers. Polaroid photographs of the event greatly aided public relations.

By the time everyone had drifted away after the dances, it was getting darn cold. Although we were almost on the equator, we were also more than 800 meters (2,600 ft.) above sea level. Since we had no sleeping bags, we curled up under thin blankets wearing every article of clothing we had brought along in our bags.

Trek to Long Nawang

We decided in the morning to head to Long Nawang, the district administrative center, to check in with the police and the district head, called the *camat*. Shortly after dawn, the

chief arrived with a most welcome pot of hot tea, into which he dumped heaps of sugar. When we told him our plans, he shook his head. There were no canoes available, either with an engine or just human paddle-power.

But, the chief told us, a good trail had been hacked to Long Nawang, and the walk, mostly along the river, would take us some five hours. Porters could be arranged for our luggage. The headman warned us, however, that the walk was not easy. Some Indonesian bureaucrats had tried it recently, he said, and collapsed from exhaustion. They were eventually rescued by canoe.

By the time we left, the sun was scorching hot. The path was wide enough for a jeep, but not well enough compacted or graded to support a vehicle. As the trail followed the curves of the Kayan River, the ground was level. After an hour, we crossed a tributary and stopped for a drink and a cigarette. That was the end of the party. The rest of the way was through hill country, and involved lots of climbing. The path had been cleared of trees on both sides to keep the mud dry, and we found no shade under the tropical sun. We lowered our heads, ignored the scenery, and trudged ahead in a bath of perspiration.

After a couple of hours the trail cut back down to the river's edge and we took a break. Life became easy again. We crossed a couple of streams, just when we were becoming thirsty. The trail then opened onto a recently cleared and burned *ladang*, and we met a family eating their midday meal in a lean-to. After declining their hospitality several

*Opposite: A woman at Long Nawang strings beads for a baby carrier. These carriers are often decorated with the family's collection of heirloom beads, old coins, and other items. The claws and teeth of wild animals, honey bears and clouded leopards, are added to protect the tender young one inside. **Above:** These sun hats are topped by excellent Dayak beadwork.*

times—as good manners required—we allowed ourselves to be persuaded to join in. The man had killed a wild boar that morning with his spear and dogs. Refreshed and satiated, the rest of the walk, over level ground, was a breeze. We checked in with the police and the *camat,* and the latter offered us hospitality and a tour of Long Nawang.

Long Nawang, with a current population of 800, was the seat of the former Dutch colonial administration for the Apokayan. A contingent of Indonesian soldiers is quartered here. As part of the current policy of cooperation between the army and the people, military engineers built a solid bridge over the Kayan River at Long Nawang. The next morning we crossed this bridge and headed for Nawang Baru.

Nawang Baru

On the way to Nawang Baru, we met two Dayak women whom I convinced to pose for my camera. Heavy metal rings stretched their earlobes. A bit further on, we passed a cemetery for aristocrats, where the tombs were marked by carved and brightly colored wooden markers, curving up to well over three meters. Chopping back a bit of grass at the base of one of these "tombstones" revealed a snarling wooden feline.

We reached Nawang Baru by crossing a rickety, swaying suspension bridge, which was perfectly safe, but still brought on some

adrenaline. The *camat* led the way to a nearby longhouse, the spacious front porch of which served as the village meeting hall. The back wall was covered in a long, complex painting, and a large wooden sculpture of a Dayak warrior sat in the center.

The decoration of the roof here was traditional—a baroque mass of loops and swirls. The sides of a communal rice barn nearby were painted in the same traditional Kenyah style. Most of Nawang Baru's population lives in several longhouses, but these traditional shelters are beginning to give way here to individual family dwellings.

We arrived during rice-planting season, and Nawang Baru was almost deserted. In our stroll around the village, we saw an old man weaving an all-purpose basket from strips of rattan, and a woman who was crafting a tiny mosaic of beads for the back of a baby carrier.

The *camat* told us that the village of Nawang Baru split from Long Nawang in 1952 as a result of a religious schism. Those who settled Nawang Baru wanted to retain the traditional faith, but they are all Christian now. A similar split occurred earlier, in 1930, when a group from Long Nawang established the village of Long Temunyat, just a few minutes' walk past Nawang Baru.

We walked to Long Temunyat with the *camat,* and although there is not much art there, the wall painting in the longhouse's

meeting hall is itself worth the short walk. When we returned to Long Nawang, there was still enough time for a look at the grave of the region's paramount chief. A path was cleared for us, and the dilapidated tomb appeared in its macabre splendor.

Two massive coffins rested on a high platform raised three meters above the ground on thick ironwood posts. One of the coffins had broken open, and a skull hung down, suspended somehow by a rotting strip of cloth. Time and the termites had done their jobs well.

Built in the early 1940s, this was the tomb of a high aristocrat (and his wife) who had been the chief of traditions for the entire Apokayan region. Some 45 years after what must have been a splendid burial, the structure was on the verge of collapse. We saw one clue to the status of the deceased: a large Chinese dragon jar was lying, broken, under the platform.

By river to Long Betaoh

The next morning we eased ourselves and our cameras into a long, slim craft. The gunwales of the canoe couldn't have been more than a couple of millimeters above water level. Soon the motor roared to life and our boatman eased the shaft of the horizontal outboard into the swiftly flowing water. As soon as the propeller bit we picked up speed and the craft stabilized. We could then relax and shift about a bit without the constant fear of overturning.

The first leg of our journey took us about an hour downstream on the Kayan River. We shot through several minor rapids with our lookout in the front expertly pushing the bow off dangerous rocks with his pole.

At one particularly bad set of rapids, our guide had us get out—not because he didn't think he could manage, but because he was afraid his passengers might panic in the rushing water and upset the boat.

We turned off the Kayan and motored up the Betaoh, one of its tributaries. Our travels took place at the end of the dry season, and the river was too low in several places for the loaded canoe. At these we got out and tromped ahead through the shallow water. Despite the slippery footing, this provided a welcome break, as our backsides had been numbed by the hard planks. We took the opportunity here to have a smoke and wolf down a pack of uncooked instant noodles.

Rounding a bend in the river, we saw sev-

eral canoes on the bank and glimpsed a few roofs above the vegetation—we had reached Long Betaoh. We were taken first to the chief's stilted house. News of our visit must have spread fast, and in just a few minutes the house was full of people.

Long Betaoh

As I chatted with the chief, everyone listened politely. The chief said he and his people were very pleased to welcome us, especially since we were the first outsiders who spoke Indonesian ever to visit Long Betaoh. Soon a couple of plates heaped with rice and pork materialized. I gave the chief our instant noodles along with several packs of cigarettes, which are always a welcome gift in out-of-the-way places.

The headman told us that there were only about 100 people left in Long Betaoh, as just about everyone in the area had left several years ago to settle in Sarawak, where supplies were available and much cheaper than in the Apokayan. Sarawak also offered relatively well-paying jobs, especially with the logging companies.

Opposite: *The longhouse at Long Ampung. The Kenyah are famous for an art style that features spiraling designs that are abstract "god-faces" or asoq, the dragon-dog.* **Above:** *The Long Ampung longhouse's roof decorations provide a bit of comedy and a modern touch.*

Now that the population had thinned out, however, the remaining people no longer planned on moving, he said. There was now plenty of good land available close to the village for growing rice, and with many fewer hunters, game was beginning return to the forest. Supplies such as soap and kerosene could be obtained with an occasional trek into Sarawak or, he said, they could just do without.

Both Irene and I wanted to stay, feeling the goodwill and warmth of this village. But our boatman was getting anxious to leave, because he wanted to be back before dark. The whole village came down to the river to see us off, waving until we disappeared behind the first bend.

After a few minutes the engine was turned off, as our canoe man was afraid of damaging the propeller on the rocks. He shifted forward and started paddling, his muscles rippling under Irene's admiring gaze. Having learned a few things about beads in spite of myself, I teased my partner that had she but arrived a few years earlier, she could have paid the headman one of her finer beads and bought that whole hunk of brawn for her personal slave.

The silent ride was a treat after the infernal din of the engine. We glided under a canopy of trees whose branches reached from one bank to another to form an enchanted tunnel. Unseen birds called out singly or joined in chorus with their kin. An occasional fish broke the surface.

Because we were anxious to visit other villages, the next day found us buzzing upstream. After a couple of hours, we passed Long Ampung, above which the shallows became more frequent. At Long Uro the canoe could go no further, and we found porters to the next village. On the way, we stopped to visit a cemetery where the tombs were topped by an assortment of grave markers including such modern touches as an air-

plane and a chainsaw, among the more traditional birds and fish.

Lidung Payau and a strange statue

We found the chief at Lidung Payau and talked with him for a while. Most of the village's 322 people, he said, slept in the five longhouses. Only the schoolteacher and two families had opted for individual residences. An aristocrat occupied the central and most spacious apartment of each longhouse. A wide, communal front porch runs the length

of the longhouses, and is where most of the village activity takes place—husking rice, playing with the children, stringing beads and weaving, and just chatting. Even the dogs choose the porch for their naps.

Before turning in for the day, we asked the chief to arrange for a couple of porters for the following day to take us to the last village upstream, and to the site of an old stone statue we had heard was nearby. The porters were no problem, but the chief was noticeably reluctant to talk about the statue. Furthermore, his estimates as to the statue's distance seemed to change from four hours to eight hours as soon as he found out that we had to be back in Lidung Payau that same evening to catch the week's only flight back to the coast. Strange.

We woke at dawn, and our two porters were already squatting nearby, anxious to get started. A few handfuls of cold rice and we were on our way.

As soon as we were out of the village, I

Above, left: *Kenyah grave markers in the cemetery between Long Uro and Lidung Payau. One is topped by the traditional hornbill; the other by the not-so-traditional chainsaw.* **Above, right:** *This mysterious stone carving, near Lidung Payau village, was probably worshipped until recent times.* **Opposite:** *This talented hunter, who had taken a deer with his blowgun and dogs, saved us from yet another dinner of rice and bony fish.*

told our guides that I wanted to see the statue on the way out. They suggested we try to find it on the way back, probably hoping that we would be too tired for the detour. I insisted obstinately that it be on the way out. Sometimes hard-headedness gets results. In a few minutes the guides told us to wait and went off in a new direction, chopping a path through the growth.

A quarter of an hour later they returned, claiming that they could not find the statue and we should get going to Sungai Barang. Never mind, I said, let's go as far as your new trail. This took us to the Kayan River, which we forded on slick stones. Scampering up the far bank, the guides stopped, and in a bid for time, pointed out several leeches on Irene and myself. We pulled them out. "Look for the statue!" A few minutes later they returned with sheepish grins—the statue had been found.

The statue was worth the effort (see photo opposite). Dayak art in stone is unknown. This figure, perhaps a cross between a man and a monkey, sits on top of a meter-high base. Large eyes stare out in space and time. The lines are simple, yet powerful.

The clearing revealed an unexpected bonus: several other stone carvings. Off to one side, a feline-like figure was crouching, ready to spring. Two flat slabs of stone nearby showed badly eroded human figures. The small clearing looked like a ritual area, and it couldn't have been abandoned too long ago, as no trees had yet grown there. But the sculptures had no elements of Kenyah style. It could be that these stone objects are the remains of an ancient megalithic culture here. Our guides were no help at all, claiming that they had never seen this place and were told where it was by fellow villagers.

Back on the main trail, we pushed uphill at a good clip, trying to make up for the time "lost" with the side-trip to the sculpture. We would occasionally traverse a low-lying area with walkways of slippery logs set in mud, but most of the trail was uphill until we started to approach the village.

The last village

We smelled the smoke before we saw a huge *ladang* which had just been burned. The buzz of a chain saw quickly explained how such a large area could have been cut. We pushed quickly over the still-smoldering black ground, and were soon refreshed again by the tree umbrella and a slight breeze. The level ground made walking a pleasure and soon our path passed a lake just outside Sungai Barang.

We saw that the lake had been formed by a man-made dam. To our surprise, a stream of water shooting out from the dam was turning a large wooden water-wheel fixed to the side of a house. A set of belts connected the water-wheel to a vibrating device which

women were using to hull their rice. The women told us that a Westerner, who once lived in the village for about a year, had designed the apparatus.

We settled down on the porch of a longhouse, and a dignified elderly man soon came out to greet us. We sensed right away that he was an aristocrat, and soon found out that he was the village chief. He gave some orders and a few minutes later a meal appeared.

The chief confirmed that Sungai Barang was the last village on the Kayan River. The closest village was a two-day walk, and it was located on a tributary of the Mahakam River. This was the direction thousands of Kenyah had followed over the past three decades in their migration downstream, to be nearer to services and goods from the coast. Now, with the airstrip at Sungai Barang's ensuring communications with the coast, the exodus had effectively been ended.

In Sungai Barang, only a few scattered buildings are left of what must have been a large village. We visited the Roman Catholic church. The church was small, but it had a lively feel to it. The walls were covered with colorful painted Kenyah motifs.

During our sight-seeing stroll, we passed a man and his wife on their way back home with a large basket full of deer meat. The man carried a spear-tipped blowgun, with which he had brought down the deer. Remembering the previous night's meal—a bony eel—Irene insisted on buying a couple of kilos of the meat. A wise move.

We stopped next to one of the longhouses to photograph a wide, woven leaf hat covered with excellent beadwork. Seeing our interest in the hat, a woman brought out her baby carrier, the best we had yet seen. The unusually fine mosaic of tiny beads was set off at the top and the bottom by strands of valuable ancient beads and coins from the colonial days. Claws and teeth of bear and leopard almost completely covered the center of the beaded back panel.

On the trail back, taking advantage of some untapped reservoir of energy, I got ahead of the rest of our team. Coming to the top of a hill, breathing hard and looking down for footholds, I glanced up to see a deer less than five meters away. I was startled, but the deer must have been really shocked. It gave out a curious, loud noise and crashed off into the bush. The sound gave away the species: this could be none other than the muntjac or "barking deer."

As we settled into the longhouse for a well-deserved sleep, a committee of women came by with armfuls of traditional clothes and ornaments. They wanted to dress Irene up as a Kenyah aristocrat. Although bone-tired, my friend submitted to the well-meant attention. As I watched sleepily, Irene was transformed amidst a chorus of giggles from a worn-out art dealer to a resplendent Chinese-Kenyah princess. Satisfied with their handiwork, the ladies finally left her to sleep.

The next morning, we hoped that at Long Uro a canoe would be ready for us, as I had requested. It was, with four paddlers. The quiet river ride in the early morning was like a dream. With no engine, we did not have to get out as our boatmen pulled and shoved the craft over the shallows. And the silence was

welcome as we glided along. We arrived at the landing strip with time to spare—enough, in fact, to worry that there might be no plane that day. But the plane showed up, late but better than never.

We took off in a swirl of dust and flew over now familiar territory. From our comfortable seats, the trails below looked easy. We wanted to traipse around, discover more stone statues, sit and chat in more longhouses. There had not been enough time, but there never is in Kalimantan.

Above: *A Kenyah Dayak chief at a festival in the Apokayan. Judging from his age and decoration, it is likely that he took heads in his youth, although he is now too ashamed to talk about this.*

Apokayan Practicalities

There are several ways to reach the Apokayan by a combination of hiking and canoeing, but this takes a week under the most ideal of circumstances, and could take several times as long and cost you a bundle as well. We suggest flying in on one of Merpati's scheduled once-weekly flights from Samarinda to Long Ampung, ($40 one-way) into the heart of the Apokayan. It's about 350 km. and the flight takes 1.5 hours. In Samarinda, make your reservations and pay for the ticket as soon as possible. Cancelled flights are not unusual.

The gently rolling terrain of the Apokayan is an average of 800 meters (2,600 ft.) above sea level. This means that you could get damn cold at night in spite of the equatorial latitude. Keep in mind you will be sleeping in a longhouse where only woven leaf mats are provided. The trails between the main villages along the Kayan River are quite wide, which means you acquire fewer leeches, but the sun can quickly fry you to a sweaty frazzle. The same goes for canoe travel on the river. Especially during July and August, the driest months of the year.

7-10 days is about what it takes for a look at some of the villages of the central Apokayan, from Long Nawang to Long Sungai Barang, all on the Kayan River. You can also spend less time, check out a couple of places, and return to Samarinda by the next Merpati flight. Travel both by canoe and foot to get a sense of the two environments and modes of travel.

What to bring

While the central Apokayan does not require the planning necessary for a trek of several days, some preparations are needed. There are a couple of small shops in Long Nawang stocking a few essentials such as D-cell batteries for flashlights, salt, some basic food, tobacco, soap and toothpaste. Prices are considerably higher than on the coast. Bring your own caviar and champagne, as well as: long pants and shirts, hat, insect repellent, boots or tennis shoes, foot powder, mirror, disinfectant, malaria pills, suntan lotion, chapstick, toilet paper, canteen, flashlight, blanket, light sleeping bag, a couple of sarongs, and a knapsack or a couple of soft bags. No need for a tent. A waterproof something (perhaps a plastic garbage bag) can come in very handy for cameras and clothes during river travel or in unexpected rain.

Bring some gifts for potential hosts: sugar, canned milk, tea, coffee, perhaps clothing, inexpensive perfume, *kretek* cigarettes, a discreet bottle of booze. For yourself, a bit of basic food: processed cheese, a few tins of meat, fish or vegetables, fresh fruit. Out of season, there is little fruit and hardly any vegetables in the Apokayan.

Costs and transport

Count on about $5 a day for room and board, $7 per man for porters/guides. For outboard-powered canoes, $20-$40 for a half-day ride, if gasoline (horrendously expensive here) is available. While you might be able to purchase a local backpack with removable sides or a rattan strip basket with great patina for $5-$20, few locals make these items for sale and need them for their everyday use. Even more difficult to purchase are incredible baby carriers, covered with fantastic beadwork. If, by miracle, any are for sale, they could run from $200 up to absolutely astronomical figures.

The villages of the Apokayan are concentrated in four locations: around the district capitals of Long Bawang and Data Dian, the Boh and Ogah Rivers (which flow to the Mahakam) and the Kayan Iot, a tributary of the Kayan. Internal communications are by foot, canoe or unscheduled MAF planes to seven landing strips: Mahak Baru, Lebusan, Sungai Barang, Long Nawang, Long Ampung, Data Dian and Long Sule. Missionary Aviation Fellowship's only scheduled service (depending on the weather and other factors) is a twice-weekly flight between Tanjung Selor and Long Nawang for $60. MAF Flights to other places are either very expensive (charters for special flights) or unavailable.

Motors on canoes began their noisy but efficient jobs in 1980, and there are about 20 of these *ces* or *ketinting* in the region. But the high cost of petrol favors the paddle as the principal means of moving on the water. Strong backs and legs are still indispensable here.

Some river crossings consist of high suspension bridges of rattan, wire and rotting planks. Grab whatever you can while apprehensively shuffling across the swaying contraption. Let go only when a nasty colony of fire ants resents your disturbing their siesta. The Dayaks bound across effortlessly, not even bothering to use their hands.

Etiquette and dress

Underpants for men and sarongs for women are the basic bathing suits. Follow the local custom. Of course, you will have an audience of children with a few adults sneaking peeks into how the strangers manage, especially the tricky part of changing into dry clothes without baring one's private parts. With experience, you can preserve your decency and disappoint the fans. In addition to providing a place for washing bodies and clothes, the Kayan, like all other rivers in Kaltim, serves as a huge toilet. Just squat in waist-deep water and hope no one is looking. Or wait until nightfall.

PART IV

Introducing The Mahakam

The Mahakam is the principal waterway through central Kaltim, receiving major tributaries from north and south. Its sources lie some 650 kilometers (400 mi.) inland of the river delta. Along this huge basin, larger boats travel to where the land begins to rise and rapids begin, and small outboard-powered boats pick up from there.

The headwaters

The Mahakam River springs to life among the 1,500-2,000 meter (4,900-6,700 ft.) Müller Range in central Borneo. Picking up tributaries—the Apari, Hubung and Kasau Rivers—the Mahakam rushes downward for 100 kilometers (60 mi.) before reaching the first Dayak village, Long Apari. It then passes a couple of dozen highland villages before it drops below 150 meters (500 ft.) above sea level, tumbling as it winds through a series of dangerous rapids that choke off all traffic except for the occasional roaring *longbot*.

The Dayaks of the uprapids region subsist on slash-and-burn agriculture, with occasional income from collecting bird's nests, rattan and a bit of panned gold. Essential goods such as salt, sugar, gasoline for engines, soap and clothing command outrageous prices, because of the high transportation costs over the rapids. It is not uncommon for freight canoes to overturn, losing the merchandise and, occasionally, the valuable engines as well. Drowning is a very real occupational hazard of being a boatman on the Mahakam.

The middle reaches

Long Bagun village, 300 kilometers (190 mi.) from the river's source, is the upper limit of year-round cargo boat traffic. From here, the Mahakam passes through 150 kilometers (90 mi.) of valleys to Long Iram, a little town just about halfway between the mountains and Samarinda. Long Iram is also the terminus of the scheduled, deep-draft mixed cargo and freight riverboats. During most of the year, some of these boats will run upstream as far as Long Bagun. But a dry spell in the inland mountains can quickly lower the water level, preventing freight from passing Long Iram.

To the sea

From Long Iram, the Mahakam drops through the lowlands, widening and meandering, casting its water in lazy, cream-brown loops. As the hornbill flies, it is about 175 kilometers (110 mi.) from Long Iram to Samarinda, but because of the twists and turns, the river route takes twice this distance. As one chugs downstream, the small villages hugging the riverbanks gradually become small towns.

A major tributary enters the Mahakam at Muara Pahu, where a long row of riverside food stalls greets hungry passengers. A few hours downstream, the great river twists between four large lakes.

Just beyond the lakes, between Kota Bangun and Muara Kaman, the Mahakam snakes north, and is met by its two most important tributaries, the Kedang Kepala and the Belayan, which drain a huge basin north and northwest of the Mahakam.

The riverside food stalls of Senoni, some 30 kilometers (19 mi.) downstream from Muara Kaman, are often a scheduled boat stop. Cold beer is sometimes available here, and huge crayfish—this is a place for celebration when you return from upstream.

By the time it reaches Tenggarong, the administrative capital of the river basin, the Mahakam becomes a busy highway of coal barges, log rafts and boats of all sizes. The lively activities finally end in Samarinda, where the boats meet the ocean-going traffic steaming towards the Straits of Makassar.

Overleaf: *Dawn on Lake Jempang, near Tanjung Isuy.* **Opposite:** *The floating market on the Mahakam River at Muara Muntai specializes in vegetables brought in by nearby Dayak farmers.*

DAYAKS OF THE MAHAKAM

The People of East Kalimantan

Although there are many linguistic and cultural differences among the various Dayak groups in East Kalimantan, there are at least as many similarities. Almost all of the region's 400,000 Dayaks are subsistence farmers, who ensure their basic livelihood by planting rice. The rice-based diet is supplemented by fishing or hunting with dogs and spear-tipped blowguns. All the villages are on riverbanks. Almost all Kaltim Dayaks are Christians or follow the Kaharingan religion; very few are Muslims. The cash economy in the Dayak areas is minimal, and gathering rattan and working for timber companies are the most important sources of income.

Particularly among the older people, traditional Dayak dress and body decoration is still followed by members of many of the Dayak groups. It is not unusual to see people with tattoos and grandmothers with dozens of large earrings in each distended lobe. Styles of traditional dress, the use of beads, personal adornment and the form of some dances, especially war dances, show degrees of resemblance among all the groups.

The Benuaq and Tunjung

On the far side of Lake Jempang, the Benuaq community of Tanjung Isuy puts on a well-rehearsed cultural show for paying tourists. Nearby, at Mancong village, there is a spanking new longhouse, built with government funds as a tourist attraction. Both the Tunjung and Benuaq groups still perform their quite spectacular funerary rituals.

The Tunjung Plateau, shared by 25,000 Benuaq and 20,000 Tunjung, is the only upland area with relatively dense centers of population. The low agricultural yields gleaned from the tired soil here have begun to increase under the influence of Javanese transmigrants. Improved farming technologies include using water buffalo to plow under the grass cover and the addition of fertilizers. This way, after a four-year fallow cycle, dryland rice can be grown for three consecutive years. The first year produces 80 times the amount of rice planted, the second year 60 times, and the third year 40-50 times the amount sown.

The government collects no information on its census of the number of followers of the Kaharingan religion, but it is estimated that over half of the Benuaq, and almost half of the Tunjung, profess this recently accepted form of an ancient traditional religion. The rest of the Tunjung Plateau Dayaks are Christians, about evenly split between Catholics and Protestants. Despite the efforts of the churches, the incidence of illiteracy and stillbirth among the Benuaq is the highest of all Kalimantan's Dayak groups.

The Bahau

The settlements of the Bahau, a large and diverse ethnic group of the Kayan culture, begin around Long Iram and dominate the Mahakam upwards through the district of Long Pahangai. There are probably 50,000 Bahau in the region. The Bahau living above the rapids are called Busang and speak a dialect slightly different from that of their downstream kin.

The Bahau are excellent wood sculptors and painters, and some still turn out an array of utilitarian and decorative pieces. Several churches in the Bahau area are adorned with superb traditional decorations. Most Bahau are Roman Catholics, a faith noted for its respect for local traditions. Thanks to the tolerance of the Catholic Church, the Bahau still perform rituals in veneration of Hunai, their ancient rice goddess. Masked performers, wearing banana leaf robes, represent supernaturals who entertain the goddess in ceremonies prior to rice planting.

The Kenyah

Ending their long migration from the Apokayan region in the early 1970s, several thousand Kenyah settled among the Bahau villages lining the Mahakam between Long Iram and Long Pahangai. The largest Kenyah village in the region is Data Bilang, with more than 3,000 people. Other sizeable Kenyah villages scattered through the middle reaches of the Mahakam basin are: Miau Baru, Gemar Baru, Long Segar, Long Noran, Rantau Sentosa, and Ritan Baru.

Opposite: *The wife of an Aoheng Dayak aristocrat adjusts her husband's headdress. The couple are from Long Pahangai on the upper Mahakam.*

According to oral history, the Kenyahs' original territory was the Usun Apau highlands in Sarawak. Overpopulation and inter-tribal warfare probably led to their dispersal. Today, some 38,000 Kenyah (30,000 in Kaltim, 8,000 in Sarawak) are split into 40 groups living in 110 communities. Each of the named groups traces its origins to a longhouse in the Usun Apau ancestral land.

The cohesion of the Kenyah people is largely a product of the aristocracy, which still wields considerable power. The bright, baroque artwork of the Kenyah, still seen on meeting halls and rice barns, is the most exuberant of any Dayak group.

Most of the Kenyah today have been converted by the Gospel Tabernacle Christian Church of Indonesia, an American mission known by its Indonesian initials, KINGMI. As a consequence, the Kenyah no longer hold traditional celebrations in a ritual context. However, they can occasionally be induced to organize dances and ceremonies for visitors. Many other Kenyah have settled on the middle and the upper reaches of the Belayan River. Their most important village there, Ritan Baru, has a population of 2,500.

The Kayan

The Kayan, a complex and diffuse group, live in scattered villages in the middle and upper Mahakam, such as Long Melaham and Long Kuling, as well as along some the the major tributaries, such as the Kelinjau. Of Kalimantan's 30,000 Kayan, some 25,000 live in Kaltim. (10,000 Kayan live in Sarawak.)

The Kenyah and Kayan share a large number of cultural traits. Basic art forms are similar, although motifs are quite distinct. Of all of Borneo's Dayak groups, the Kayan and the Kenyah had—and still have—the most rigid social structure, with strict divisions among nobles, commoners and slaves. Both groups were accomplished head-hunters and warriors, greatly feared by their neighbors for their skill at taking heads and slaves. Only the Iban provoked greater terror.

Kayan villages always consisted of a single longhouse, while the Kenyah villages often had several. Among both groups, the highest ranking aristocrat took the central apartment, which was decorated with motifs exclusive to his class. There was regional organization as well, and the village chief was subject to the authority of an area leader.

While the Kayan culture is relatively homogeneous, the Kenyah are split into many clans, speaking different dialects and adhering to local variations in customs. For both groups, "foreign" relations and lucrative trade contacts were reserved for the aristocrats. Intermarriage between Kayan and Kenyah was not rare, although class standing was always respected. Marriages, both internal and external, were a frequent way of cementing or repairing political alliances.

The Modang

The Modang group is linguistically related to the Kayan, and claims the Kejin highlands (the Apokayan) as the group's ancestral homeland. Since the 18th century, Modang groups have migrated into a number of river basins: the Mahakam, the Kelinjau, the Telen-Wahau, the Kelai-Segah and the lower Kayan. There are many Modang subgroups, including the Long Gelat, Long Bleh, Long Way, Wahea and Menggoe.

The Modang cultural heritage includes superb art and important harvest festivals along with a men's house, unique among the Dayak groups, called the *eweang*. Although they maintain many of their traditions, the Modang unfortunately are among the poorest of the Dayaks of Kaltim.

A concentration of about 6,000 Modang people can be found in the district of Muara Wahau on the uppermost reaches of the Kedang Kepala, a major tributary of the Mahakam that flows almost due south. The Long Gelat, a Modang subgroup, live in the village of the same name. There are other Modang villages located on the Telen River and Belayan River, Kembang Janggut. Long Tuyoq, on the upper Mahakam, also belongs to the Modang.

Other Dayak groups

The Aoheng (also called Penihing) dominate the uppermost inhabited reaches of the Mahakam, and many of this group live in the downrapids villages of Long Bagun and Ujoh Bilang. This 2,000-member tribe spreads between Tiong Ohang, the *kecamatan* capital, to Long Apari, the last upstream village. Seputan and Bukat groups have also settled into this same stretch. The government is trying to consolidate all these scattered villages in Tiong Ohang.

Above the rapids, 3,500 Busang, a heterogeneous group, are scattered in 11 villages.

Various Punan groups have, within the past two generations, given up their nomadic lifestyle in the strands of primary forest deep in the interior to settle in permanent villages, especially on the Belayan River.

Dayak Migrations

The history of many Dayaks in the Mahakam basin is closely tied to that of the Apokayan, the region around the headwaters of the Kayan River, northwest of the Mahakam. Some informants say that back in the 18th century, the Kayan people—who include the Bahau, the Modang, the Long Gelat, and the Busang—inhabited the Apokayan as well as the upper reaches of the Pujungan and Bahau Rivers.

Then, in the second quarter of the 19th century, the Kayan began to move out of their homeland in response to territorial pressures from shifting populations of Kenyah, who were then migrating into the Apokayan. The Kenyah were leaving their downriver settlements in Sarawak to put a greater distance between themselves and the Ibans. It is said that the scrupulous Kenyah sometimes paid the Kayan for land rights when they moved into Kayan territory.

Leaving the Apokayan in increasing numbers, the Kayan invaded the upper Mahakam, driving out or enslaving the Ot Danum and the Tunjung peoples. Many Ot Danum fled to the Barito River basin, while the Tunjung settled further downstream on the Mahakam.

The Bahau followed the initial invasion, forcing the Tunjung further downstream. Then came the Busang and, in the early 19th century, the Long Gelat, a tough bunch led by a chief named Bo Ledjo, whom the Europeans called the "Kayan Napoleon." The Long Gelat forced the Busang to accept their leadership, then engaged in devastating head-hunting raids all the way to the Kapuas and Barito Rivers.

While these Kayan headed for the Mahakam, their Modang cousins, another tough bunch, muscled their way to the upper Telen, Belayan and Kelinjau Rivers.

Then the Kenyah, now established in the Apokayan, began a war against the Busang, forcing them to abandon their settlements along the Ogah and Boh Rivers, tributaries of the upper Mahakam. The Kenyah had a much harder time with the Modang. The latter were eventually expelled from the upper Belayan River but avenged themselves in 1906, when they gave a sound thrashing to the Kenyah in the Wahau district. By then, thanks to sheer force of numbers, the Kenyah had driven the other Modang downstream to Kembang Janggut.

Even today the Modang are not particularly friendly with the Kenyah. In the 1960s, when the Kenyah began leaving the Apokayan, the migrants had to sign a peace treaty with the Modang whose land they crossed.

Opposite: *A water buffalo is sacrificed at the climactic moment in a Benuaq funerary ritual. Part of the Kaharingan traditional faith, this ritual was enacted at the Erau festival.*

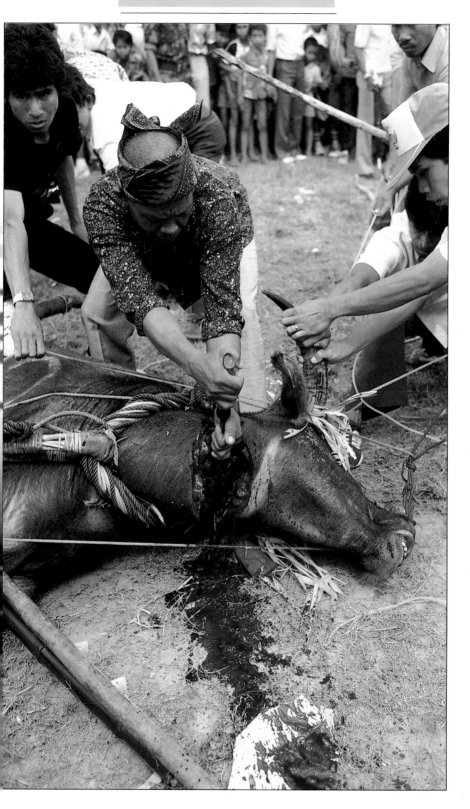

THE LOWER MAHAKAM

Busy River Meanders Past Dayak Villages

The lower reaches of the Mahakam River, from Tenggarong to Long Iram, are convenient to the coast and provide an opportunity to sample Kaltim's Muslim past as well as the traditional Dayak way of life.

The city of Tenggarong, the former capital of the Kutai sultanate, now serves as the administrative headquarters of the huge Kutai *kabupaten*. The chief attraction here is the Mulawarman Museum, which is located on the site of the old palace of the Sultan of Kutai. For anyone interested in the history and culture of Kaltim, this museum is worth several hours' visit.

The museum's building was erected in 1936, after the splendid old wooden palace burned down. By the late 19th century, thanks to the discovery of coal and oil in East Borneo, the sultan of Kutai was a very rich man, the wealthiest on the island. After the

fire, a Dutch architect designed the current palace, a neoclassical structure more in line with Dutch notions of what kind of building a wealthy ruler should live in than local building traditions.

The sultan's splendid palace

Foreign visitors to Tenggarong before 1936 came away stunned and impressed by the sultan's wealth and taste. The palace was huge and splendid, and looked out over the great Mahakam River. The sultan's furnishings were the best and most luxurious that could be found in the world, Chinese and Japanese porcelains, thick Belgian carpets, and polished ironwood floors. A 1910 account by W. O. Krohn describes the palace:

"The verandah opens directly into the great throne room, a high-ceilinged, baronial hall with impressive proportions, its dimensions being sixty by one hundred and twenty feet. On the dais against the farther wall stood the throne of the Sultan and Sultana, and immense cut-glass chandeliers were suspended from the ceiling, while numerous tiger-skins covered the mosaic floor. These tiger skins were marvelous specimens and were arranged on radiating lines in a semicircle, their heads pointing towards the throne."

In addition to a thriving harem and a private yacht, he kept such technological marvels as an ice machine, an electric generator,

and three automobiles. A 1924 audit revealed more than three million Dutch guilders in the Tenggarong treasury, and with the near limitless largess, our informant states, "Croesus, at his prime, never made a more prodigal display of wealth than met my eyes this day in the Sultan's palace at Tenggarong."

The Mulawarman Museum

A tall, finely carved Dayak totem pole, (*belawang*) topped by a hornbill bird guards the museum entrance. Inside, you will see typical sultan's regalia such as gamelan instruments, sacred kris daggers and finely made aristocrat's clothing. Take a close look at the beadwork in the royal bedchamber, and the chairs of deer antlers and composite mythological animals.

Although a good number of the best pieces have been taken to the National Museum in Jakarta (or have been given to prominent politicians), there is still plenty to see at the museum. Be sure to check out the examples of the first known specimens of writing in Indonesia. The cone-shaped, grayish "tablets" in the museum are paper mâché replicas. The stone originals, which date from the 4th century A.D., are safely stored in the basement archives—not on display—of the National Museum. The writing, in Pallawan script, celebrates King Mulawarman's generosity in a ritual sacrifice performed by Brahman priests.

While there are some samples of Dayak crafts in the museum, the best Dayak art has been moved to an inconvenient location at the edge of town. There you will find fine carvings, mostly associated with Benuaq and Tunjung funerals. Behind the garden lies the royal cemetery of Kutai's sultans. Since Muslim doctrine forbids human or animal representations, the carvings are restricted to floral designs and geometric patterns, as well as flowing script from the Koran. Before completing your visit to the museum complex, walk around back to see if any of the flowers in the orchid garden are in bloom.

The Mulawarman Museum is usually open every day—except Monday—from about 10:00 a.m. to 2:00 p.m. If the museum is closed, try the tourism office on Jalan Diponegoro 2, just above an art shop selling new Dayak crafts. The tourism office keeps regular government hours, and an employee could get the museum opened for you, even on Mondays, for a small contribution.

Local dances are sometimes performed in the museum's main hall on Sundays. These dances, or Dayak dances, can be arranged almost anytime with a day or two of advance

Opposite: *Heading upriver on the Mahakam, a passenger lounges on an obstetrical chair destined for a local clinic.* **Below:** *On a slow boat up the Mahakam, this woman has arranged a tidy little hammock to rock her grandchild to sleep.*

notice, for about $50-$100. The museum has inherited the sultan's fine collection of porcelains—assessed at $450,000 in 1910—and this is usually only available for viewing on Sundays. But a contribution can usually get a keeper to unlock the door on other days.

The passenger boats traveling up and down the Mahakam River do not stop long enough at Tenggarong for a proper visit to the museum, so you have to stop either before or after a trip inland unless you travel with an organized tour. A stop at the museum is scheduled in all tours.

Upriver to Tanjung Isuy

Several hours out of Tenggarong, all boats bound upriver tie up at the floating foodstalls of Senoni. Try the huge crayfish and a beer-on-the-rocks. The next stop, Muara Kaman, was the capital of the ancient Hindu-oriented Mulawarman Kingdom. Muara Kaman is also the port of entry for the tributary systems heading north and west (See "Kedang Kepala," page 122.)

A couple of hours from Muara Kaman, the boats reach Kota Bangun, a town of some 10,000 inhabitants stretched out along the Mahakam's north bank. Kota Bagun marks the beginning of the flat lake country of the lower Mahakam drainage area. Swampy terrain and large, shallow lakes—Semayang, Melintang and Jempang—landmark this region. The town of Muara Muntai is the

regional center for all trade, market activities and communications.

At the Sri Bagun Lodge in Kota Bangun, check to see if David Boyce is around. David, a chunky Australian, has spent many years here, loves the place and has written a book on the history of Kutai. He, or someone else at the lodge, can arrange for a boat to see the interesting freshwater dolphins, birds and long-nosed proboscis monkeys that live in the area. The best time for a wildlife tour is early morning or late afternoon, and because the animals are so shy, guides can only guarantee that you will see birds. These nature rides are usually arranged ahead of time, but if their boat is around and not busy, you can try to schedule something for the next day, or even persuade them to make your trip to the next stop—Tanjung Isuy village—into a guided wildlife tour.

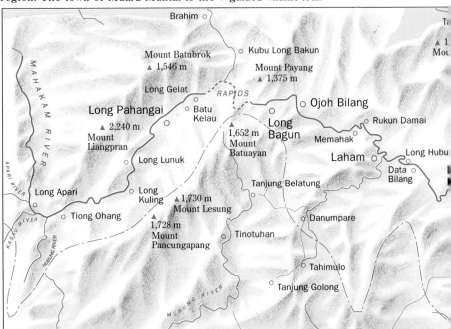

Tanjung Isuy

On the way to Tanjung Isuy from Muara Muntai, you will probably see colorful kingfishers, herons and other birds, especially if you get an early start. Less than an hour into the ride you pass the village of Jantur, which marks the beginning of Lake Jempang. You motor right up Jantur's main "street," and pass numerous waterside streets and a mosque. The colorful houses are perched on stilts, and you may see fishermen casting their nets. From Jantur, it's another one-and-a-half hours to Tanjung Isuy at the far end of Lake Jempang.

Upon arrival, contact the *camat* or the *kepala desa* to arrange a ritual welcome and dance. The performance will cost $50 or more, depending on the number of performers and dances you want to see. Tanjung Isuy is the Dayak village most frequented by visitors, and the performances here have lost some of their flavor and authenticity. A visit is still worthwhile—the costumes are great and you can photograph at will—but don't expect a full-blown traditional ritual. And this is probably the best you will see, unless you have the time to travel inland.

Even if you do go inland, in which case you can probably find—with enough luck—a "real" ceremony, most likely the participants will be wearing Western clothes.

Tanjung Isuy is one of the last places in Borneo where traditional vegetable fiber cloth is still woven. In accordance with the village's development as a tourist site, traditional weaving is maintained here, and visitors should ask to see the weaving operation and have it explained.

There is a *penginapan* at Tanjung Isuy, but you can also stay at the village's longhouse-cum-meeting house. The villagers all live in single-family dwellings. Meals are available, and if you spend the night, report

Opposite: *Tunjung Dayak dancers at the Erau Festival in Tenggarong.* **Above:** *A woman at Tanjung Isuy villages weaves traditional vegetable-fiber cloth. This village has been planned as a tourist attraction, which perhaps takes some of the charm out of it for visitors. The weaving of this cloth, however, had been a dying art until Tanjung Isuy was shined up for foreign tourists.*

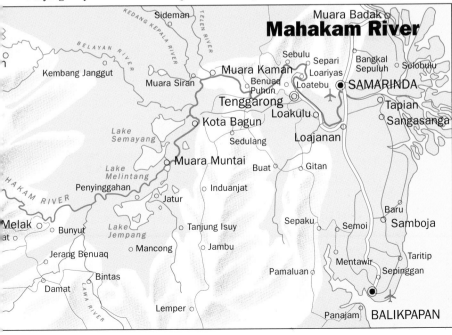

Mahakam River (map): Sideman, KEDANG KEPALA RIVER, TELEN RIVER, BELAYAN RIVER, Kembang Janggut, Muara Badak, Muara Kaman, Muara Siran, Sebulu, Separi, Bangkal Sepuluh, Selobulu, Loariyas, Benuaq Puhun, Loatebu, SAMARINDA, Tenggarong, Loakulu, Kota Bagun, Lake Semayang, Sedulang, Loajanan, Tapian, Sangasanga, Lake Melintang, Muara Muntai, Buat, Gitan, HAKAM RIVER, Penyinggahan, Jatur, Induanjat, Baru, Melak, Bunyut, Lake Jempang, Tanjung Isuy, Sepaku, Semoi, Samboja, Jerang Benuaq, Mancong, Jambu, Taritip, Bintas, Mentawir, Sepinggan, Damat, LAWA RIVER, Pamaluan, Lemper, Panajam, BALIKPAPAN

to the police with your passport—or a photocopy thereof. It's just a formality.

The people of the nearby village of Mancong have just rebuilt their longhouse, thanks to development funds made available by the provincial government. Mancong is 9 kilometers (6 mi.) from Tanjung Isuy, and you can walk there in about three hours (bring a hat and canteen, it's a hot walk). You can also hire a local driver to take you there on the back of a motorcycle on the bad, but passable, road for about $10 round-trip.

A third way to go there is by *ces,* or small motorized canoe, which takes about three hours but passes up a small river where you will see lots of birds and monkeys. If you are planning on going further into the interior of

East Kalimantan, the longhouse here is not really worth seeing. But if this is your last stop, make the trip.

On to Melak

Muara Pahu, the next upriver town from Muara Muntai, sits at the confluence of the Mahakam River and the Pahu River—which drains the Tunjung Plateau to the south. Heading up this little-traveled river system, you will find villages practicing the traditional Kaharingan religion. (See "The Dayaks," page 40.) This faith, along with other cultural influences, entered the area from south-central Kalimantan. You could hire a guide and trek to the Barito River basin, and from there float down to Banjarmasin in Kalsel.

Melak is the next population center after Muara Pahu. It sits at the head of a road network which reaches north to Tering, on the Mahakam River, and south, on logging trails, to the Barito basin. There are several *losmen/penginapan* at Melak, and food stalls offering simple meals. From Melak, you can rent a jeep or the back seat of a motorcycle for the 16-kilometer (10 mi.) ride to the Kersik Luwai Orchid Reserve. Some 112 species of orchids have been catalogued here, including the famous "black" variety, which is unique among these colorful beauties. According to informants, the greatest number of species are in bloom in April.

From Melak, head away from the river to the *kecamatan* center of Barong Tongkok, across some 18 kilometers (11 mi.) of good dirt road. Although everyone in the district dresses in Western-style clothes, there are plenty of Dayaks here who follow the traditional Kaharingan religion. Ask at the *camat's* office in Barong Tongkok if there are any rituals coming up.

The most dramatic Kaharingan rituals are the funerals, in which water buffalo are sacrificed, but weddings, agricultural rites and shaman healings are also fascinating. There are many longhouses in the area, which are decorated with carvings to scare away evil spirits. Some of the local cemeteries also have interesting carvings.

There is a lot of basket-weaving in this area, as well as smithing operations. The blacksmiths use hand-operated bamboo blowers to heat scrap metal from which they forge long knives, agricultural tools and household items.

The more traditional local villages include Mengimai, Eheng, Papas and Engkuni. All can be reached by motorcycle or jeep from Barong Tongkok or Melak.

There is a very primitive *losmen* in Barong Tongkok, called Wisma Tamu Anggrek. You could also stay in one of the longhouses. To stay in a longhouse, common courtesy requires you to ask the permission of the village chief (*kepala desa*). We suggest paying about $3 or so a day for room and board, and more if special food (chicken or meat) is prepared for you.

From Barong Tongkok you can either try to catch a ride to Tering, walk there (about six hours) or return to Melak and hop the next boat going upriver.

Above: *A hirsute Dayak at the Erau Festival.*
Opposite: *Tanjung Isuy on Lake Jempang.*

ERAU FESTIVAL

Dancing, Dragons and Water Fights

The Dayaks were a tough bunch from a long way up the Mahakam River. They certainly did not look like they had put on their leopard skins, beaded headdresses, and huge earrings for the benefit of gawking tourists. In fact, aside from myself, the only white faces around were those of a couple of expatriate French oil workers' wives who lived in nearby Balikpapan.

Although there were few tourists, local Indonesians were busy with their video cameras, and a national television crew had come from Jakarta to film the five-day Erau Festival, an extravaganza of dancing, food, boat races and much more in the district capital of Tenggarong in East Kalimantan.

The Erau Festival celebrates the founding of Tenggarong, and the continuation of the tradition is partially thanks to government encouragement, partially to the residual respect which some Dayaks still feel for the royal family in Tenggarong. The festival includes traditional Dayak dances and ritual displays, as well as coastal Muslim ceremonies and dancing.

On September 28, 1782, the sultan of Kutai moved his court upriver to avoid conflict with the Bugis immigrants from South Sulawesi who had settled there in large numbers. The celebration used to be a yearly event, and now occasionally takes place at the government's discretion. Since the district treasury foots the bill, the decision to hold the festival is based on the state of the district coffers. The events last from September 24 to 28. In recent years, the Erau was held in 1982, 1986 and 1988. The decision to hold the show is usually not made until just a few months before the event.

Speeches, games and races

A series of speeches kicks off the events, including a keynote address by the governor. A huge parade follows, with marching bands, majorettes and some muscular Dayaks, these last quite amused by the show as they are mobbed by amateur and professional wielders of cameras and handycams.

After the V.I.P.s go home, the festival settles down to a routine of sports competitions and games of skill. One of the traditional team sporting events consists of players spinning heavy tops into a ring. During the deliv-

ery the players try to knock out their opponents' tops, and the one whose top remains spinning the longest is the winner. Government officials and Dayaks, children and adults, join in this game, all shouting and gesticulating like rowdy boys. Another game, played with a hollow rattan ball, combines elements of soccer and volleyball. There are blowgun competitions, and lots of canoe races. The light, narrow canoes, sometimes profusely decorated, are, in some races, powered by teams of 25 paddlers. Races are also held for canoes with small motors.

Dances and rituals

At a recent festival, each day saw Dayak dances and ritual enactments, all performed by men and women in full ceremonial costume. The participants looked splendid in their leopard skins, beads and feathered headdresses. In 1986, in addition to the dances and regalia, the festival included two spectacular recreations of traditional events.

The first recreation was of a funereal ritual, in which the Dayak group raised a carved ancestral pole, and then, after a frenzy of dancing, slaughtered a water buffalo. Next was a chilling reinactment of the ritual that in the past would have accompanied a successful head-hunting raid, with an orangutan skull substituting for the real goods. This ritual was performed by the Dayaks who had traveled the furthest, from a village many days upstream. They looked wild and tough, and it was easy to imagine that they longed for the good old days of real raids.

The atmosphere at the end took a strange turn, as the chief of traditions submitted to an interview for Indonesian national television. Even a Dayak chief gets 15 minutes of fame.

An interesting contrast to the Dayak celebrations were the shows put on by the Muslim people of Kutai. The performances included a marriage and several dances, all conducted in traditional attire—beautiful,

embroidered silks. In the best of the dances, the brother and the oldest son of the last sultan of Kutai joined in stately steps with government officials, all wearing brilliant, Kutai-style silk outfits, accompanied by an expert gamelan orchestra.

The free-for-all

The last and culminating day began with prayers at the grave of Haji Imbut, the founder of Tenggarong. And later, the two ritual dragons that had served to insure the festival's

success were dragged out. Each dragon was 8 meters (26 ft.) in length, and was fashioned out of rattan and covered with colorful cloth. A committee of men in full Kutai finery took the dragons in a boat out to the middle of the Mahakam River. After due ceremony, the dragons were lowered into the water, to be released and floated downstream to the ocean. Just before they were set free, two young men jumped in to chop off the dragons' carved heads, which were to be saved for the next festival. The bodies then floated off downstream.

The severing of the dragon heads was the signal for a free-for-all water fight to begin. All of a sudden the whole riverfront erupted in spray. Boats with power pumps and nozzles soaked the crowd along the river bank, but the people had already done a good job of plastering each other with tossed bucketfuls and plastic bags filled with water. Some of the boats engaged in pitched battles, sweeping their opponents' decks with water cannon. Photographers, be warned: carrying cameras by no means guarantees staying dry.

Opposite: *The climax of the Erau Festival comes when the head of the dragon is severed and his body sent downriver to the ocean. The head is believed to bring prosperity.* **Above, left:** *Modern influences play a role at the festival, as this drum majorette shows.* **Above, right:** *A Kenyah Dayak chief grants an interview to a Jakarta TV crew.*

MIDDLE MAHAKAM

Long Iram Upriver to Long Bagun

Traveling up the Mahakam River, the Long Iram area marks the beginning of the villages occupied by more traditional East Kalimantan Dayaks. Although many have been converted to Christianity, the Dayaks of the middle Mahakam have for the most part retained their old ways and beliefs. The Bahau are mostly Roman Catholics, but the church's tolerance has allowed them to retain their traditions, and the Benuaq and Tunjung groups have been influenced by the Kaharingan faith, a government-approved traditional religion (see "Kaharingan Faith," page 152).

Long Iram

Just before Long Iram, there are three villages clustered along the Mahakam River called, collectively,Tering. Tering Baru and, just upstream, Tering Seberang, are on the south bank, and Tering Lama is on the other side of the river. Tering Baru has been a Roman Catholic missionary center since the 1920s, and the resident Dutch priest maintains an excellent health clinic and school. There is a large meeting house at Tering Lama, decorated with Dayak motifs, as well as a few interesting post carvings left over from a long-gone longhouse.

In Tering Lama stop by the four fine antique statues, covered by a tin roof, that gaze across the Mahakam. Here a woodcarver creates traditional Bahau Dayak carvings, particularly shields, for sale in the regional capital of Samarinda. You can watch his work, and perhaps even commission a carving.

Just upriver from Tering is Long Iram, the *kecamatan* center and the terminus of scheduled river traffic from Samarinda. There was a recent gold rush here, but since the government forced out the 6,000 mostly Banjarese who were panning the lower Kelian River a few years back, the place has lost its boomtown atmosphere. An Australian joint venture company has set up large-scale gold mining at the Kelian River's headwaters.

For accommodations in Long Iram, we suggest the Wahyu—clean and owned by a still hard-working haji. It's $3 a night, a small fan along with egg-bread-coffee breakfast included. There are two cheaper *losmen* in town, including the Parida, which is in a floating boathouse above a store. The balancing act that you must perform every time you go

ashore is compensated by the view from the *losmen*'s balcony, which overlooks the Mahakam. The boathouse is used by neighbors as a bathing and clothes-washing platform. No enclosed bathing space for guests.

The only restaurant in town, the Java Timur, serves simple, tasty Javanese-style dishes, and has beer (with ice if the plant is working). The place is clean but locals will often sit at nearby tables to gawk at the foreigners. At the *warungs* and stalls, which serve snacks and drinks, the staring is worse, particularly for women. In the evening, try the local fried bananas—*pisang goreng*—sold along the main (and only) street in town, which runs parallel to the river.

The Long Iram Dayaks

Benuaq and Tunjung Dayak lands reach inland to Long Iram, where they converge with Bahau territory. There are also several large Kenyah villages between Long Iram and Long Bagun, a result of large-scale migrations from the Apokayan in the 1960s and 1970s. Each of these villages was founded by a single, well-organized group under the leadership of their aristocrats.

The Dayak groups along this part of the Mahakam have retained many of their traditions, even though partially Christianized. The Benuaq and Tunjung, of different languages but similar culture, have been strongly influenced by the Kaharingan religion which reached them from Central Kalimantan. This faith has been included by the government in its "Bali-Hindu" category of approved religions, although you won't see anything like a Balinese temple festival around here.

The Benuaq are the largest group in the Kutai district, living mostly along the southern tributaries of the Mahakam. They are perhaps the most traditional group in East Kalimantan. The Benuaq consider themselves a subgroup of the Lawangan Dayaks, who live along the Barito River in Central Kalimantan.

Among all Kaharingan believers, funerals are of utmost importance. This is usually a two-phase affair, the first taking place just after death, and the second, a much more elaborate event, taking place later. It is in the second stage that the soul is sent off, the bones of the deceased being cleaned and placed in an elaborately carved coffin.

The Benuaq add a third stage—called *kwangkei*—which includes dances for the spirits and food offerings to the ancestral skulls. A carved pole is erected during this

ritual. A slave was formerly tied to this pole, then sacrificed. A water buffalo is substituted today. The reason for its upcoming death is carefully explained to the animal by the high priest and then the buffalo is then speared to death. The men who sacrifice the buffalo sometimes carry cloth-wrapped ancestral skulls on their backs. The Benuaq and Tunjung also perform the blood-letting ceremony called *behempas,* a traditional fight using rattan staffs and wicker shields.

The Bahau Dayak, under the sway of Roman Catholicism, have retained many of their beliefs and rituals thanks to the church's tolerant policy of trying to reduce the trauma of breaking with old traditions. The most spectacular of the Bahau ceremonies is the *hudoq* dance, conducted by male dancers wearing huge, grotesque masks and banana-leaf robes. This dance is part of a series of rites performed at rice-planting time, anytime from mid-September to late October, depending on the local forecast for the arrival of the rainy season.

The Kenyah, recent arrivals to the Mahakam River, are all converted Protestants.

Opposite: *A typical passenger/cargo boat makes a pit stop at a riverside bathhouse on the Mahakam.* **Above:** *Father Ding, a Roman Catholic priest and a Bahau Dayak, encourages his flock in Long Hubung to maintain some of their traditions. The father dons the* hudoq *mask himself.*

Their proselytization was begun in the 1920s by the Dutch, and they were later strongly influenced by strict American fundamentalists, who held no sympathy for Kenyah tradition. Nevertheless, Kenyah art has survived, and recently, thanks to government encouragement, the Kenyah have resurrected some of the old rituals.

The most spectacular of these is called the *mamat,* in its original form a nine-day, multi-purpose affair honoring successful head-hunters and purifying the village. Some Kenyah can be persuaded to put on a cut-down version of the *mamat,* lasting from a half-day to three days. The celebrants don full regalia, including leopard skins, shield, and—for warriors only—ear plugs. The ceremony consists of dancing, singing and the sacrifice of pigs and chickens.

Upriver from Long Iram

Past Long Iram, the traveling becomes more difficult. There are many fewer boats going this way and delays are frequent. It is still inexpensive, however, all the way to Long Bagun, where the traffic stops because of the rapids just beyond. To travel upriver from Long Iram, check continuously at the dock to find out when a boat is leaving, and get yourself and your gear on board early, as things tend to get crowded.

If there has been little rainfall inland, the larger boats cannot manage because of several shallow spots. If this is the case, the only option is to hire a longboat—*longbot*—a wide canoe usually equipped with a strong outboard motor. These can take up to eight passengers with luggage, but with fewer people on board you can stretch out during the long hours ahead. Remember to bring a hat and have a jacket handy in case of a sudden squall. Longboat prices depend on distances and number of days required.

Whereas regular boats take as long as three days to travel from Long Iram to Long Bagun, a longboat can zip you there in 8-10 hours, although the cost is steep: $150-$200. The real advantage of chartering a longboat is that this allows you to stop in some of the villages along the way, and stay as long as you wish, even overnight. This won't add much to your cost, because most of the fare goes to covering the very high price of fuel. Don't worry about the return trip, the longboat has to come back to its home base in Long Iram and this is included in the price.

In addition to the boatman, bring along a helper and stock up on food and drinks in Long Iram, as you will find no restaurants along the way. The very few stores you might see will probably be out of stock. A four-to-six day round-trip journey to Long Bagun, with two boatmen and one cook, should cost around $300. Not too expensive when split among 3 to 5 travelers.

We do not recommend taking small canoes, although they are quite cheap. There are too many horror stories of travelers in these being swamped, either from the wash of a big riverboat or just from lack of experience, and of course losing their cameras and bedding to the river.

Data Bilang

About one-third of the way to Long Bagun, the large village of Data Bilang appears on the south bank of the Mahakam. All of the more than 3,000 inhabitants of the village are Kenyah of the Uma Jalan Uma Bakung subgroups, who originally migrated here from the Apokayan. They are a progressive and well-organized group, taking advantage of government programs, including irrigated rice-growing techniques.

Above: *This boy, a Bahau Dayak, is the proud winner of the grease-pole climbing contest. He displays his prizes before giving them to dad.*
Opposite: *Two Benauq Dayaks near Long Iram perform a ritual fight with stick and shield, formerly used to train warriors for battle.*

There are no longhouses in Data Bilang, but the two huge communal buildings and some of the raised rice barns are decorated in traditional Kenyah motifs. At one end of a large, open field, an intricate carved pole was erected to commemorate the visit of President Suharto, who inaugurated the new village after the resettlement from the Apokayan was completed. This pole, on which a dragon and warriors are carved, also serves as the occasional site of a *mamat* ritual, in which pigs are sacrificed. The older women of the village still wear their huge earrings, and many are tattooed. Check to see if there will be a dance in the meeting hall on Sunday evening. Ask the *kepala desa* to help you find a place to stay overnight.

A short way upstream from Data Bilang, the Bahau village of Long Hubung makes a worthwhile stop. See if Father Ding, Catholic priest, is around. He is a Bahau himself and promotes traditional cultural events in the village. He can arrange for a *hudoq* dance performance with himself taking one of the leading roles. Further upriver, Rukun Damai, a Kenyah village, has two longhouses, and the residents occasionally hold Sunday dances.

Long Bagun

Along the final stretches of the Mahakam before Long Bagun, hills crowd the river and the scenery is spectacular. Sheer limestone cliffs sprout from the luxurious tropical vegetation. These formations sometimes hold the caves where edible-nest swiftlets build their precious glutinous nests.

Ujoh Bilang is the seat of the *kecamatan* Long Bagun, and has a police station, a health clinic (don't count on them stocking medicines), a *camat* and several stores, which also serve drinks and snacks. No *losmen* however. When you check in with the police, they will help you find a place to sleep. The inhabitants of Ujoh Bilang are a mixed lot, with Bahau, Modang, and Aoheng Dayaks, Kutai Malays and Javanese.

Five kilometers upstream from Ujoh Bilang is Long Bagun, actually three villages set close to each other: Long Bagun Hulu (upstream), Long Bagun Tengah (central) and Long Bagun Hilir (downstream). The inhabitants of Long Bagun Hilir are mainly Aoheng Dayaks, and there are some traditional carvers in the village. Make sure you see the riverside graves here. A few minutes upstream, next to a lumber camp, there is a stone statue, of mysterious pronvenence, of the sacred Hindu bull Nandi.

Longboats will occasionally make the trip through the rapids to Long Pahangai and beyond, and if a boat is going rapid-running, the fare is about $30 as an ordinary passenger. You could also charter a rapids runner, if the river level is right and there is a craft available and willing, for about $300 for a full day of excitement.

UPPER MAHAKAM

Past the Rapids and to the Interior

The upper Mahakam is cut off from the coast by a stretch of difficult rapids just upriver from Long Bagun. Although there are other parts of Borneo which are similarly sealed off, either the rapids are less severe than those on the Mahakam or, as in Sarawak, turbocharged river craft have tamed the white water. Only the Apokayan is more isolated than the upper Mahakam.

During a 15-month trek across Borneo in 1897-1898, Dr. A. W. Nieuwenhuis became the first European to visit the headwaters of the Mahakam. By treating the malaria and syphilis that was afflicting the people of the region, Dr. Nieuwenhuis won their confidence. Medicines and fear of recurring raids eventually won the Dayaks' peaceful submission to Holland. Kwing Irang, a Kayan chief from this area who was also Dr. Nieuwenhuis' interpreter, pressed strongly and persuasively for the Dutch takeover. He clearly foresaw the benefits of protection from both Iban head-hunters and the coastal Muslims.

At the turn of the century, conditions beyond the Mahakam's rapids (Nieuwenhuis calls them "waterfalls") were not good for the area's Dayaks. Kayan and Bahau Dayaks lived here, and Aoheng settled on the river's uppermost reaches. Although the sultan of Kutai's political power did not reach into this area, he had a lock on trade—jungle products heading downstream were heavily taxed, as were essential commodities going the other way. At the time, salt in the upper Mahakam sold for over 15 times its cost in Samarinda.

Kutainese and Bugis merchants settled just below the rapids, elbowed in on the trade in jungle products and began to exploit the Dayaks through gambling and outright robbery. A few severed heads reestablished an equilibrium of sorts, but the Bugis were tough folks and by the time Niewenhuis arrived, preparations were afoot for large-scale confrontation. Dr. Nieuwenhuis' assistant, J.P.J. Barth, was given the position of controller and established his headquarters at Long Iram in 1900.

The next year, the Dutch established an outpost, and armed it with imported Javanese soldiers. In the face of armed authority, tensions between the Muslims and Dayaks eased and large-scale head-hunting disappeared. Dutch price controls on salt helped a

great deal. The sultan of Kutai eventually traded his tenuous upriver claims to the Dutch for a yearly cash payment.

Ethnic wars

The complex ethnic situation in the upper Mahakam traces its roots back to the 18th century, when well-organized Kayan tribes invaded the area from their homeland in the Apokayan. It is perhaps the case that the Kayan themselves had been chased out of their homeland by the Kenyah.

Be that as it may, the Kayan forced a group called the Pin (related to Kalteng's Ot Danum) from the upper Mahakam, and became the region's dominant force. The Kayan traded with nomadic Punan groups, some of whom settled down to at least a partially sedentary existence. These former nomads continued as part-time gatherers of jungle products.

In 1885, several thousand Iban—probably the largest single war party Borneo had ever seen—swept into the upper Mahakam, severing heads, gathering booty and wreaking havoc. The Iban burned every Kayan and Aoheng village. No wonder the Dayaks of the upper Mahakam turned to the Dutch colonial authorities for help. In 1907, the area came under Dutch colonial administration, and the first missionary school opened its doors at Batu Ura in 1927.

Art and tradition

The Roman Catholicism that has taken hold in this region is tolerant of traditional belief, unlike the Protestant missions in Kaltim and elsewhere. The priests do not berate their parishioners for a continuing belief in spirits, magic or shamans, and are confident that superstitions will eventually disappear, even if it takes several generations. Nor do the church leaders disapprove of planting or harvest rituals nor of other traditional festivals.

Although most of the old wood sculptures have withered away or been snapped up by enterprising art dealers, there are still excellent carvers in the region. They sculpt ancestor poles, canoe figureheads, wooden baby carriers, and a variety of utilitarian and decorative items.

Today, blacksmiths seldom fashion the beautiful inlaid work of old. But metal tools, especially *mandau* blades, still come well tempered from the forges and anvils, and are decorated with graceful swirls at the top of the blade, and even an occasional inlay. These *mandaus* now perform the mundane tasks of the *parang* or machete, or serve as a traditional fashion accessory when finished off with a carved horn handle and embellished with all sorts of decoration.

Beads are still highly esteemed in the region, and rare, very valuable ones are still occasionally seen. Beads, together with old Chinese trade jars, ancient gongs, locally made cloths and *mandaus*, are essential ingredients in the bride price, as traditional weddings are still performed in addition to the ceremony offered by the Church.

The upper Mahakam today

When available, basic necessities in the upper Mahakam cost several times more than in Samarinda, and the region is dependent on goods from the coast. For example, it is not unusual, in the few months preceding the harvest, for rice imports to be necessary to stave off famine. Travel here depends on gasoline to power the little outboards used here, and the stuff is outrageously priced.

The people of the upper Mahakam, like most of those in Borneo, practice shifting slash-and-burn cultivation of staple rice. Poor, acidic soils, steep slopes and animals erode the output figures. Fish brings protein to the table. Deer and wild pigs are hunted with dogs and spears, and blowguns with poisoned darts bring down monkeys.

Forest products, including rattan, bird's nests, some panned gold, and other rare finds—such as bezoar stones—provide some cash, as do jobs in Sarawak. Long Apari, the first village over the border— where there are no immigration or customs officials—is a three- or four-day walk. Monthly wages in a lumber camp in Sarawak can earn a Dayak up to $1,500, an incredible figure, and much higher than any similar work in Kalimantan. At any one time, up to one-quarter of the men from the last upriver villages on the Mahakam could be working on the other side of the border.

They return over the mountains lugging outboard engines, instant cameras, radios, T-shirts and even an occasional television, this last quite useless since there is no electricity or signal reaching the interior of Borneo.

In spite of these money-making opportunities, the area has suffered from depopulation, some 2.5 percent per year recently. Many of the brightest youngsters go away to school, get used to city lights and comforts, and never return to their home village.

Opposite: *Rapids-running, Dayak style.*

Visiting the upper Mahakam

Regular passenger and cargo vessels travel up the Mahakam only as far as Long Iram, 409 kilometers (253 mi.) from Samarinda. Some of the smaller mixed cargo boats reach Long Bagun, 583 kilometers (361 mi.) from the sea. But from here on, reliable river travel comes to a complete halt. There are only two ways to travel further than Long Bagun—to wait for an occasional twin-motor outboard, laden with merchandize and planning the rough trip through the rapids. Or you can charter a longboat yourself, if one is available, for around $300.

An uncomfortable but exciting two or three days could be spent bouncing the 140-odd kilometers to Long Pahangai, the next upstream stop. Part of the excitement comes from the fact that, depending on water levels, the longboat could turn right around and go back to Long Bagun. Even if all goes well, over the most dangerous rapids all the cargo has to be unloaded to lighten the boat. With no load and two engines running wide open, the craft can only inch its way through the worst of the white water. Overturning is always a frightening possibility. Between Long Bagun and Tiong Ohang, as many as 800 liters of the expensive fuel can be consumed.

Running the Mahakam's rapids, exciting as it is, may well take too much time or money. You might have to wait several days, or even weeks, for a longboat to make a cargo and passenger run. Although you miss a great travel experience, taking an airplane to Data Dawai from Samarinda makes everything much simpler.

Data Dawai, the name of the landing strip, is located about a few minutes' walk from Long Lunuk, a village central to the uprapids Mahakam region. From here you can travel upriver to Long Ampari, the last village on the Mahakam, or downriver to Long Pahangai, where occasional longboats leave to run the rapids downstream to Long Bagun.

Since the opening of the scheduled flights to Data Dawai in 1985, tourists have begun to make their presence felt in the region. Motorized canoe prices could be ridiculously high, and Dayak hospitality occasionally takes a back seat to fleecing travelers.

Check with your fellow airplane passengers to see if any are going up or downstream from Long Lunuk. There are usually boats meeting family members returning home from Samarinda. Even if no one seems to be heading your way, walk right away (after reconfirming your return flight with the agent) from the landing strip to the river to check if canoes or a longboat are ready to leave shortly.

The upriver villages

If there are any canoes or longboats leaving Long Lunuk, they will likely be heading for one of the two *kecamatan* centers: Long Pahangai, downstream, or Tiong Ohang, upstream. Report to the *camat* and the police, then ask whether there are any special events coming up—a dance, perhaps, or a pig hunt.

At Long Pahangai, you can also check with the Catholic mission. The church there has great Dayak motifs blended into the interior design. The village also has a somewhat dilapidated longhouse, with some old carvings and a huge drum. A talented young sculptor, who does mostly commission work, lives near the Pahangai River.

Hire a canoe and paddlers for a quiet ride on the Pahangai River, really more of a stream. The silence is wonderful after all the noisy river craft, and the scenery and birds are spectacular. There are 3,600 people in the Long Pahangai *kecamatan,* or just 1.2 people per square kilometer (.46 per sq. mi.).

Tiong Ohang, the other *kecamatan* center here, is also on the bank of the Mahakam, and has a store and a couple of interesting longhouses. The villages strung out along the other side of the river are more traditional, and are better places to explore once your business with officialdom is finished. This district has a population of some 2,300, with a density of only .3 inhabitants per square kilometer (.1 per sq. mi.).

If you want to walk from here across the Müller Range to the Kapuas basin, which drains West Kalimantan, you can arrange the trek at Tiong Ohang or Long Apari. (See "Trek Across Borneo," page 58.)The former village has some good art on display and a wonderfully solid longhouse, and makes a fine place from which to make short trips into the forest or up river tributaries.

Although each of these little villages has its own elementary school, just about everything else—stores, churches, clinics, high schools, radio transmitters, police, military, officials—is concentrated in Long Pahangai and Tiong Ohang. Recently, however, Long Lunuk, halfway between the district centers, has gained prominence with its airstrip.

Opposite: *Two Aoheng Dayak fishermen display their morning's catch of giant river catfish.*

KEDANG KEPALA

A Trip Up 'Cut-Off-Head' River

My feet were muddy and slippery, and I struggled upward in the dark. The crude ladder steps were hacked out of a log, which leaned against a hut perched on stilts. The last rung led directly into a small room, the far corner barely lit by a tiny lamp. The crowd of bodies shifted to make space as I wiggled inside. From the far corner, where a gaunt figure stood over a child, a high-pitched chant pierced the quiet. A Dayak curing ritual was in progress.

The chanting continued in a clear, female voice. Burhan Mas, the headman and my host, whispered that the *belian*—a lady shaman—was invoking the spirits to heal her patient. The *belian*'s silhouette, tall and thin, was barely visible, and she seemed to float over the child. The healer's long hair was loose, and she was wearing only a dark skirt. She stroked the child's body with leaves, and then rolled an egg over her.

Soon, all the flashlights were directed towards a plate where the egg was broken. Along with the yolk, a worm, a bit of root and a sliver of fish all slid onto the plate. The *belian* said that the child's stomach problems had been caused by eating fish which had incurred the anger of a spirit. She then directed that the egg and its contents, which the spirit had pulled out of the body thanks to her intervention, be thrown into the river.

Traveling to Ben Hes

The Dayak village of Ben Hes is far inland in East Kalimantan. To reach the village, one must travel on one of the major tributaries of the Mahakam River, the Kedang Kepala. Translated into English, the name of this river is the none-too-reassuring "Cut-Off-Head," a subtle local reference to a practice that was once widespread here.

On the several days' trip to Ben Hes by riverboat, I became somewhat used to scampering up and down the various wobbly planks which lead from the riverbank huts down to the rafts where the boats moor. All clothes washing and toilet activities take place on these floating docks. They cannot be mounted more firmly because it is not unusual for the water level to fluctuate a couple of meters or more overnight. In the morning, the banks are often slick with mud deposited the night before.

Simply walking down to a raft for something essential like boarding your boat becomes a confidence-shaking experience. The local people bound up and down effortlessly, of course, having developed a master gymnast's sense of balance during childhood. After a while, I could climb up most of these contraptions but coming down was always a problem, especially when the staircase was just a log with perfunctory notches. Going down, I always gave my camera bag to a sure-footed local with the feeble joke that my cameras could not swim.

Long Noran

Our boat chugged through the dark, its way lit by a powerful spotlight, and sometime during the first night out of Samarinda we turned off the Mahakam just past Muara Kaman (see map page 102) and headed up a wide tributary called the Kedang Kepala. We spent the second night tied up to the riverbank by the village of Batu Ampar. In the morning, it became clear why we had not proceeded the previous night. Just above Batu Ampar, the river narrows, and here the current was rushing through, turbulent and threatening. With the throttle wide open, we were barely making any headway at all, and—for a few breath-taking seconds—we once came to a complete stop. By gradually edging closer to one bank, which was lined with boulders, our captain somehow guided his boat through the dangerous passage.

A few more hours upriver, and I saw the first evidence of Dayak carving: a tall, colorful "totem" pole, topped by a sword-wielding warrior. The boat stopped for a half hour to allow me a closer look. The *hampatong* (A Dayak word for some kinds of statues) was firmly planted in front of a large meeting

Overleaf: A Dayak blacksmith on the upper Mahakam fashions a mandau, now used for cutting vegetation rather than heads. The mandau originated in this part of Borneo, and was later adopted by the other groups. **Opposite:** *A woman shaman in Ben Hes who has "cleaned" this sick girl's body with an egg breaks it to see what has caused the illness.*

house which rested on sculpted wooden pillars. The spacious interior was a riot of multi-colored, arabesque carvings, and a few strange, stylized faces could be made out in the abstract composition. A photo of President Suharto, although in a prominent spot, was lost in the wild decoration.

The village of Long Noran and nearby Long Segar are recently established, founded by the Kenyah Dayaks who moved here from their ancestral homes in the Apokayan region. The first group of several hundred people wandered for six years, planting crops and waiting for them to ripen before settling in their current location.

Leaving Long Noran, our boat chugged past several lumber camps worked at the time by Georgia Pacific, and early evening brought us to Muara Wahau, the administrative outpost for this region. I slept at the headman's house in the village of Nehes Liah Bing (also called Slabing), just across the river from Muara Wahau.

In the morning I rented a motorized canoe. With only a couple of centimeters of freeboard, the *ces* is nerve-wrackingly wobbly at first, but as soon as the propeller bites into the water, the canoe stabilizes wonderfully. Being so low in the water gives one an exhilarating feeling of speed as the brown water rushes by. After three hours skimming the surface, we arrived at Ben Hes, the last settlement upriver.

Ben Hes at last

As I landed, a curious band of little boys gathered around—the new elementary school, built that year, was not yet open for business. I waited several hours for the headman to return from his fields, and he arrived covered in sweat and dirt. I introduced myself, and Burham Mas invited me up the ladder to his house, built on stilts some three meters above the muddy ground. His wife received us with hot tea and we sat on a linoleum floor as evening enveloped the village.

During a long, leisurely conversation, I explained the purpose of my visit: photography and gathering information. But first, Burham Mas had a few questions of his own. He had had problems in the past with visitors, and sought to avoid any unpleasant situations. His first query was about my religion. It was obvious that I was not a Muslim, so I could eat pork and guzzle booze, both essential adjuncts to Dayak hospitality. His next questions were more basic: could I sleep on the hard floor? eat the local food? use the river for both bathing and toilet purposes? When all these questions were answered in the affirmative, backed by anecdotes of prolonged stays in places where living conditions were much more lean than at Ben Hes, Burham Mas invited me to stay with him as long as I wished.

His wife soon had a meal ready: wild pig,

two kinds of vegetables with hot sauce and noodle soup. We sat on the floor and ate the delicious supper with our hands. I was a bit reluctant to take a third helping, but Burham Mas urged me on, remarking that he enjoyed seeing me eat copious quantities because now he could see that feeding his guest would be no problem.

Most of the people of the village, including Burham Mas himself, had converted to Catholicism three years ago, he told me. There was still no church erected there, and the Indonesian priest who occasionally visits Ben Hes lives more than 200 kilometers (125 mi.) away from the village.

The ancient beliefs still govern many aspects of the villagers' lives, such as marriages, funerals and healing rituals. When I asked if I could observe and photograph some of their traditional dances, Burham Mas replied that this would unfortunately be quite impossible. The music for these dances is provided by sacred gongs, which can only be sounded at prescribed times.

Working the fields

Every morning during my stay at Ben Hes, families jumped into their canoes to paddle or motor to their fields, called *ladang*. These are chopped out of the forest, using the slash-and-burn technique in which the ash from the bush and trees enriches the soil. Cutting and burning the fields is the usual activity in August, the dryest month of the year.

Because the soil is thin and poor, the fields can be cropped only once or twice before requiring a fallow period of seven years or more. Each of the 71 families in Ben Hes cultivates at least one *ladang* in widely scattered locations. Due to the yearly necessity of shifting one's fields to avoid soil depletion, many families have to travel for hours to reach their plots, which can be ten or more kilometers away.

We eased ourselves very gently into the headman's canoe early one morning. Sidling his way around obstacles was child's play for Burham Mas as we zipped upstream for a half hour before turning into a narrow tributary where the vegetation from each bank met overhead. A few more minutes brought us to several canoes tied to the shore, with a slippery log providing the way up and out of the water.

Nearby was a cleared area where everyone was sitting in a small, open hut built on stilts. There were some 15 adult men and women, and a few children in the hut. As we

waited for the owner of the field to show up, everyone chatted in the local language, and I smiled a lot.

The women were preparing a mixture of glutinous rice, corn and coconut milk—later to be our lunch. The paste was poured into bamboo tubes and set to cook over a fire. One of the men asked if I wanted a drink and I happily accepted. A large bamboo tube was hauled up to the hut. It contained *tuak*, a mildly alcoholic brew made by fermenting the sap of a palm tree. When the owner of the *ladang* eventually showed up, it was time to start working.

The men grabbed their dibble sticks while the women filled bamboo tubes with seed rice. Standing a meter or so apart, the men slammed their planting sticks into the ground, leaving holes about 40 cm. (16 in.) apart. The women followed behind, dropping a few grains of rice into each hole.

Later, as the men sat in the comfortable hut, the ladies served lunch. A table of leaves was laid down on the raised floor and the

Above: *The chief of traditions of Ben Hes village, now a recently converted Catholic. He determined that a traditional dance could be performed using a tape recording, instead of the sacred gongs which could only be sounded at special times.*
Opposite: *Wearing a shirt of barkskin, an elder Modang Dayak from Ben Hes performs a bird dance using hornbill-feather wings as props.*

bamboo tubes were split open. We were each given a plate with pieces of wild pig along with a soup of vegetables and palm trunk into which we dipped chunks of the rice mixture. The meal was superb, especially since we were all starving after a hard morning's work planting.

Night entertainment

That evening, Burham Mas had some good news for me. One of the men at the *ladang* that day had been the *kepala adat,* or chief of traditions. After our noonday meal, they had discussed my request to see some traditional dancing. Although the *kepala adat* was adamant that the sacred gongs, the usual accompaniment to these dances, could not be touched, he suggested a clever alternative.

During the previous year's post-harvest rituals, one of the men had made a tape-recording of the gongs. The *kepala adat* decided there was nothing taboo about playing the tape for the dances as long as the sacred gongs were left alone.

I bought three dozen bottles of a locally distilled booze called "gin" to lubricate the proceedings and to put everyone in a cheerful mood. Some elderly ladies were the first to arrive, most sporting the distinctive large hoops in their earlobes. Among them was the shaman who had invoked the spirits in the healing ritual I had observed earlier. She was elegantly dressed in traditional finery, and shot an occasional coquettish glance at the younger men.

The village secretary, a young man whom I had seen earlier in spiffy western clothes, had pulled a change of attire and personality. He appeared transformed before me now, in full warrior regalia, ready and competent to chop off enemy heads. He performed a war dance, graceful and virile.

This act was followed by a dance performed by the girls, whose restrained, elegant movements imitated the flight of birds. Then came another warrior dance, but in this one there were two men, the one serious and fierce, and the other a natural comic who sent the audience into fits of laughter.

Then the chief of traditions and the shaman, a well-matched, picturesque couple if there ever was one, danced gracefully together. These two were followed by a group performance, in which everyone held hands as they stepped through the harvest dance. I joined in, and the seemingly shy girls on either side of me each gave my hand a squeeze. Did this have an ulterior motive?

I sat down to rest with a full glass of gin next to a pretty girl whom I had photographed many times while they were planting the rice. I offered her some of my gin, but she just smiled and touched my hand, then the glass of gin, and then her chin. What did that mean? I didn't ask, preferring to leave it a titillating mystery.

Mahakam Practicalities

Visitors go up the Mahakam River to see the Dayaks, hoping for a glimpse of the exotic. Frustrations are common. For the most part, the Dayaks of East Kalimantan seem quite ordinary—most wear Western clothes, most are Christians, very few live in longhouses and, of course, no one hunts for heads anymore.

But such outward signs do not mean that Dayak tradition is a thing of the past. If you explore the upriver villages, you will meet Dayaks in traditional dress and—with a bit of luck and initiative—you will be able to witness interesting funerary and agricultural rituals. Just remember that the days of the wild head-hunters of Borneo are over; what can be seen in Kalimantan is a people with a rich culture, trying to maintain as much of it as possible while entering the modern world of medicines, education and jobs.

There are both advantages and disadvantages to visiting the Mahakam in either the wet or the dry season. Agricultural rituals are held at planting time, September and October, and harvest time, February and March. During the driest months, July to September, the larger boats cannot make it as far upstream as they can in the rainy season, but in the rainy season, especially November to January, flooding may prevent travel. And dry spells or heavy rains can come any time.

ACCOMMODATIONS AND DINING

Up to Long Iram, commercial accommodations and meals along the Mahakam are inexpensive and usually available—just don't expect luxuries like hot showers, flush toilets, fancy food or ice. Everywhere else, Dayak hospitality and schoolteachers or other government officials are the only practical means of survival, unless you happen to be a jungle-trained commando. Gifts of salt, tobacco and sugar are greatly appreciated. Although in some villages you may be offered lodging *gratis,* expect to pay some $6 a day for room and board. Agree on a price before settling in to avoid unreasonable demands when leaving. For all journeys off the beaten path, you must be able to speak at least a little bit of Indonesian, and be adaptable and self-reliant.

TRANSPORTATION

Boat travel on the Mahakam could well become one of the highlights of your journey, if you are more interested in sights than creature comforts. There are several river craft with Western-style amenities, but these are owned and operated by travel agencies for group tours. (See "Agency Tours" below.) If money is no object, you could charter one of these, along with an English-speaking guide.

Most travelers take one of the ordinary riverboats for moving up and down the Mahakam. A few of the larger ones, making the day-and-a-half run from Samarinda to Long Iram, have bunk beds and a kitchen. Most boats are mixed passenger cargo, making innumerable stops. Passenger-only river taxis ply back and forth from Samarinda to Kota Bangun and at times to Muara Muntai.

All boats must stop at Tenggarong to check in at the river-traffic control post. But if you are planning a long river journey, especially on a smaller boat or during holidays, it might be a good idea to board at Samarinda (instead of Tenggarong) to stake out your territory before all the best spots are taken.

The following fares, times and distances are from Samarinda. Times on regular boats can vary tremendously. Speedboats hold 4-6 passengers and their fares below are for round-trip, unless you linger at your destination.

Destination	Distance	Reg. Boat	Speedboat
Kota Bangun	160 km	$1; 10 hrs	
Tanjung Isuy	240 km	$1.60; 16 hrs	$240; 5 hrs
Muara Muntai	200 km	$1.25; 14 hrs	
Muara Pahu	270 km	$2; 18 hrs	$240; 6 hrs
Melak	325 km	$4; 24 hrs	$300; 8 hrs
Long Iram	410 km	$5; 30 hrs	$400; 11 hrs
Data Bilang	470 km	$5; 37 hrs	$500; 14 hrs
Long Hubung	480 km	$5.50; 38 hrs	
Long Bagun	525 km	$6; 40 hrs	$600; 16 hrs

From Muara Muntai on the Mahakam River to Tanjung Isuy on Lake Jempang, it's 40 km. By regular boat, 30¢ and 3 hrs.; by motorized small canoe, $1.50 and 2 hrs.; chartering one's own canoe for the trip, $15 and 2 hrs.

Tenggarong

If you decide to spend the night in Tenggarong, there are several inexpensive *losmen* ($2-$7) on Jl. Diponegoro running parallel to the Mahakam just downstream from the main dock or, in the same direction, across the bridge on Jl. Sudirman. All are within easy walking distance from the dock unless you are overloaded with luggage. There are plenty of motorcycle "taxis" or *ojek,* but first agree on the price (30-60¢). The dock area also holds several restaurants serving mainly Indonesian and Chinese dishes. Try venison brochettes at the **Tepian Pandan**, overlooking the river.

SHOPPING

Check out the **Karya Indah Art Shop** on Jl. Diponegoro next to the docks. Lots of Dayak craft items here, some genuine antiques but no really top pieces. There are new Dayak baskets, *mandaus* and carvings in the shop under the tourist office (**Bapparda**) across the street from the Karya Indah. If you are around during the morning hours, stroll through the **Pasar Pagi**, the town's main market, located next to the bridge on Jl. A. Yani. Some Dayak crafts here also. Careful shoppers with some time should check art shops in Balikpapan, Samarinda and Tenggarong to see what is available and at what prices. Craft items can also be purchased in upriver Dayak villages at cheaper prices if you are good at bargaining. But you can't count on finding what you want in the villages, and if you see a nice piece, people are usually very reluctant to part with it.

Kota Bangun

There are several inexpensive *losmen* ($1-$4) but if you can afford it, stay at the **Sri Bangun Lodge**, the only Western-type accommodations on the Mahakam beyond Samarinda. The spread holds a tennis court and rooms have hot water as well as AC for $24 a night. Meals are extra but the portions are large and the price is a reasonable $4.50.

Muara Muntai

Muara Muntai is 9-12 hours by river taxi from Tenggarong, perhaps 14 hours from Samarinda. There are several small *losmen* here.

Muara Muntai is the cheapest and most convenient point of departure for Tanjung Isuy. There are a couple of large boats heading there each week from Muara Muntai, but these trips are canceled if the lake level is too low, often the case during the summer months. Smaller craft usually head out every morning, taking 4-5 hours and charging about $2 a head.

We recommend travel to Tanjung Isuy by small motorized canoe, saving time and enjoying the scenery at your own pace. The people at your *losmen* can help you find a canoe—locally called a *ketinting* or *ces* (pronounced "chess")—to rent. Bring a hat or make sure that your canoe can put up a roof. The 2-hour trip will set you back $15-$25 one-way, depending on the size of the engine and your ability to bargain in Indonesian. You can hire the boat out of Muara Muntai for the round trip (less than two one-ways) or rent another one for the return trip out of Tanjung Isuy. If you plan to spend just one night in Tanjung Isuy, rent your craft out of Muara Muntai for the round trip.

Long Iram

If you are interested in having a ritual/dance performed especially for you in the Long Iram area, you can contact the *camat* or Pak Sadik (alias Adi Surya) who runs an outfit called the **Meranti Group**, located downriver at the edge of town. Ask both the *camat* and Pak Sadik if there are any traditional happenings going on

either at the moment or sometime during your planned stay.

If you want a ritual for yourself or group, this can be arranged with several days' advance notice. Costs vary according to the number of participants and degree of elaboration, which includes musical instruments. Count on at least $50 for a short, small-scale affair and up to $1,500 for a two-day *mamat* with dozens of participants and hundreds of local spectators. Pak Sadik can also provide fast longboat transportation to the sites.

Uprapids Mahakam

Not too easy to get here. We suggest trying to fly on one of Merpati's twice-weekly Twin Otters, $40 to Data Dawai. Bad weather often forces cancellations. During holidays, flights are crowded. On arrival, make certain the agent at Data Dawai confirms your return flight. If you can't get out of Long Lunuk the day you arrive, there is a rudimentary *penginapan* for $3/night and several well-stocked stores. Stock up on supplies and let the word out as to where you want to go—be ready to bargain. Remember that gasoline for the outboards is scarce and horrendously expensive. As a very general rule, a small canoe might charge $30-$50 to Long Pahangai, a bit more to Tiong Ohang, and $60-$100 all the way to Long Apari. The large longboats, much faster and roomier, could charge 2-3 times this amount.

COMMERCIAL TOURS

The standard shorter tours (2-4 days) usually include the museum at Tenggarong, river travel up the Mahakam and across Lake Jempang to the village of Tanjung Isuy for dances, traditional meals and overnight stays in a longhouse modified for foreigners. Agencies usually insist on a minimum group of 4 for this and other tours. Based on parties of 4-6, costs run from $290-$395/person. In groups of 10 or more, costs drop to $228-$245/person.

Candra Wirapati. Jl. Antasari 5, Balikpapan, Tel: (542) 21762.

Tomaco Tours. Benakutai Hotel, Balikpapan. Tel: (542) 21747. Also Jl. Thamrin 9, Jakarta, Tel: (21) 347453.

Longer tours go further up the Mahakam River. These stop at Melak, with the nearby Kersik Luwai Orchid Forest (where the black orchids flower in March-April) and Eheng, a Tunjung Dayak village. Further upriver, tours stop at the Kenyah Dayak villages of Rukun Damai and Data Bilang, as well as Bahau Dayak villages including Tering. Traditional meals and dances are included. These tours last 6-8 days, costing around $575/person in a group of 4-6 and $375-$450/person in groups of 10 or more. There are also longer planned tours, further upriver. (See "Coast Cities Practicalities," page 68, for more agencies.)

PART V

South Kalimantan

The province of Kalimantan Selatan—Kalsel—is the smallest of the four administrative divisions of Kalimantan. This was not always the case. Until the late 1950s, Kalsel included all of what is now Kalimantan Tengah—Central Kalimantan. Then, after a vicious little guerilla war, the Dayaks of Kalteng demanded and received their own province, independent of heavily Islamic Kalsel.

The geography of the region is shaped by the Meratus Mountains, which form a long, broad range covering most of Kalsel north to south. The mountains are not high, the tallest peak being Puncak Besar, 1,892 meters (6,200 ft.). The Barito River and its major downstream tributary, the Martapura, remain important means of communications and trade with the interior, in spite of a paved highway which runs from Banjarmasin to Balikpapan. Near the coast, the province is covered with tidal swamp, some of which has been successfully reclaimed by rice farmers.

Kalsel is Kalimantan's most densely populated province, with 2.4 million inhabitants living in its 37,660 square kilometers (14,000 sq. mi.). The people of Kalsel are Banjarese, as ethnically mixed a group as one is likely to find. Their ancestors include four Dayak groups—the Ma'anyan, Lawangan, Bukit and Ngaju—as well as Malays from Sumatra, Javanese, Sundanese, Arabs, Chinese and Buginese. The Banjarese dialect is closely related to Malay.

The kingdom of Negara Dipa

The Banjarese trace their origins to a legendary Hindu kingdom, and the first raja's wife sprang, fully formed, from a gigantic mass of white foam, making her dramatic Venus-like appearance to an awed audience. In a less flattering version, she emerges from the mud. Her birth was assisted by the grand vizier, Lambung Mangkurat, remembered today in many place names such as the main street of Banjarmasin and the province's museum. This vizier hung around for three generations to help build the new Hindu kingdom called Negara Dipa.

A scattered set of Hindu-style ruins called Candi Agung (not really worth visiting) have been found inland, and the site is extolled as the province's original foundation. Little evidence backs this claim. There is another Hindu temple in ruins called Candi Laras (not worth a visit either), in the Tupin district.

At the end of the 13th century, the region's history is on more solid ground. Ampoedjatamaka, the son of a merchant from India's Coromandel coast, established a settlement which became the state of Banjarmasin. Three generations later, the ruler's daughter and sole heir married a Majapahit prince from Java. At this point, and it is unclear why, the kingdom changed its name from Negara Dipa to Banjar. The royal marriage made Banjar a vassal state of the powerful Majapahit Empire.

Javanese craftsmen were brought to build the new palaces, and Majapahit laws supplanted the local ones. The cultural remains of this period include *wayang* puppet figures, gamelan orchestras, art and dance styles, *topeng* masks and ornamental metalwork. Though the old Javanese-style objects are still honored, Islam soon dominated the Banjarese, as it did most of the archipelago.

In 1620, a local power struggle for the throne was resolved with military aid from the Javanese kingdom of Demak, and the price for this was conversion of Banjar to Islam. Art and lifestyles changed to conform to Muslim mores. Thanks to the Islamic network, existing trade picked up with Java and the Gujerati coast of India. Pepper bushes were planted to compete in the spice trade. The region of Banjarese political control and

Overleaf: *The floating market at Banjarmasin.*
Opposite: *Small boats on the Barito River are dwarfed by the majestic Bugis schooners.*

English, and you can either hire them or sign on with an agency to visit the Dayaks of the Loksado area (the Dayaks are not worth it, but the trip itself is) or the Tanjung Puting orangutan reserve in Kalteng.

Air communications are good and a paved road from Banjarmasin reaches all the way to Balikpapan. By river, one can reach Palangkaraya, the capital of Kalteng, or motor to a couple of towns by the Barito River, from where you can explore the far interior of the island.

Skilled farmers

Historically known as a producer of black pepper, Banjarmasin now thrives on the large surpluses of rice and other crops that farmers coax from the region's rich alluvial soils. Although the soil is rich, the land has not always been suitable for farming. In what has been called "one of the world's major experiments in marginal land utilization," Banjarese farmers have been pioneers in swamp reclamation, skillfully converting tidal regions into rice paddies, tangerine and orange groves, and vegetable gardens.

And Kalimantan can well use these technologies. Not counting Irian Jaya, which contains the world's largest continuous swamp, 43 million hectares (106 million acres) of the Indonesian land mass is mangrove or tidal swamp, more than one-quarter of the nation's total land area. Almost half of this swamp is in Kalimantan—18.7 million hectares (46 million acres)—and about one-fifth of this area has agricultural potential. Now the land use consists chiefly of one-shot logging operations, which offer zero long-term benefits. In the long run, fisheries and farming would be much more profitable.

Despite its diminutive size, Kalsel leads Kalimantan in land reclaimed from tidal swamps, over 100,000 hectares (250,000 acres) to date. In 1939, the first government-sponsored transmigration settlement, for farming rice in swamplands, was established at Purwosari, near Banjarmasin.

Most Banjarese remain rice farmers, although recently corn has been planted in a big way. Improved breeds of cattle, introduced through livestock programs, have helped to put cash in farmers' pockets. The government has been active in introducing

tribute-taking expanded from the small sultanates on the south coast to include a measure of influence in Sukadana, Sambas and Sanggau in the west-central portion of the island, and Pasir, Kutai and Berau in the east. This was the Golden Age of Banjar.

After a war with the Dutch, the Banjarese sultanate fell. Internal political strife had already weakened the throne when Holland installed an unpopular puppet to rule the Banjarese. In 1860, Holland declared the end of the sultanate, and set up her colonial headquarters for all of Dutch Borneo in Banjarmasin. A faction, led by Pangeran Antasari, fought against the Dutch between 1860 and 1864, and pockets of resistance remained until the end of the 19th century. (See "Islam and the West," page 30.)

A bustling capital

The capital city of Banjarmasin is the most interesting urban center of Kalimantan. There are docks where graceful Bugis schooners moor, a beautiful new mosque, and busy floating markets. Nearby islands, in the Barito River, are populated by troops of monkeys. Inland, carts drawn by water buffaloes amble along the paved road to the diamond fields at Cempaka, or to Martapura, where the gems are cut and polished.

Banjarmasin has hotels of all categories and many good restaurants. There are plenty of freelance guides here, speaking some

Above: *In Banjarmasin, modern lumber mills are rapidly replacing the small riverside shops where logs are sawn into planks by hand.* **Opposite:** *The river serves as highway, market and even bathroom for the inhabitants of Banjarmasin.*

new, high-yield varieties of rice that grow well in swamps. Irrigation programs result in two or more crops a year. Recently, a novel technique has been used to plant two new varieties of rice directly in the swamplands, increasing production. Since water levels here sometimes reach two meters, boats are used to harvest the crop.

Thanks to the modern methods, new seeds and close to a half-million hectares under irrigation, rice production has shot up over the last few years. Most of the surplus is exported to Central and East Kalimantan.

A rich range of exports

As in the rest of Kalimantan, the wood industry dominates the local export economy. In 1987, over $332 million worth of plywood and sawn timber was shipped out, mainly to Japan and the United States. There are 13 plywood factories in Kalsel, and 43 sawmills, employing mainly Javanese. The Banjarese prefer farming or trade, and will not put up with the living and working conditions at the mills.

Rubber, the most important cash crop for the villages, is shipped mainly to Singapore and is the second-most valuable export: $41 million in 1987. About $30 million worth of rattan is shipped to Japan, and $10 million worth of frozen shrimp and crayfish head to Japan and Singapore. The rattan shipped Central Kalimantan is processed in Kalsel into carpets and furniture. The town of Amuntai is the traditional rattan center, but the big "factories," mainly employing women and girls, are in Banjarmasin. Other export items include frog's legs, snake and lizard skins, a kind of tree bark used in making joss sticks and insect repellent, roots for *jamu* and other traditional medicines, and *gaharu*.

Sawn timber, dried fish and recently, coal from the Batu Licin region are exported to other islands in the Archipelago. Crude oil from the inland Tanjung region is piped to Balikpapan for processing.

Over 160,000 fishermen make a living from Kalsel's open inland waters, more than anywhere else in Kalimantan. In contrast, there are only 5,000 sea fishermen, compared to 15,000 in Kalbar, 48,000 in Kalteng and 19,000 in Kaltim. Taiwanese experts are now designing commercial aquaculture systems here.

The pepper harvest, barely 500 tons a year, is a minor part of the economy today, but valuable cash crops such as cacao and *illipe* nuts are commanding increasing acreage. Although there are many small coconut plantations in the region, this crop is chiefly for local consumption.

There are large known deposits of iron ore, kaolin and limestone in the Meratus Mountains waiting for investment. The diamond fields of Cempaka provide several hundred jobs, but even more pan for gold on a small scale basis.

BANJARMASIN

Picturesque City on the Barito River

Banjarmasin is the only city in Kalimantan that is worth visiting for its own sake, rather than as a place from which to hop upriver. In the city and its environs, which cover 72 square kilometers (28 sq. mi.), one can visit the busy floating market, monkey islands and low-tech diamond mining operations.

Banjarmasin is just 22 kilometers (14 mi.) from the Java Sea, and since portions of the city are below sea level, the city rises and falls with the tides. Where it passes by the capital of Kalsel, the Barito River is a full kilometer wide. The Martapura River, much narrower, snakes through the city, a busy "main street" for a bewildering variety of boats.

City on the river

Banjarmasin was founded at the junction of the Martapura and Barito Rivers on September 24, 1526. This happened just after Pangeran (prince) Samudera overthrew his uncle with the help of an army from Demak in Java. As a condition of Demak's help, the prince accepted Islam and took the name of Sultan Suriansyah. The area's old capital during Hindu times had been at Negara, a fair ways inland, on the Negara River. Banjarmasin remained the region's capital until the outset of the Banjarmasin War in 1860, when the Dutch moved their headquarters to Martapura. (See "Islam and the West," page 30.) After independence, Banjarmasin resumed its pre-eminent role.

Originally, the city was completely river-oriented, and much of this characteristic is still evident today. Houses on stilts, called *lanting,* line the waterways, which crisscross the capital. Taking a small motorized boat— *klotok*—around the rivers and canals, especially during the early morning and late afternoon hours, shows the city from the inside: Banjarese bathing, washing laundry, buying fruit, vegetables or fish from women vendors

in tiny canoes, gossiping.

The floating vegetable and fruit market is a colorful bustle of boats where produce from upriver is wholesaled to shopkeepers and restauranteurs. There are also two fish markets—one for freshwater fish, the other for the saltwater species. At the schooner dock on the Martapura river, dozens of these majestic Bugis vessels tie up to one another, making a splendid photograph that seems to have come from the age of sailing ships. Just downriver from the dock is a shipyard where these graceful vessels are still built. For about $120,000 you can commission a Bugis schooner of your own, fully equipped, including a powerful engine.

The city's industrial strip is along the Barito river, close to downtown. Here are plants where workers saw thick logs into planks, in some cases by hand. The modern plywood factories here face the river so they can receive the huge rafts of timber that float down from the interior. Among the lumber plants are huge shed-like buildings where crumb rubber is processed for export.

Pulau Kembang Island, just off Banjarmasin, is the home of dozens of semi-tame monkeys. The island, which is an attraction for Banjarese and visitors alike, gets very crowded on Sundays and holidays. Further downriver is an island nature reserve, Pulau Kaget, where there are proboscis monkeys, birds, and other wildlife.

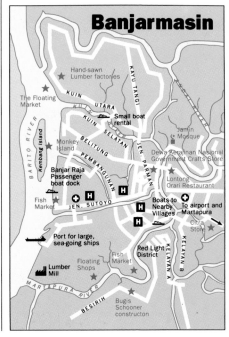

Opposite: *Banjarmasin's Grand Mosque.*

Banjarmasin has one of the most splendid mosques in all of Kalimantan. The Grand Mosque, the Sabilal Muhtadin, is set on a 10-hectare plot in the center of the city, and it faces the Martapura River. The mosque is named for the great writings of Sheik Mohammed Arsyal Al Banjari, a Muslim scholar who lived from 1710 to 1812. The inside of the mosque is top-quality marble, with exquisite calligraphy from the Koran gracing the walls. A watchman is always around to open up the mosque for visitors. While the front gates to the mosque area are often closed except at prayer times, the enclosure is usually open in the back.

The floating market

Klotok can be rented at the bridge near Kuin Pertamina for $2-3 an hour. They are usually powered by an 6 HP engine and can take six to ten passengers in comfort. Get an early start: the floating market starts at first light and it is pretty much over by 8:30 a.m. Best to start out around 6:00 a.m. to be there at the first light of dawn.

The floating market, *pasar terapung,* is a busy, colorful gathering of small boats and canoes. The larger craft bring fruit or vegetables at wholesale prices. Tiny canoes, called *jukung,* are paddled by turbaned women in colorful dress. They buy their stock of foodstuff from the stationary wholesale boats, and then take their buys to their riverside customers. Along the river, stop at one of the floating mini-restaurants for a refreshing cup of hot tea or coffee, and a sweet cake.

For photographs, ask your *klontok* boatman to maneuver as close to shore as possible to have the best light on the crowd. A few women might turn away from the camera, but most don't mind. Some of the men assume outrageous poses and beg to be photographed. Bring lots of film along, with both a telephoto lens for portraits and wide-angle to capture the colorful scenery.

After shopping, many of the women hitch a ride up- or downriver. As many as a dozen of their little canoes can be seen tied to a motorized boat for the trip back home.

To Flower Island

From the floating market, it is a quick hop to Pulau Kembang—"Flower Island"—now full of common long-tailed macaque monkeys of all sizes. They are believed by some to hold spirits who must not be offended.

The monkeys wait for you right at the dock, hoping for a handout of peanuts which you can buy in a nearby stall. If you want any of the little fellas to get a peanut, pitch it to him accurately, as the big male raja monkeys will otherwise hog all the food in sight. An old man, whose family used to own the island, will want you to sign the guest book and make a contribution—Rp 500 is about right. The place gets awfully crowded on

Sundays and holidays. A stone shrine on the island is believed by both the Chinese and Buginese to have magical powers, and flower offerings and prayers here bring good health and business success.

Continue your trip around Pulau Kembang, past the Trisakti port for large vessels, coast by the towering rubber-processing mills and plywood factories, and enter the Martapura River. A short ways in, you will see colorful riverside shops, open to customers arriving by canoe. Houses, shops, even gas stations are on floating platforms. Further upriver, you will see dozens of the magnificent Bugis sailing ships. Swarming dock hands load and unload these ocean-going vessels, the backbone of inter-island commerce.

The strange proboscis monkeys

Pulau Kaget, literally "Startling Island" is 12 kilometers (7 mi.) south of Banjarmasin in the Barito River. The name comes from the island's reputation as a haven for ghosts. The trip by *klontok* from Banjarmasin takes about one and a half hours, and the round-trip charter should cost around $10-$20. Don't forget to bring a hat and a cool drink.

To see the proboscis monkeys, it's best to be there at dawn, around 6:30 a.m., which means that you should get started at around 5:00 a.m. Later in the day, the monkeys move to inaccessible places in the swamps, and return to the shore at dusk. It is not difficult to spot the monkeys, but getting within telephoto range requires silence, time, patience and lots of luck. You will need at least a 300 millimeter lens, high-speed film and steady hands. Best to forget the photos unless you really know what you're doing. The animals have a healthy fear of man, especially if your boat engine is still running.

Pulau Kaget is actually two islands, the larger one covering 24 hectares (60 acres). The best spot for viewing *Nasalis larvatus* is the river inlet heading into the interior from the south shore of the first, northernmost island. At low tide, this mini-river becomes too shallow to navigate, another factor to consider when planning your visit. A guide could be very helpful in arranging this jaunt, if he has had the experience.

I arranged for a guide, and left while it was still dark. The air was cool enough that I needed a jacket. My reward for this early departure was the sight of dozens of proboscis monkeys performing superb acrobatics in the trees. These curious fellows are not at all afraid of the water, and would on occasion fling themselves from the trees into the water or mud, splashing and thrashing into the swamp. We also saw black gibbons, swinging from arm to arm through the canopy, and a variety of birds, including several colorful kingfishers.

Below: *A riverside store in Banjarmasin.*

VISITING KALSEL

Hill Dayaks, Gem Fields and Monkeys

Banjarmasin is an ideal base for exploring the surrounding attractions, as there is plenty to do in town while you arrange your visits to the vicinity. The most popular short trip from Banjarmasin is to the diamond fields of Cempaka, the gem-cutting center of Martapura, and the provincial museum, which is on the way. Colorful oxcarts, called *keroba sapi*, ply the roads. Other recommended trips, to visit the Dayaks in Loksado and to see the orangutan rehabilitation center at Tanjung Puting, require several days.

The gem fields

The Cempaka diamond fields are about 45 kilometers (28 mi.) from Banjarmasin, near Lake Riam Kanan. Here teams of men and women dig vertical, well-sized shafts up to 5 meters (16 ft.) deep to bring up the clay. Rocks and pebbles are picked from the raw, gray muck, the clay is washed, and then panned by members of the team. For hours on end these folks sit in the muddy water, waiting for Lady Luck in the form of flakes of gold, an occasional sapphire, an amethyst, a garnet or maybe even a tiny diamond.

Once in a great while it is boom time, and a monster, such as the 167.5-carat Trisakti Diamond brought up in 1965, is found. (See "Trisakti," page 140.)

According to records, the largest diamonds found here were: in 1846, three diamonds of 12, 13 and 20 carats; in 1850, two whoppers—one 106.67 carats, the other a measly 77 carats; in 1965—in addition to the Trisakti—one of 29 carats; in 1968, one of 26.5 carats; in 1970, one 13-carat gem; and in 1987, three big ones of 14, 33 and 50 carats.

Ten percent of the value of all the gems goes to the owner of the land who parcels out plots to the various teams. If you don't mind picking your way through the mud and water, you can see all the phases of work from up close. b You can buy a raw diamond or some other precious stone on the spot.

Near the diamond fields, in the village of Cempaka or the town of Martapura, the gems, called *galuh*—"lady"—are cut and polished. A one-carat, clear diamond will cost you about $2,500. (See "Kalsel Practicalities," page 142, for details on diamond buying.)

The Lambung Mangkurat Museum

This museum, covering the history and culture of Kalsel, is worth a short visit. If you are really interested in the area's history you could stay longer, but then you would need an English-speaking guide. A good way to see the museum is to stop there on your way to or from the diamond fields.

Unfortunately, the museum has only copies (the originals are in Jakarta, as usual) of large bronze pieces from the Hindu period, and a model of Candi Laras, a temple from that time. There are also a large-scale model of the sultans' wood palace, palace clothing, model ships and fishing gear, a red-sugar processing apparatus, the royal gamelan and Javanese-style masks, weaving tools, and various old armaments. There is even a genealogical chart listing all the past rulers of Banjarmasin.

There is some Dayak art here too, including some funerary pieces and carvings. There are a couple of dragon heads on display, which were used in weddings and were presumably a carryover from pre-Muslim times. Parked just outside the main building

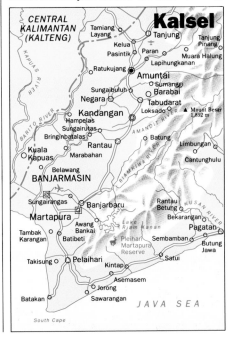

is an elaborate ruler's canoe, called a *tambangan,* covered with decoration. A separate building holds an exhibition by Gusti Sholihin Hassan, a locally famous painter of semi-abstract portraits.

The museum is on the main highway in the town of Banjarbaru, close to Martapura. Entrance fee is Rp 200. Closed Mondays. All other days, open at 8:30 a.m. until 2:00 p.m. on Tuesday, Wednesday, Thursday and Sunday, until 11:00 a.m. on Friday, 1:00 p.m. on Saturday. Shoes must be removed to visit the upstairs part of the museum. Traditional dances are occasionally performed here on Sundays and holidays.

Dances and weddings

A rich variety of dances is performed in Kalsel, usually during Muslim rites of passage, as entertainment for visiting V.I.P.s, and to celebrate important public holidays. The dances include the *hadrah,* a dance of Arabic origin performed to escort the bride to the groom; the *rudat,* originally from Persia, danced in connection with various Islamic ceremonies; the Dayak *gintor* or welcome dance, a flower dance; and the *mumenggung,* an elegant masked step which welcome spectators to the all-male dramas performed in villages after the harvest. These dramas, or *mamada* plays, often include topics from *The Thousand and One Nights,* integrated with Malay themes. Javanese influence shows in many other dances and in the occasional *wayang* performances.

Weddings here are complicated affairs. The bride's family is ritually offered a traditional bride price of antique porcelain, gold rings and cash (up to $300). The *hadrah* and the *rudat* are often danced, and old dragon (*naga*) heads, owned by clans, escort the bride and groom around the village. These *nagas* are a carryover from Hindu times, and must be covered with a yellow cloth and treated to offerings of flowers and eggs when stored or sickness will result. The *naga* heads are believed to originate from an underwater kingdom, and bring luck and happiness for the newly wedded couple's life ahead. Marriages are usually held during the two months or so after the Idul Titri Lebaran, which fell on April 17 in 1990 and will fall 11 days earlier on each succeeding year.

The Dayaks of Loksado

The Dayaks of South Kalimantan are not the most remote in Borneo, and the combination of trekking, rafting and overnighting circuit in the Dayak "home-stays" of Loksado has been broken in by many visitors. Still, it could be the highlight of your trip to Kalimantan if you take your time. Trips to Loksado usually start from Kandangan, four to five hours by bus north of Banjarmasin on the main road to Balikpapan. Either on the way there or the way back, you might stop at

Margasari (not far from Rantau), which is a handicraft center.

There are several trails to Loksado, the shortest one 8 hours, the longest perhaps 24 hours of hiking, spread over several days. The best trail for jungle scenery and animals starts at Batu Ampar. During the dry season, four-wheel-drive vehicles can sometimes make it all the way to Loksado ($90-$120). But this way you do not see much along the way and miss all the suspension bridges. And the engine scares away all the wildlife. Kalsel is rich in animal life, with 500 species of birds, more than 200 kinds of amphibians and reptiles (including 150 snake species) and over 700 varieties of freshwater fish.

The Bukit or Meratus Dayaks practice a form of ancestor-spirit worship called Kaharingan (see "Kaharingan Faith," page 152). After harvest, around the end of July, they celebrate the *Aruh Ganal* to thank the spirits, and a month later, perform a follow-up ceremony called *Aruh Biasa*. During the rainy season, when there is lots of sickness, the *belian* or women healers perform exorcism rites that sometimes last several days. The Dayaks here do not perform rituals for tourists, and unless a ritual is taking place, the villages here are not really worth visiting.

There are over two dozen village "long-houses" in the area, with the largest, in Melaris, holding 165 people. These communal *balai* are not the longhouses familiar in other parts of Borneo, with the communal veranda stretching the structure's entire length and sleeping quarters in the back.

The *balai* are large, slightly rectangular buildings, some 30 by 40 meters (100 by 130 ft.), with family units on all four sides and a communal space in the middle.

Unless your Indonesian is relatively fluent and you are an experienced trekker, we recommend either an organized tour or at least an English-speaking guide from Banjarmasin. A sanitized agency tour runs about $400; a guide with some English skills, perhaps $15/day plus his expenses.

Bring a sleeping bag, air mattress, some food, insect repellent, good hiking shoes and sandals, but keep the weight down. Either carry a backpack yourself, or hire a porter—expect to pay about Rp 750 per kilo, per day. For an overnight stay in a Dayak longhouse, plus meals, pay $3.

There is a very basic bamboo cottage guesthouse in Loksado, without bedding, for a bit over a dollar a night, and *warungs* for simple meals. Wednesday is market day and

ALAIN COMPOST

the Dayaks from the hills gather to sell, purchase and socialize. Loksado's population is a mixture of Malays and Dayaks.

Instead of staying in Loksado, continue on to Melaris village just three kilometers away. You can sleep there and the weather is cooler. A short distance away, there is a bamboo-and-rattan suspension bridge to cross and a waterfall.

The return trip is by bamboo raft, through the rapids of the Amandit River. From the raft you could see big monitor lizards sunbathing on the riverside rocks, otters, black monkeys, and perhaps proboscis monkeys as well as butterflies, an occasional snake and lots of birds, including hornbills.

These rafts are used by the local farmers and rubber tappers to take their produce to market in Kandangan. There they sell the craft as well, for its bamboo. From Loksado to Kandangan is 12 hours, but travelers usually offboard after the thrilling rapids (between Lumpangi and Muara Hariang) at Muara Hariang, a 45-minute walk from Mawangi. Here year-round land transportation is available to Kadangan.

Opposite: *This riverboat, plying the route between Banjarmasin and Palangkaraya, sports a large TV antennae to entertain its passengers.*
Above: *With a little luck, the shy but very interesting proboscis monkey can be seen on an island a short boat ride south of Banjarmasin.*

TRISAKTI

The Story of a Monster Diamond

The ground was muddy with scattered pools of water, and branches and logs served as the only walkways. Bits of plastic sheet and a few leaves offered some meager shade from the tropical sun. Several dozen laborers, men and women, were busy with the various phases of diamond extraction at the Cempaka fields.

Some were digging shafts the size of wells, and others were working shafts already constructed, handing up rattan containers full of clay. Gasoline-powered pumps chugged and spewed water from the bottom of the shafts. The loads of clay brought up were packed into a wooden sluice and mixed with water by the tromping feet of two men.

This slurry was then poured into conical wooden pans which were spun, casting the lighter material to the pan's edge and concentrating the heavier bits—diamonds?—in the center. The concentrated matter in the middle was then saved for later close inspection.

I sloshed over to one of the stalls hoping for a cold beer, but settled for hot tea instead. One of the diamond buyers sat down next to me and we chatted.

The work groups, he said, are made up of teams of 10-30 men. Each receives an equal share of any diamond found, after a percentage has been deducted for the owners of the land and the pump, and the provider of the supplies. On a long-term basis, the workers earn an average of about $2.50 a day, the buyer said, but there is always the possibility of a windfall if a large gem is found.

'Thrice Sacred'

What was the biggest diamond ever found here? The buyer stopped talking and looked at a group of men who had gathered to listen to our conversation. A boy ran off to call someone. He returned with Haji Samlan, a strong, middle-aged man of open and cheerful countenance. He looked as tired as everyone else, and I invited him to a glass of tea. I repeated my question.

He took a sip of tea, looked at me, said nothing. Then he reached down to pick up a clump of earth the size of a bird's egg. It was like this, he said. Or, pointing to his work-toughened big toe, like this. This was the size of the raw diamond, which was a bit smaller once cut: 166.75 carats.

The man who first saw it, Haji Sukri, was working at the bottom of a 12-meter (39 ft.) shaft, which is deeper than most. Flooding usually prevents digging deeper than 10 meters (33 ft.). Sukri picked up the stone and put it in his pocket to show later to members of his team. It didn't even cross his mind that it might be a diamond, but he hoped it would turn out to be a semiprecious stone.

The market burns

Samlan remembers the time very well: 12:00 noon on Thursday, August 26, 1965. How could he be so sure of the exact time? Easy, he said, the market in nearby Martapura burned to the ground at this time—the price of finding the diamond. It is said that every time a major diamond is found here, a building burns down.

Coming out of the pit, Sukri sat down for tea. He showed the stone to a friend on his team who also hoped that it would be a semiprecious stone. Then Samlan came up to the pair and looked at the stone. The hair on the back of his neck stood up, he recalled. He knew it was a diamond and, in a trance,

grabbed it up and ran to his house to keep it safe, the others following, shouting out, "Diamond! Diamond! Diamond!"

Several diamond brokers came over to Samlan's house and identified the stone, which was bigger than any of them had seen before. Soon, a line of villagers more than one kilometer long had formed, all wanting to see the marvel. Samlan said he remembers the time very well.

His mind was strangely blank, and he had trouble falling asleep. Many times during the night he would awaken, find himself levitating above his bed, and then come crashing down. He could think of nothing, as if he were in a trance.

This, he said, was how the diamond, known as the Trisakti—"Thrice Sacred"— was found.

Politics and the diamond

Late the same afternoon the gem was found, a delegation from Cempaka took Trisakti to the nearby town of Martapura to show it to the *bupati,* the chief district official. The chief of police (probably hoping for official favor) said that the diamond must be taken to the nation's president. So, the next day, eight local V.I.P.s and two miners took the gem to Jakarta.

Samlan was supposed to go along, but he literally fainted at the airport at the thought of his first plane ride. He pulled himself together, and finally got up the courage to fly to the capital the next day with four other members of his digging team.

The year 1965 was not an ideal one in which to find a big diamond in Indonesia. The government was in the throes of a coup attempt, and government officials were too busy to meet with the miners. Eventually, the miners received an advance, which was divided among the team. Samlan received just enough to build a modest house.

Six months later, the government paid for the team members to make a pilgrimage to Mecca, together with their wives and suppliers. Shortly after they returned, the men were given another modest payment. Once the diamond was cut and appraised in Holland, the men were told, they would receive final payment.

Over the next several years, small groups of the original team traveled to Jakarta at their own expense to try to find out something about Trisakti and their shares from the profit. Each time they were shuffled about from office to office, until their money finally ran out.

They never received their final payment.

Sweat

We had all sat spellbound by the story. When Samlan finished, he took the last sip of his tea, thanked me and said that it was time to return to the mud.

Somewhere in the fields sleeps another Trisakti. With sweat, perseverance and luck, one of the men or women toiling out in the heat and mud may find it.

Opposite: *A worker pitches mud from a deep shaft to his partners so it can be washed and panned for gems.* **Above:** *Diamonds and semiprecious stones from the Cempaka fields.* **Right:** *Haji Samlan, a Cempaka diamond miner, remembers vividly the day a member of his team found the 167-carat Trisakti diamond.*

Kalsel Practicalities

Unless otherwise noted, prices in US$; city code for Banjarmasin 0511.

The airport is 27 km. (17 mi.) from Banjarmasin. After collecting your luggage, buy a taxi coupon for $4 which will get four passengers to any location in Banjarmasin. Alternately, if you don't have a lot of gear, walk out to the main highway (around 2 km.) and catch a public bus to town. They are usually crowded and stop at the station on the outskirts, from where you have to switch to one of the yellow minibuses.

ACCOMMODATIONS

Banjarmasin has a good selection of hotels from two-star to bare-room *losmen*. See map opposite for locations. For AC and attached sit-down toilet, you'll pay $12 and up.

Maramin. Jl.Lambung Mangkurat 32, Tel: 8944. 72 rooms, all rooms AC, color TV with video and parabolic antenna, fridge. Restaurant with Indonesian food, $2-$4, and European, $6. Located right downtown. Daily disco, souvenir stand. $35 S; $43 D.

Fabiola. Jl. A. Yani, Tel: 2707. Name has changed as of 1990. 74 rooms, located on the airport road, about 3 km from downtown. Tennis court, usually free on mornings, and pool. Coffee shop open 24 hours, Continental breakfast, $2; American $3; steaks at $4, burgers $3 and Indonesian dishes $2. Supper Club with a greater variety of food, more expensive. Also a barbershop, beauty salon, souvenir shop, drug store and boutique. $30 for standard AC room.

Sampaga. Jl. Sutoyo 128, Tel: 2753, 2480. 25 nice rooms, motel-style layout, about 1 km from downtown. Restaurant features large crayfish at $4.50, fish at $2.50, chicken $1.50, noodles or fried rice $2. $16 w/AC and attached bathroom.

Sabrina. Jl. Bank Rakyat 21, Tel: 4442. 18 rooms. $13 w/AC; $11 w/fan and attached bathroom; $8 basic w/fan.

Perdana. Jl. Katamso 3, Tel: 3276. 31 rooms. Restaurant with Chinese and Indonesian dishes $1.50-$3. Pleasant atmosphere with lots of plants, located downtown. $12.50 w/AC.

Kuripan. Jl. A. Yani 126, Tel: 3313. 38 rooms. Has a *warung*-like restaurant. Room price includes light breakfast and afternoon snack. $12 w/AC and attached bathroom; $5.50 w/fan and attached bathroom; $4.50 basic.

Metro. Jl. Sutoyo 102, Tel: 2427. 30 rooms. Quite close to the Grand Mosque and downtown. $11 for standard room w/ AC.

Rahmat. Jl. A. Yani 9, Tel: 4322, 4429. 55 rooms. $7 w/fan and attached toilet; $4 basic.

Beauty. Jl. Haryono 174, Tel: 4493. 20 rooms, next door to the similar Mestika. $3-5 according to room size, fans and attached bathrooms.

Mestika. Jl. Haryono 78, Tel: 4159. 20 rooms. Relatively clean and the price is right. $2 for basic room; $3 w/ fan and attached toilet.

Accommodations outside Banjarmasin

The larger towns have hotel/*losmen* type accommodations, usually clean and cheap.

Amuntai: 6 *losmen,* including the **Abadi** on Jl. Abdul Azis.

Banjarbaru: 2 hotels, 4 *losmen.*

Barabai: 8 *losmen,* including the **Bhima** I on Jl. Bhima and the **Garuda** on Jl. Garuda.

Kandangan: 4 *losmen* with the **Santosa** a good, clean, inexpensive choice on Jl. Antasari.

Kota Baru on Pulau Laut Island: 14 *losmen.*

Marabahan: 3 *losmen,* including the **Bhatera** on Jl. Pang. Wangkang.

Martapura: 3 *losmen* with the **Mutiara** on Jl. Sukaramadi 121.

Pleihari: 4 *losmen.*

Rantau: 1 *losmen.*

Tanjung: 9 *losmen* with the **Diyonie** on Jl. Penghulu Rasyio.

LOCAL TRANSPORTATION

In Banjarmasin, omnipresent yellow minibuses go just about everywhere for 10¢. Taxi hire in town is about $2.50/hour, with a 2-3 hour minimum. *Bajaj,* motorcycle-driven cabs, run about $1.25 per hour (bargaining), depending on distances covered, or 80¢ to most in-town destinations. *Ojak*—on the back of a motorcycle—about 15¢ to most places. Try to bargain for an hourly rate of about $1.

Intercity buses all leave from the Terminal Taksi Antar Kota, 6 km. out of town. It is about 1 hr. to Martapura—30¢. To Balikpapan, it's 12-18 hrs., perhaps more during the worst of the rainy season in December and January— $6 for a tiring ride.

Taxis to out-of-town destinations charge $4 to the airport, $9 for the 40-km. round-trip to Martapura, adding $6 to include Cempaka and the diamond-mining area for a total of about 4 hrs. No AC taxis available.

To go cheaply to the airport, first make your way to the intercity bus station. From there you can take a public minibus to the airport for 90¢. Tell the driver before you start that you want to be dropped off at the terminal.

Boat trips around town

You can rent motorized *klotok* all day at Kuin Cerucuk in a section of town called Kuin Pertamina. Everyone knows the place. The *klotoks* charge $2-3 per hour. You can also find them from morning until early afternoon under the A. Yani bridge. Speedboats can be rented at the Dermaga pier near the Sabilal Muhtadir mosque—$16-$20/hr., or about $30 for a tour

But the *klotoks* are better, because they are small enough to get you through the more interesting canals and right into the action at the floating market.

DINING

There are lots of *warungs* serving Indonesian dishes and also an abundance of Padang style restaurants in Banjarmasin. You can find Western food at some of the better hotels.

The Rama Steak House is the best restaurant specializing in non-Indonesian dishes. It is in the Arjuna Plaza on Jl. Lambung Mangkurat. Open 10:00 a.m. to 11:00 p.m. Local steaks $4-$5, imported ones $10. Hot dogs $1.50, hamburgers $2. Japanese dishes, $7-$13.

The Shinta Restaurant, in the same building as the Rama and also on the third floor, is the city's finest Chinese restaurant according to local gastronomes. Same hours as the Rama. Both are very quiet during the day, and business booms at night. Shark's fin or bird's nest soup $20; pigeon, chicken, pork, fish, shrimp, crab, beef and frog dishes, $4-$8. Also simple dishes for $1.50-$2.50. Both the Rama and the Shinta provide live music at night.

The Blue Ocean, Jl. Hasanudin 49, also specializes in Chinese food. Much less variety than the Shinta and cheaper. Depending on the dishes, count on $2.50-4 per person for a full meal but without any of the expensive goodies.

For typical Banjarese cuisine, try out the **Kaganangan** on Jl. Pangeran Samudera or the **Cenderawasih** across the street. About $3 per person to fill up. Huge crayfish at $1.50, fish-egg brochettes 30¢, various kinds of riverfish, including the *peperan ikan* wrapped in banana leaves and roasted. No beer.

Lots of *warungs* serve the well-known *soto banjar,* a rich chicken- and duck-egg soup or stew, often served with *lontong,* rice cooked in banana leaf. We particularly liked the *soto banjar* they sell at a little place called **Acil Inun** (no sign, though) on Jl. Haryone, just north off Jl. Samudera.

For a Padang meal, try the **Kobana**, Jl. Pangeran Samudera 93A. About $2-$4 per person with a soft drink or two over ice. Good Indonesian and Chinese food at the **Jakarta Restaurant** on Jl. Hasanudin at $2.50-3.50.

For free entertainment with your meal, try the **Bobo** on Jl. Pasar Baru 234. Right next to a roller-skate disco by the same name. $3 entrance charge for men, $1.50 for women. Open 9:30 p.m. to 12:30 a.m. (to 1:30 a.m. on Saturday nights). Beer at $3, chicken, shrimp dishes $3, simple Indonesian food $2.

For night owls looking for local atmosphere, try the **Lontong Orari** in Kampung Melayu, open from late afternoon until around 2:00 a.m. It's shoes off at the entrance and sitting on the floor. Your right hand is the only utensil. The main dish is *lontong* and coffee or tea. The Banjarese come here to meet friends, chat. Late night coffeeshop atmosphere. We saw no women around. Best after 10:00 p.m.

AGENCY TOURS

The only agency with experience handling foreigners is **Adi Angkasa Tours**, run by Pak Hariso, who speaks fluent English and Dutch. They offer three basic tours. The shortest, 3

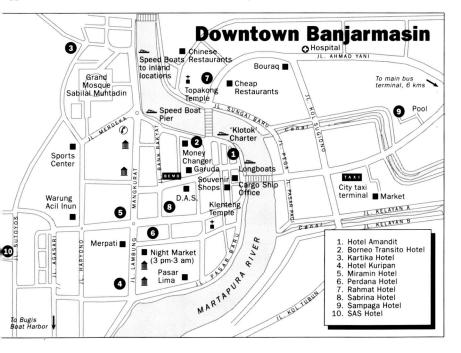

Downtown Banjarmasin

1. Hotel Amandit
2. Borneo Transito Hotel
3. Kartika Hotel
4. Hotel Kuripan
5. Miramin Hotel
6. Perdana Hotel
7. Rahmat Hotel
8. Sabrina Hotel
9. Sampaga Hotel
10. SAS Hotel

days and 2 nights, includes river life, especially the floating market and Monkey Island, as well as diamond fields and polishing centers. All for $135 per person.

On a longer tour, 6 days and 5 nights, they take you to the Dayaks near Loksado. One-way there by four-wheel-drive from Kandangan (dry season only) and return by bamboo raft, 4 hrs. to Harantang on the Amandit River. $400 per person. This tour also includes everything on their local tour.

Another tour takes you to the Tanjung Puting orangutan rehabilitation center in Kalteng, 5 days and 4 nights, all-inclusive from Banjarmasin for $1,250 per person.

Adi Angkasa Tours, Jl. Hasanudin 27, Tel: 3131, 3040.

Guides

A local guide association of some 30 young men also sets up tours. The official fee is $9 per day in town, $15 out of town plus expenses. Their level of English varies greatly. You can go to the Tourism Office to ask for a guide but one will probably show up at your hotel shortly after you check in. Make sure he is licensed.

If you want a guide, we recommend Johan Yasin. Johan specializes in inexpensive tours. Although he can arrange an AC hotel room for you, he usually recommends home stays. Land travel is by (crowded) public bus, but he can also provide taxis. His 6:30-9:00 a.m. river, canals and floating market tour is $4.50/person. (Note: whether you go with Johan or on your own, you must get to the floating market early—by 8:30 a.m. it has petered out.) The diamond mining and polishing tour, including a simple lunch, costs $7.

For the Kaget Island proboscis monkeys (either early morning or late afternoon), Johan charges $12 for a single guest, $9/person for 2 or more. The Loksado Dayak trip, 3 to 5 days, runs $70-85. His Tanjung Puting orangutan tour, 4 days, costs $200-300, depending on the number of people and level of accommodations they require. The price includes round-trip air fare from Banjarmasin. Johan can also arrange long treks, such as the 5-day hike from Muara Teweh on the Barito River to Tering on the Mahakam. He is a very pleasant young man who speaks passable English, and has plenty of experience.

Tourism Office. Jl. Panjaitan 23, Tel: 2982.
Johan Yasin. Jl. Pos 123, Tel: 3674.

REGIONAL TRANSPORTATION

Garuda. Jl. Hasanudin 11A, Tel: 4023, 3885. Two direct daily flights to and from Jakarta ($70) and 2 a day to and from Surabaya ($43). Three flights weekly to Balikpapan ($33).

Merpati. Jl. Haryono Tel: 4453, 4307. Twice daily to Surabaya ($34) and 5 times weekly to Palangkaraya ($21).

Bouraq. Jl. Lambung Mangkurat, Tel: 2445,

3285. Twice daily to Palangkaraya ($21), 3 times daily to Sampit ($30), 2 daily flights to Pangkalanbun ($36), daily to Kotabaru ($25), 3 times daily to Surabaya ($34), daily to Semarang ($48), 3 times daily to Balikpapan ($26).

DAS. Jl. Hasanudin, Tel: 2902. Twice daily to Kotabaru ($27), twice daily to Sampit ($31), twice daily to Palangkaraya ($23), daily to Muara Teweh ($34), daily to Pangkalanbun ($37).

Airline offices are theoretically open from 8:00 a.m. to 4:00 p.m. Lots of local flights are cancelled or delayed. The planes eventually leave, but take the waiting time into account when planning your trip.

By sea

Pelni Line's large *Keli Mutu* calls at Banjarmasin every 2 weeks on the following routes: Semarang–Banjarmasin–Surabaya–Padangbai (Bali)–Lembas–Ujung Pandang–Bima–Waingapu–Ende–Kupang and back the same way. A first-class ticket to Surabaya costs $33, second class $26, economy class $15. To Bali, it's $45/$38/$20. To Kupang, $89/$70/$38.

You can also try going to Surabaya or Jakarta on a Bugis schooner, deck passage, price negotiable. To obtain information on sailing dates as well as the necessary permit, go to the harbor master's office (*Kantor Syahbandar Pelabuhan I*), Jl. Barito Hilir. This is at the Trisakti dock.

Cargo ships to Surabaya also take passengers—no permit needed. The ticket office is near the Antasari Bridge (see map). The trip to Surabaya takes 20 hrs. and costs $10.

River transportation

Passenger speedboats leave from the Martapura river, near the main mosque (see map). Engines vary from 40HP to 200HP and they carry 12-28 passengers. Departure is whenever the boat is full. There are usually 2 a day to Palangkaraya, $10, 4-6 hours depending on engine size and if there is a meal stop. There are also speedboats to Negara ($7), Martapura ($5) and Antasari ($9). Very rarely, one will go to Muara Teweh ($20). To charter a speedboat to Muara Teweh, it's $300.

Regular boats, called *bis air* or "water bus," dock at the terminal Banjar Raya (see map). Though crowded—100 to 200 passengers—they're cheap. A 2-day, 2-night trip to Muara Teweh in Kalteng on the Barito River costs $4.50 plus $1.25 for a mattress and pillow, well worth the extra. Depending on water levels, these boats may be able to continue as far as Purukcahu. The ride to Palangkaraya, the capital of Central Kalimantan on the Kahayan River, costs $2.75. The trip usually takes about 18 hrs., but could last up to 36 depending on water levels. No bedding on these boats.

All the *bis air* carry a *warung* for simple meals at 75¢. Almost all have video programs for those tired of the scenery, i.e. all local passengers. The very basic toilets have long waiting lines at key hours. All the boats are quite clean. Frequency of departure varies, but usually there are 1-2 a day to Palangkaraya, 2-3 a week to Buntok, and less beyond there. Most destinations are on the Barito River.

BANKING AND MONEY EXCHANGE

Official sources state that the following banks change travelers' checks and some currencies, but only if the bills are in perfect condition. Have your hotel phone them before you go to make sure that they will change your brand of travelers' checks and during what hours. You can also try the money changer just off Jl. Pos.

Bank Bumi Daya. Jl. Lambung Mangkurat 31, Tel: 4939, 4298, 22339, 2316 and 2636.

Bank Dagang Negara. Jl. Lambung Mangkurat 8, Tel: 4012, 4286, 3987 and 4095.

Bank Expor-Impor. Jl. Lambung Mangkurat 16, Tel: 2755 and 3435.

Bank Negara. Jl. Lambung Mangkurat, Tel: 4532.

Bank Rakyat. Jl. Pangeran Samudera 98, Tel: 4363.

Overseas Express Bank. Jl. Hasanudin HM, Tel: 2856,

Panin Bank. Jl. Simpang Kamboja, Tel: 3622.

LOCAL MARKET DAYS

Rantau	Tuesday, Friday, Sunday
Martapura	Friday
Negara	Friday and Monday
Barabai	Saturday
Kandangan	Tuesday and Friday
Amuntai	Thursday
Pleihari	Monday
Tanjung	Sunday
Pagatan	Monday

SHOPPING AND SOUVENIRS

There is not much in the way of local crafts: the odd rattan basket and quite handsome examples of *batik sasirangan*, a tie-dyed cloth of many designs. Several tiny factories produce this textile, and a guide can take you to one of them (see map). Cloth prices vary from $3 to $15 (the more expensive are silk) per meter, with a standard sarong cloth going for $4 to $8. The widest selection is available at the **Toko Citra** on Jl. A. Yani near the Fabiola Hotel. The designs of these cloths were formerly believed to be able to drive away evil spirits and cure diseases.

For general souvenir shopping, try the stalls between Jl. Samudera and Jl. Sudimampir, close to the bridge. The **Toko Permata** specializes in beads of all kinds. Other little shops are full of ships-of-the-dead made from hard rubber coming from Kalteng. They go for $3 to $20, depending on size and degree of elaboration. *Mandaus*—Dayak swords—run $10 to $18. There is a bit of antique porcelain around. Bargaining is expected. If you go into any store

with some guides (not all of them), prices could go sky high, as your "friend" gets a cut.

For strictly local craft (Kalsel only), we recommend the (low) fixed-price **Dewan Kerajinan Nasional** on Jl. Panjaitan 18. Open 8:00 a.m. to 6:00 p.m. (closed 1:30 to 2:30) except Sunday. There are colorful bamboo crafts and baskets, rattan wall hangings, lots of woven fiber bags and purses, *sasirangan* cloth (but the **Citra** has a wider selection and more ready-to-wear clothing made from this textile), lizard- or snake-skin belts ($10), purses and shoes (men's $24, women's $12); gold-plated silver jewelry of traditional Banjar designs, handsome lamp shades, Dayak swords ($5 and up). Also the most god-awful goatskin shoes.

Shopping for gems

Semi-precious stones and diamonds can easily soak up all your spare cash. Obviously, buy gems from a well-established dealer with a reputation to uphold. In Banjarmasin, try **Toko Banjar Baru**, Jl. Sudimanpir 61, Tel: 4076 or 8565. In Martapura, either the **Kayu Tangi**, in the back of the market (diamond cutting and polishing on the premises) or, best of all but a bit out of the way, the **Penggosokan Intan Pekauman** at Kampung Melayu Ilir No. 251A. This last store is the oldest one around, established in 1940, shortly after the diamond fields of Cempaka started production. The cutters and polishers used to work for an Amsterdam firm. You can also try the official, government-run, fixed-priced **Penggosokan Intan Bank Indonesia**, 2 km. before reaching Martapura when traveling from Banjarmasin.

While the amateur diamond buyer can expect a fair deal at these stores (no glass fakes, as in some other places), the more one knows about jewels, the better bargains one can strike—up to a point. Remember that the stones you buy in Kalsel will almost certainly need some re-cutting and re-polishing.

The largest stones you can expect to find for sale are in the 2-carat range. For a top-quality white one, $8,500 to $9,000. One carat of similar quality runs $2,500, half carat $425-500. Yellow ones fetch up to $900 for one carat, $300 or less for a half carat. Try bargaining, perhaps 15% of the asking price. Diamonds here cost 30-50% less than in Jakarta where, however, they are better cut.

LOCAL EVENTS CALENDAR

In **April**, the Mappanre Tassi festival is held at the beach of Pejala and Pangatan (*kecamatan* Tanah Bumbu Selatan).

August 17th is Indonesian Independence Day and **September 24th** is the anniversary of the founding of Banjarmasin.

In **September** and **October**, post-harvest kite-flying contests and *bagasing* (top spinning) contests are held in *kecamatan* Tapin.

Check the tourism office for exact dates.

PART VI

Central Kalimantan

Central Kalimantan is a huge province, covering south-central Borneo from the Schwaner Mountains to the Java Sea. Kalimantan Tengah—Kalteng—is the least visited region on the island. But the Dayak peoples of this region are perhaps Borneo's most traditional, and the Kaharingan religion, a government sanctioned faith that has spread to other Dayak groups in Kalimantan, has its roots here. For the visitor, Central Kalimantan requires initiative and the ability to travel like a Bornean, by small airplane, and on speedboats, slowboats and canoes.

Kalteng has 153,800 square kilometers (59,382 sq. mi.) of swamp, jungle and forest which are split by a series of roughly parallel rivers flowing from the Schwaner and Müller Ranges in the north to the Java Sea in the south. Most of the *kabupaten*s follow Kalteng's major river systems inland to where the rapids make the transition to the highlands and mountains. Two special districts incorporate the vast, sparsely populated northern region of the province. The total population of the province is 1.3 million.

The coastal extremities of the river systems are also thinly populated, because of the swamplands, choked with nipa palms and mangroves that extend in some places 30-100 kilometers (19-60 mi.) inland from the coast. The exceptions are the towns of Kumai, Pangkalanbun, and Sampit near the coast.

History of Kalteng

For centuries, much of Kalteng was under the sway of Banjarmasin. When the Banjar elite converted to Islam at the beginning of the 17th century, the coastal kingdoms followed suit and proselytized the Dayaks living in the vicinity. The diffusion of Islam among the Dayaks was slowed considerably during the 1830s by the colonial administration and the first Protestant missionaries.

A Dutch geologist named Schwaner carried out the initial exploration and mapping of Kalteng. Between 1841 and 1848 he made his way up the Barito, Kahayan, Kapuas and Katingan Rivers, recording village locations. To honor this explorer-geologist, the mountains that separate Kalteng from Kalbar were named the Schwaner Range. During the decade from 1880 to 1890, the Dutch opened communications across the southern section of Kalteng by cutting five canals, connecting the Kapuas, Barito and Kahayan Rivers in the southeast corner of the region.

After Indonesia won its independence in 1949, the region was still controlled from Banjarmasin, and conflict arose between the traditional Dayaks and the heavily Islamic Banjarese. In the late 1950s, the Dayaks of Central Kalimantan sought autonomy, and the combination of small-scale guerilla actions and support from Jakarta resulted in the creation of a separate province, Kalteng.

A wealth of resources

Most of Kalteng's economy is still controlled by Banjarmasin. Imports and exports go through this port city, with heavy waterborne traffic on rivers and canals between Palangkaraya and Banjarmasin. But the political focus has shifted to Jakarta while airplanes are helping to "liberate" Kalteng.

The huge tropical forests of Kalteng produce logs which are floated downriver and processed into timber and plywood at Sampit, Pangkalanbun and Kuala Kapuas. Over 100 companies, including ten joint ventures with Korea and Japan, are involved in Kalteng's timber industry.

The next most valuable product is rattan, processed mostly in Kalsel. Rubber, which was introduced from the Amazon at the end of the 19th century, is third, with fishing and shrimping (the latter processed at Kumai) as

Overleaf: *Javanese transmigrant farmers motor upriver in Kalteng. Photo by Alain Compost.*
Opposite: *A Dayak woman and her child.*

fourth. The forests also produce a number of other products that bring cash into the local economy, including damar resin and *kulit gemur,* a tree bark used in cosmetics and insect repellent. Illipe nuts yield an oil which is processed into cosmetics as well.

While the timber industry had developed into large scale operations by 1974, commercial gold production has just started. Geological exploration continues, with important deposits of kaolin, quartz, iron, uranium and petroleum already discovered, but considerable investment in roads and communications must take place before mining operations can begin.

Dayaks of Central Kalimantan

As elsewhere in Borneo, attempts to group the various Dayak tribes of Kalteng usually flounder. The majority of the Dayak groups in Kalteng—the Ngaju, the Lawangan, the Ma'anyan and the Ot Danum—share common linguistic and cultural bases.

The largest group, located in south and central Kalimantan, is called the Barito, after the area's largest river. The above-mentioned groups, as well as the Benuaq and the Tunjung, are Barito Dayaks. The Benuaq and the Tunjung also live along the middle reaches of the Mahakam River in Kaltim (See "Mahakam Dayaks," page 100.) Some Ot Danum, the lesser-known Tebidah and some Limbai live in northwest Kalteng across the

Schwaner Range in the Melawi River basin, a tributary of Kalbar's great Kapuas. The rest of the Barito peoples—the majority—live inland along the rivers flowing from the Schwaner and Müller Mountains due south to the Java Sea.

All the Barito Dayaks speak related languages and practice elaborate burials characterized by a "secondary" funeral ritual, in which the bones of the deceased are cleaned and honored, often with powerful carvings and animals sacrificed amidst complex rituals. Many of the ancient beliefs are kept alive here thanks to Kaharingan, a traditional religion slightly modified to be acceptable to the Indonesian government.

Numerically and politically, the Ngaju are the most important group. Less numerous but also covering a huge territory, the Ot Danum (some branches of which are called Dohoi) live north, uprapids, from the Ngaju. The languages of these two groups are mutually incomprehensible although there are some linguistic similarities. The Ot Danum practice mostly subsistence farming whereas the Ngaju have long emphasized commercial agriculture. Thanks to their relative isolation, the Ot Danum are more traditional in both religion and general culture.

The Ngaju

The Ngaju are the best-known of the Barito Dayaks. Although the group does not have a

tribal-wide organization, the Ngaju were largely responsible for the creation of the province of Kalteng by the Indonesian central government. The Ngaju speak several dialects of which one, Kahayan, has become the region's *lingua franca*. Most Ngaju adhere to either the Protestant or the Kaharingan faiths, although the Bakumpai Ngaju converted to Islam over a century ago.

Community meeting houses, used also for rituals, substitute for the typical Dayak longhouse which is very rare among the Ngaju. Their funerary artwork, including wooden coffins, raised tombs, ships-of-the-dead and tall memorial sculptures, place the Ngaju among the island's best artists.

The Ma'anyan

The Ma'anyan Dayaks speak a language very similar to that spoken in Madagascar, establishing a cross–Indian Ocean link between the two islands. It is likely that the Ma'anyan lived nearer the coast around the 3d and 4th centuries, when Madagascar was first populated by Austronesians.

The Ma'anyan groups maintain contact with each other and with the towns on the Barito River through periodic markets. Their main export, in high demand among the Banjarese, are finely crafted dugout canoes. In former times of warfare, extended family households lived together in dwellings perched up to 7 meters (23 ft.) off the ground on ironwood pillars.

Many Ma'anyan adhere to the Kaharingan faith. They practice spirit propitiation, agricultural rites, and elaborate death ceremonies, and call shamans to cure their sick. Funerals and graveyards testify to the former importance of classes: the ossuaries of the nobles, the most elaborate, are located upstream, followed by those of the warriors, the common people and, furthest downstream, those of slaves.

In spite of all the transfer of wealth in the form of ceramic jars, bronze gongs, beads and cash, traditional marriages require a five-year period of residence and service with the wife's family. Extra payments to the mother-in-law can reduce this time.

The Ot Danum

The Ot Danum, whose name means "upriver region," inhabit the area to the north of the Ngaju, along the rivers to the Schwaner and Müller mountains, as well as the upper Melawi basin, to the north of the Schwaner Mountains in West Kalimantan. Their home-

land covers a 300-kilometer (200 mi.)-wide swath of land just south of the equator.

The Ngaju consider the Ot Danum their cultural ancestors, yet there are some striking differences between the two groups. The Ot Danum live in longhouses raised 2-5 meters (7-15 ft.) on ironwood posts. This was perhaps picked up from the Kenyah or Kayan, along with a modified form of social hierarchy, head-hunting and art patterns on shields and *mandau* blades.

Although the Ot Danum religion resembles that of the Ngaju (a majority now call themselves Kaharingan), the secondary funerary ritual is much simpler, and their carvings are not as elaborate.

Cash crops

Most Dayaks base their livelihood on subsistence farming of rice in slash-and-burn fields. The Ngaju Dayaks of Central Kalimantan have pioneered the growing of cash crops, and the practice has spread to other areas. Rattan is planted in the rice fields just prior to harvest, then cut 8-10 years later. The current harvests of cloves, palm oil, coffee, pepper and cacao can be expanded.

Opposite: *Dr. Gary Shapiro with boisterous young orangutans at the Tanjung Puting Reserve (his wife snaps a photo). Shapiro has taught sign language to the apes.* **Above:** *Closeup of an old Ot Danum sepunduq, a funerary carving.*

KAHARINGAN FAITH

Traditional Religion and Dayak Identity

The Ngaju, living along the middle and upper reaches of Central Kalimantan's great rivers, are numerically and linguistically the dominant Dayak group in the region. Even in pre-European times, the Ngaju of the Kahayan River basin were the most responsive group of Dayaks to outside technologies and cultural influence. When the Dutch arrived, many of them became Christians, and today these form the province's elite.

During the 19th century, a Ngaju consciousness, or sense of cultural identity, was awakened by German and Swiss Protestant missionaries, and reinforced by the Dutch policy of keeping Islam out of Kalimantan's interior. The Protestant missionaries, who first arrived in the 1830s, set up excellent schools which helped train a local elite. Even today a very sizeable minority adhere to the traditional religion of their ancestors.

Kalteng independence

During Indonesia's struggle for independence against the Dutch, the Dayaks of Kalteng, mostly Ngaju, fought under Major Tjilik Riwut. Riwut, a parachutist, first fought in the revolution on Java before going home to continue the fight in Kalimantan. Major Riwut was a Ngaju Dayak who practiced the traditional faith.

When the republic was finally at peace, the central government in Jakarta decided to combine into one province the heavily Islamic area of Banjarmasin and the Dayak-dominated region to the west. The Dayaks, especially the Ngaju, objected to this, wishing to be in control of a province of their own. Led by Tjilik Riwut, who had gained considerable fame in the revolution, the Dayaks took limited guerilla action. Many of his fighters were adherents of the traditional religion, and official acceptance of this faith, called Kaharingan, became one of the demands of the Ngaju struggle.

The demand was not independence from the nation, just for a separate province and state recognition of the Ngaju religion. Perhaps because Tjilik Riwut had been a loyal comrade, the Indonesian army leadership did not want to escalate the fighting. In 1957, a presidential decree established the province of Kalteng.

But, after outlawing the Communist party,

the matter of religion became a complex and delicate matter in Indonesia. State ideology calls for belief in One Supreme God and membership in one of the "accepted" world religions that recognizes a holy book. The flexibility of this policy showed in the official acceptance of the Hindus of Bali. In Bali, as in Kalteng, religious recognition was closely tied to cultural identity. After a little theological legerdemain, Kaharingan was finally recognized as part of the sanctioned "Bali-Hindu" religion in 1980.

Festive funerals

The religion of the Ngaju focuses on a supernatural world of spirits, including ancestral spirits. Like some other Dayak groups, the Ngaju hold a secondary funeral, usually months (sometimes years) after the initial rituals. This secondary funeral is essential if the soul is to reach the highest place in heaven.

During the secondary rites (*tiwah*), the bones of the deceased are exhumed, cleaned and placed in a special mausoleum (*sandung*) alongside the remains of ancestors of the same family. Both the primary and the secondary funerals are essential to protect the living from evil supernatural forces.

The primary funeral, which ends in either burial or cremation, is performed right after death. Masked dancers keep nefarious spirits away from the body. Kaharingan priests chant, accompanied by drums, to send the soul to a multi-layered heaven in a splendid ship full of helpful spirits. Although in heaven, the soul cannot ascend to the highest level until its family performs the *tiwah*. The soul waits in the lower part of heaven until summoned for the secondary funeral.

The *tiwah* is a grand, complex, long and very expensive affair. It can cost anywhere from $6,000 to $120,000. Because of this it is usual for several families to join together to sponsor a collective *tiwah,* which involves the sacrifice of many water buffalo and pigs. Up to 200 souls have been sent off in one gigantic secondary funeral.

Word that a *tiwah* will be performed spreads long before the ritual starts, and entrepreneurs arrive and set up food stalls, open-air shops and, at a discreet distance, gambling boards. The ritual becomes a carnival in the jungle.

After the bones are have been cleaned, they are placed in the *sandung* alongside those of other ancestor-kin. The mausoleums, carved in the shape of a bird or water snake, are often decorated with scenes of the

upper world. Unfortunately, prefabricated concrete *sandung* are now beginning to replace the traditional carved ones.

Adapting a religion

Concrete *sandung* are not the only recent changes in Kaharingan. In the effort to make the religion acceptable to the government, a 16-member supervisory council was formed to exercise some control over the theology and rituals of the approximately 330,000 followers of the Kaharingan religion. Some 90 percent of this council are Ngaju, and other Dayaks make up the rest. None of the 78-odd *basir upu,* or top ritual specialists, is a member of the council. Nor are any of the more than 300 lower-level Kaharingan priests.

The council emphasizes aspects of the Kaharingan which show ties to the establishment religions. Even before the council formed, Jesus Christ was identified with Tempon Telon, one of the most important local deities. Borrowing from Christianity and Islam, the council tries to instill the concept of individual salvation and accountability to the Supreme Being. This de-emphasizes the traditional pantheon of supernaturals.

A 300-page *Study Book of the Kaharingan Religion* was written in 1981. In its attempts to make Kaharingan more like Christianity or Islam, the council sponsors weekly services in specially built Hindu-Balinese Kaharingan meeting halls, complete with sermons, prayers and hymns.

The council insists on registering and coordinating each *tiwah* (there are between two and 10 each year in the Palangkaraya) before it gives the go-ahead to the police to issue a permit.

Opposite: *A Ngaju mausoleum,* sandung, *holds the bones of a kinsman whose spirit watches over the village.* **Above:** *A ship-of-the-dead, made of gutta-percha, depicts the spiritual entourage that accompanies the soul to Paradise.*

VISITING KALTENG

Up the Rivers into Central Kalimantan

The capital of Kalteng, Palangkaraya, was hacked out of the jungle after the province was created in 1957. The Soviets, at the time allies of Indonesia's President Sukarno, chipped in with 40 kilometers (25 mi.) of pavement. The road follows the Kahayan River, from the village of Pahandut, which was to expand to become the capital, to the upstream village of Tangkiling. Transmigrants from Java have now settled along this road, which has been extended for a total of 85 kilometers (53 mi.) to Kasongan on the Katingan River, linking together two riverhighways. A dirt road of sorts heads from Kasongan to Tewah and beyond.

Palangkaraya is about two meters above sea level, 130 kilometers (80 mi.) from the Java Sea in a straight line, and by boat twice as far by the twisting Kahayan River. Thanks to government jobs, developing trade and transmigrants, Palangkaraya has become the province's largest city, recently overtaking Sampit. In 1980, Sampit's 60,000 inhabitants still represented double Palangkaraya's population. Today, taking into account transmigrant Javanese, there are some 100,000 people in the capital.

The busiest part of the city remains the Pahandut area, along the Kahayan River and reaching a short way inland to Jalan Ahmad Yani, a broad avenue of hotels and shops. Beyond this area are government buildings and houses, with plenty of room to grow. Monuments around the city often combine themes of the revolution against the Dutch with Dayak designs.

The museum of Kalimantan Tengah, devoted to Dayak carvings and other artifacts, displays scale models of different-style longhouses, fine agricultural and fishing tools, and some old Chinese porcelain. The best pieces here are some fine, old, weathered pole carvings. At the time of this writing, there were two buildings housing local art and crafts, and a third was under construction to house objects from other parts of Indonesia. The museum is on the outer edge of town, near the Pasar Kahayan bus terminal.

Other than the museum and some riverside activities, there is little in the capital to hold a visitor's interest. Best to head upstream to Tewah and beyond, to the rapids and Dayak villages. Speedboats and slower craft frequently leave Palangkaraya for Tewah.

Up the Kahayan River

If you have lots of time, say a week or two, the trip upriver is inexpensive. If you only have a few days, the trip can cost $700. The further upriver you go, the more interesting the culture and particularly the art. In the areas just north of Palangkaraya some of the traditional funerary "carvings" are now precast concrete; upriver they are hardwood.

Motoring up the river, you can walk inland a short way and see some *sandung* along with *sepunduq*—poles, the top carved into human form, to which sacrificial animals (or, in the past, slaves) are tied. The *sandung* and *sepunduq* are carved of ironwood, and will last quite a long time, unless they are stolen. Some are quite recent, others are claimed to be more than a century old.

Another unique feature is the *sengkaran,* a kind of totem pole featuring a distinct motif: a Chinese jar is skewered on a tall post, and

Upper Kahayan

Tumbang Maharoi
Tumbang Anoi — Tumbang Korik
Tumbang Sian
Tumbang Miri
Upunbatu — Kasintu
Sepinang
Tewah — Tumbang Jutuh — **Kuala Kurun**
Tumbang Samba — Tekuknyatu
Tumbang Miwan
Dahiyantambuk
Kampuri
Sepang Kota
Sepang Simin
Kasongan — **Bawan** — Pujon
Bukit Bamba
Pamarunan
Bahupalawa
Bukit Liti
Bukit Rawa
Tangkiling
Palangkaraya

SAMBA RIVER
MIRI RIVER
KAHAYAN RIVER
KATINGAN RIVER
KAHAYAN RIVER
KAPUAS RIVER

Opposite: *Braving the rapids.*

just above the jar is a dragon, its back bristling with spears, and at the very top is a hornbill bird. With sufficient notice, the people of the villages beyond Tewah can do traditional dances with gong and *gedang* accompaniment, if you pay for the feast, which requires pigs, chickens, rice and lots of rice wine. The whole celebration runs about $150.

Once past Kasintu, just about all the villages have *sandung* and *sepunduq*. The four at Upun Batu, at the base of a 300 meter (1,000 ft.) hill with a sheer cliff on one side, are excellent examples of funerary art. Tumbang Hampatung and Tumbang Kurik also offer some excellent examples. Try to find the half-buried mausoleum at Tubang Kurik, which is accompanied by four handsome statues. The best grave at Tewah is located in front of the *camat*'s office and in back of a school, a bit over a half-kilometer from "downtown." Local sources say it was made for a *tiwah* some 80 years ago.

Because its original site was eroded by the river, the *sandung* and accompanying *sepunduq* were moved to the present location. In the moving process, the mausoleum acquired an unfortunate coat of paint but otherwise is still quite handsome.

The yellow flags one occasionally sees along the river are meant to attract the attention of the spirits, to let them know that there are offerings for them below. For some reason, there are many more of these riverside offerings between Kuala Kapuas and Palangkaraya thanthere are upstream, even though the Kaharingan religion is equally spread out.

Tewah, the principal upriver town on the Kahayan, is a gold-mining center. A Canadian-Indonesian joint venture mine is located nearby, at the appropriately named Gunung Mas—Gold Mountain. The town sits on the border between the lands of the Ngaju and the upriver Ot Danum Dayaks.

The Ot Danum Dayaks

The upriver Dayak are all Ot Danum groups, linguistically distinct from the Ngaju. Most of them understand Ngaju, the lingua franca of Kalteng, but many do not speak Indonesian. If you have a guide, make sure he speaks Ngaju before you leave Palangkaraya.

Of the more than 10,000 Ot Danum who live in the Tumbang Miri district, some 70 percent adhere to the ancestral religion, and the rest are Protestant Christians. They are all subsistence farmers, although they receive a little cash from tapping rubber trees, panning for gold or cutting rattan and ironwood in the jungle. They only occasionally hold a *tiwah,* but most villages celebrate post-harvest festivals, the *pesta panen.* This takes place in March or April, and is accompanied by feasting, dancing and drinking.

The post-planting festival, the *pesta tanam,* is more of a family affair, taking place in the *ladang*s, the hillside rice fields. Guests are

often invited to share in the pigs or cattle sacrificed, and the inevitable booze. Planting is usually in September or October.

Trekking in the Kalteng highlands

Once past Tumbang Hamputung on the Kahayan, or along the upstream tributaries, the water in the rivers clears somewhat, the trees from each bank often meet overhead, and you begin to see monkeys playing above, kingfishers diving in a burst of color, and white-breasted eagles gliding aloft.

From Tumbang Kurik you can trek to Tumbang Maharoi in six to nine hours, depending on your physical shape and sense of balance. The people of Tumbang Maharoi, the last village on the Kahayan River, pan for gold and weave fine rattan baskets, creating designs on them with strips of rattan dyed black. Beyond Tumbang Maharoi, there are more Ot Danum on the Juloi River. Even further inland, locals say that there are some nomadic groups who seldom have any contact with anyone, including settled villagers in the vicinity. It is said that they live exclusively from hunting and gathering.

As you return by river, stop to see the remains of a longhouse at Tumbang Anoi, famous as the site of the great peace conference organized by the Dutch in 1894. Here representatives from 30 Dayak groups from Central Kalimantan agreed to stop large-scale head-hunting.

Kalteng's great rivers

The Kahayan River's sources go back to the Gunung Mas district in the north. The Kapuas River (not to be confused with the Kapuas in West Kalimantan) also starts in the Gunung Mas district, in lands inhabited by the Siang Dayaks. Most of the river's course is through Ngaju land, and Kuala Kapuas is the principal town in its basin. This river town is well connected by both speedboats and river taxis to Banjarmasin and Palangkaraya, thanks to the canals built by the Dutch.

The drainage area of the Lamandau River forms the Kotawaringin Barat district, the westernmost in Kalteng, bordering on southern Kalimantan Barat. The name of the district, Kotawaringin, comes from the formerly important sultanate. Today, Pangkalanbun is the district's principal town. It receives scheduled flights by small planes from Pontianak, Banjarmasin, Palangkaraya, and even Jakarta. This is the point of departure for a trip to the Tanjung Puting orangutan rehabilitation center.

River travel is possible on the lower part of the Lamandau River, while upstream areas are easier to reach overland from the coastal town of Ketapang in Kalbar and there is a road (jeeps and motorcycles only) heading inland. It forks a short distance from Pangkalanbun, and the western branch cuts through the lands of the Delang Dayaks before heading across the border to Kalbar. The road's eastern branch forks again, to Sampi and Rantau Pulut along with Tumbang Manjul in the north (see map page 154).

The Seruyan River (also known as the Pembuang) forms the backbone of the next district to the east, the *kabupaten* Persiapan Seruyan. Two parallel offshoots of the Schwaner Mountains encase the Seruyan River along most of its course. Kuala Pembuang, which is the district capital, lies at the mouth of the river, a short distance inland from the sea. One branch of the "road" system from Pangkalanbun follows the western bank of the Seruyan to Rantau Pulut, and goes almost to Tumbang Manjul, just below the heavy rapids. Most of the course of the Seruyan River cuts through the Delang Dayak lands, with the northernmost part

Above: Funerary poles, sepunduq, are found at most Ot Danum villages. A sacrificial victim— today a pig or water buffalo, in the past a slave—is tied to these. **Opposite:** A tiny dock on a quiet tributary of the Kahayan.

reaching the territory of the Ot Danum.

East of the Seruyan is the Mentaya River, draining the Kotawaringin Timur district. Sampit, the area's capital, was just recently surpassed in total population by Palangkaraya. Sampit receives frequent scheduled daily flights by small planes from both Palangkaraya and Banjarmasin. Riverboats are frequent from Sampit to Kuala Kayan, which can also be reached by dirt road from east or west. Another rough road, which starts at Kuala Pembuang, heads north then northeast to the Schwaner Mountains, almost reaching Kalbar. This is Ot Danum land, whereas the westernmost of the Ngaju Dayaks dwell downriver.

To the east of the Mentaya, the Katingan River flows from the Ot Danum highlands to Ngaju territory, then to the district capital of Kasungan and on to the Java Sea. There are three scheduled flights a week from Palangkaraya to Tumbang Sumba in the Katingan district. Kasongan is connected by 85 kilometers (53 mi.) of paved road to Palangkaraya. A dirt road from Kasongan connects to the one heading north from Sampit. Here again, it's Ot Danum to the north and Ngaju to the south.

The Barito River, navigable up to Teluk Tolo and Tumbang Juloi, is the westernmost in Kalteng. The river begins in the Murung Raya district, its headwaters separated from Kaltim's upper Mahakam by a branch of the Müller Mountains. The upper part of the Barito and its tributaries flow through lands inhabited by scattered Dayak groups such as the Ot Danum, the Murung and the Siang.

Many rapids mark this area, but the Barito becomes navigable long before it reaches the district capital of Puruk Cahu. From there it is possible to travel by land as well as on the river to Muara Teweh, the capital of the Barito Utara (North) district. There are two dirt roads reaching Muara Teweh, one from the east and the other from the south, and daily flights leave Palangkaraya and Banjarmasin for Muara Teweh.

Buntok, the capital of the Barito district, is connected by paved road to the Banjarmasin–Balikpapan road to the east, thus the economy is focused in this direction. Buntok also receives daily flights from Palangkaraya and frequent speedboats, river taxis and freight boats from Banjarmasin.

From Muara Teweh downstream, several groups of Dayaks live along the Barito. The Dusun and the Ma'anyan live on the west bank, and the east bank is the home of Ngaju, Mengkatip and the Islamicized Bakumpai Dayaks.

Just to the south of Buntok, the Barito acts as the boundary between Kalsel and Kalteng. The river divides, with the western branch flowing past Banjarmasin to the sea, and the eastern branch joining the Kapuas at Kuala Kapuas.

TANJUNG PUTING

Reintroducing Orangutans to the Forest

Some 50 orangutans, from unbelievably cute babies to huge dominant males, are the stars of the show at the Tanjung Puting orangutan rehabilitation center. Rescued from captivity, the animals are here taught how to live wild in the forest of Borneo, their natural home.

Since she established the center some 20 years ago, park director Dr. Biruté Galdikas has succeeded in reintroducing 50 orangutans to the forest at Tanjung Puting (in addition to the 50 still in the process of being weaned from their captive ways). The resettled animals join an estimated wild population of 200 of the endangered hominids in the Tanjung Puting reserve.

There are only a few thousand orangutans, *Pongo pygmaeus,* left in the forests of Borneo and Sumatra. Because of deforestation and habitat encroachment these peaceful creatures, who along with chimpanzees and gorillas are the most humanlike of all animals, are now in real danger of extinction.

The Tanjung Puting National Park is one of the very few protected areas of tropical jungle. It is unique in its diversity of ecological zones: wetlands, lowlands, swamp forest, hardwood rain forest and mature tropical heath. The park has been the site of the longest running study of orangutan behavior.

The animals that stock the rehabilitation center are confiscated pets, or animals destined for the lucrative black market. Although it is now illegal to own an orangutan in Indonesia—and many other countries—the practice of shooting female orangutans in order to capture and sell their babies as pets continues. In Europe, an orangutan can fetch up to $25,000.

Visiting the orangutans

Nowhere else on earth can you see so many orangutans in their natural setting as at Tanjung Puting's two rehabilitation centers, Tanjung Harapan and Camp Leakey. Early in the morning and late in the afternoon the apes gather at the centers for their meal of rice, bananas and seasonal fruit.

Mothers bring their children, the tiniest cradled tenderly in their mothers' great arms, the older ones riding piggy-back. Orphans and juveniles also show up at feeding time, often playing with each other as well as the wardens and visitors. One of these cute "children" might grab your hand or foot, or otherwise try to play with you.

The park regulations are strict regarding contact with the orangutans: visitors may not initiate contact with the animals, but if the apes initiate the encounter, visitors are allowed to hold and play with the creatures. It's a wonderful feeling to cradle a small orangutan or walk hand in hand with a larger one.

Beware, however, as these are inquisitive animals: they will explore your pockets, your camera bag, and even under your clothes.

Another cardinal rule at the center is that no one is allowed in who is ill, particularly with any kind of respiratory infection. It is also suggested that you spend at least two weeks in Asia before visiting Tanjung Puting to lessen the risk of introducing exotic bacteria and viruses.

Education campaign

Ever since falling in love with the "little men in red suits" at a zoo when she was a girl, Dr. Galdikas—who holds her PhD in anthropology—has dedicated her life to the study and preservation of orangutans. In the 20 years since she first established the center at Tanjung Puting, she has pioneered a kinder, gentler, more personal approach to the orangutans. If they behave, the orangutans who have been released are allowed to occasionally return to one of the two camps for a good meal and some human affection.

Galdikas' most important task is to make officials and the public in Indonesia aware of the plight of the orangutans, so that laws designed for the animals' protection will be enforced. The Louis Leakey Foundation was an early supporter of her work, and the main research camp is named after the famed paleoanthropologist. Galdikas' research is currently supported by Earth Watch and the Los Angeles–based Orangutan Foundation.

The orangutan trade within Indonesia has been largely stopped, thanks to Galdikas' efforts, but she has to keep fighting to preserve the species. There are still an estimated 1,000 orangutans in Taiwan—perhaps one-third of total population of the apes—which had been smuggled out of Indonesia. Some serve as tragic side shows and others are sold as pets for $3,500-3,800. Galdikas recently helped repatriate six mistreated orangutan babies seized by customs officials in Bangkok.

Galdikas usually spends June through December with her orangutans and teaches the rest of the year at Simon Fraser University in British Columbia.

The nature reserve

The 300,000 hectare (750,000 acre) Tanjung Puting Reserve is home to more than just the orangutans. Few of the animals are really easy to see, although you might see gibbons, big dragonflies, or the blue streak of a kingfisher. The other interesting inhabitants require patience: proboscis monkeys, crab-eating macaques, small crocodiles and false gavials, and large monitor lizards.

The boat ride to Tanjung Puting from Kumai town is itself a memorable experience, leading along the jet-black, nipa palm fringed Sekonyer River. The blackwater, rich in tannins and organic acids and poor in oxygen, reflects the sky and trees like a mirror.

The Hotel Rimba is located just upstream from Tanjung Harapan, with easy access to the orangutans by paddled canoe. This post was set up at Tanjung Harapan in 1989 as there were too many orangutans at Camp Leakey, the main upriver study center, 50 kilometers (30 mi.) from Kumai. Visitors are encouraged to stay in the Tanjung Harapan area, which is more conveniently located.

Late one afternoon, I boarded a small canoe at Pondok Ambung to look for the proboscis monkeys that usually come to the rivers edge at dusk. No sooner had I settled in the canoe than a baby proboscis monkey hopped right in the boat. In answer to my look of astonishment, the ranger explained that the little fellow, nicknamed—what else—Pinocchio, was semi-tame and loved dugout rides. Pinocchio settled on the canoe prow.

Soon enough we heard the big critters crashing around the river's edge. When she heard the bellowing of the dominant males, Pinocchio jumped on my camera bag, and peed on it in fright. Another bellow, even closer, sent her scrambling to the dubious safety of the top of my head. Later, she settled on

my lap, peeing there again as she snuggled. I never managed to get any shots of the other proboscis monkeys, but I snapped away at Pinocchio at very close range.

See page 195 for practical information on the Tanjung Puting Reserve.

To support the orangutan programs, contact the Orangutan Foundation at 822 South Wellesley Ave., Los Angeles CA 90049. The man in charge, Dr. Gary Shapiro, has taught sign language to the orangutans at Tanjung Puting and provided much appreciated background information on the park.

Opposite: Baby orangutans get bottles of formula at the Tanjung Puting Rehabilitation Center.
Above: Dr. Biruté Galdikas and her charges.

Kalteng Practicalities

Prices in US$ unless otherwise noted; city code for Palangkaraya, 0541.

Palangkaraya

Coming up the Kahayan River from Banjarmasin by speedboat or a *bis air* "water bus," you land at the Dermaga Pelabuahan Rambang (see map opposite). Young men vie with each other to grab your luggage to take you and your bags on their motorcycles. There are two inexpensive *losmen* very close to the dock. If you go further into town for accommodations, be sure to bargain—50¢ to $1 should get you to any hotel or *losmen*. Arriving by air, minibus-taxis whisk you to anywhere in town for $3. The airport is just at the edge of the city.

ACCOMMODATIONS

In Palangkaraya there is a good range of accommodations, running from close to international standards to cheap digs as low as $2.

Dandang Tingang. Jl. Yos Sudarso 11, Tel: 21805, 21254, Telex: 39286 HODATI IA. By far the best in town, with tasteful Dayak-style decorations, 23 modern rooms all AC and with ice boxes, conference room, bar and restaurant, disco on Saturday night. A longish walk from downtown but very quiet. The hotel provides free transportation to any in-town destination. In their restaurant, Indonesian dishes cost $1.50, and Western food goes for $4-$8. There is a fair variety of booze, including the local rice wine at $1 for a bottle, but watch out for the hangover. Western liquors, $3-$4 a glass. $18 to $60, discounts possible.

Adidas. Jl. A.Yani 90, Tel: 21770. 9 AC rooms, conveniently located downtown. There is a billiards room and an open-air restaurant serving grilled fish and crayfish ($1-$3), simple Indonesian dishes ($1-$1.50), soft drinks and beer ($1.70). $18-$22.

Rachman. Jl. Murjani 9, near the river and dock area, Tel: 21428. 19 AC rooms. $10-$12.

Halmahera. Jl. Halmahera 24, Tel: 21993. 19 so-so rooms, some AC, some fan-cooled. Restaurant serves common Indonesian dishes ($1-1.50), crayfish ($3) and the esteemed local fish, *jelawat* ($3.50). Beer $2 a bottle. $7-14.

Virgo. Jl. A. Yani 7B, Tel: 21265. 39 AC and fan-cooled rooms, clean place. Moderately priced restaurant serving local and Indonesian dishes. $7-$14.

Sukma Indah Permai. Jl. Sumatra 12, Tel: 21859. 26 AC or fan-cooled rooms, near the docks, $4.50-12.

Rita. Jl. A. Yani 82, Tel: 21634. 10 rooms, some AC, some fan-cooled. On the second floor, above shops. $4-$13.

Losmen Putir Sinta. Jl. Nias 15, Tel: 21132. Across the street from the Mahkota. 15 fan-cooled rooms, attached bathrooms. $4 S, $5.50 D.

Losmen Mahkota. Jl. Nias 5, Tel: 21672. 30 fan-cooled rooms, most with attached bathrooms. Very close to the docks. $2.50-$6.

Losmen Pahandut Jaya. Jl. Kalimantan 33, Tel: 21541, near the dock. 21 rooms, no AC or fan. $2-$3.50.

Sesari. Jl. Murjani 44. Small, clean, family atmosphere with 11 rooms, all cooled by small fans. No attached bathrooms; 4 toilets and 5 ladle-type baths. $1.50-$2.50.

DINING

Bukit Raya. Jl. Milono at km 2.5, Tel: 21413. Best for local grilled fish, especially the *jelawat* but located some way from downtown, past the governor's office complex. Grilled fish $1 and up, crayfish ($3), chicken ($1.50), common Indonesian dishes ($1-$1.50), beer ($1.75). Try the *sayur ambut,* a hot local speciality of fish and tender rattan shoots ($1.50).

Depot Gloria. Jl. Murjani, Chinese pork and chicken dishes $2.75 and up.

Empat Lima. Jl. A. Yani 63, specializes in grilled fish, $1.50-$2.50.

Sampaga. Jl. Murjani 100, near the Losmen Serasi, specializes in pork dishes (75¢ to $1.50). Pork and rice for about $2 per person. Try the *babi sate,* pork brochettes, $1.50.

Simpang Raya. Jl. A. Yani near the Hotel Virgo. Padang-style eat-your-fill for $1.50-$3.

Tropicana. Jl. Darma Sugondo, Chinese dishes $2.50-$3.50.

LOCAL TRANSPORTATION

Orange minibuses circulate just about everywhere for 15¢. On the back of a motorcycle or *ojek*, it is 30-60¢ to most destinations or $1.50-$2/hr. Colt minibuses can be chartered for $2/hr., minimum of two hours. For a full day in the colt, 6:00 a.m. to 6:00 p.m., $25. Jeep taxis go for $3/hr., two-hour minimum, $28 for the day. $3 to or from the airport.

REGIONAL TRANSPORTATION

Garuda. Jl. A. Yani 69A, Tel: 21411. Daily flights to Jakarta ($67) and Balikpapan ($35).

Bouraq. Jl. A. Yani 84, Tel: 21622. Daily to Pangkalanbun ($30), twice daily to Banjarmasin ($23) and twice daily to Sampit ($22).

DAS. Jl. Milono 2, Tel: 21550. Small planes twice daily to Banjarmasin, ($23), twice daily to Sampit ($21), daily to Muara Teweh ($25), daily to Buntok ($21), daily to Pangkalanbun ($30) three times weekly to Tumbang Samba ($21).

By river

Frequent boats going down the Kahayan River from the Dermaga Pelabuhan Kambang dock

Get there early for the speedboats which leave whenever full. The *bis air*, the larger and slower boats, depart more or less as scheduled.

Palangkaraya to Banjarmasin by speedboat, $10, by slowboat $2.75. To Kuala Kapuas by speedboat $8.50, by slowboat $2. To Pulau Pisau by speedboat $7.50, by slowboat $1.50. To Bahaur (on the coast) by slowboat, $2.30. To Panghoh by slowboat, $2. To Danau Panggong in Kalsel, $2.50. To Buntok on the Barito River, $6. (For boats upstream, see "Kahayan River" below.) Going up the Rungan River, it's $15 to Tumbang Jutuh in 5 hours by speedboat, by slowboat $6 and 12 hours.

By land

It is 85 km. (53 mi.) and about 1.5 hours by either public minibus ($2) or a chartered bus ($24) to Kasongan on the Katingan River. From there, regular riverboats to Tumbang Samba. By speedboat, $6.50 in 5.5 hours or river taxi at $3. Beyond Tumbang Sanba, it's either charter or wait for an occasional boat to head upriver to Tumbang Senamang. By chartered speedboat, $200-$250.

TRAVEL INFORMATION

If you speak Indonesian, try the tourism office, Kantor Pariwisata, on Jl. Supaman 21, Tel: 21416. Otherwise contact Pak Ariel Adrianus Ahat, the manager of the Dandang Tingang Hotel, Tel: 21805, 21254. He speaks Japanese, English and some French, and knows if there there are any ceremonies going on. He can find an English-speaking guide, $15 a day plus expenses. Beware of would-be guides.

AGENCY TOURS

Several agencies out of Bali and Jakarta as well as Banjarmasin offer tours to the orangutan rehabilitation center in Tanjung Puting. Although other agencies are looking over the possibilities of inland tours to Dayak villages, so far only the **Ida Dewi Sarawati** out of Kuta in Bali has sent a group there. They offer a seven-day tour, starting and ending in Palangkaraya, which goes to Tumbang Kurik and the walk to Tumbang Maharoi. $450 per person in groups of 7-10, $400 for groups of 11-15 and $375 per person for more than 15. All-inclusive and with an English-speaking guide.

MARKET DAYS

Buntok	Saturday
Ampah	Friday
Temang Layang	Monday
Kalahien	Tuesday
Pendan	Thursday
Menkatip	Wednesday
Kuala Kapuas	Saturday
Mandomai.	Friday
Pulang Pisau	Thursday

These last three have markets on the water.

SHOPPING AND SOUVENIRS

Most souvenir shops are located in the streets just in back of the dock area. Two well-stocked ones are the **Fauzi**, Jl. Madura 60 and the **Aries**, Jl. Madura 7, both a half a block from the Hotel Halmahera. Lots of rattan baskets, 60¢ to $6 according to size. The Aries sometimes has old *mandaus*, $100 to $300. They

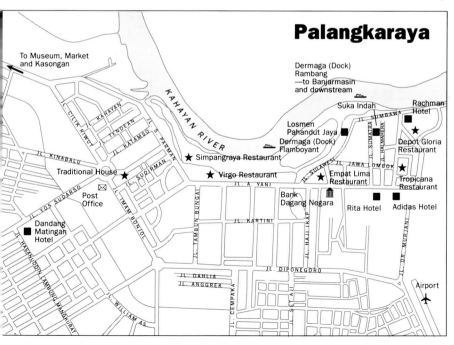

also sell many semi-precious stones, some loose, some set in rings, along with beads. Ships-of-the-dead ($1.50-$35) are excellent buys here. Bargaining is expected.

VISITING LONGHOUSES

There are 4 longhouses within reach of Palangkaraya. Several days' round trip are required for each. Tours have begun to the longhouse at Tumbang Kurik, on a tributary off the uppermost Kahayan River. You either join a tour, or hire a guide in Palangkaraya.

From Palangkaraya, travel up the Rongan River, a tributary of the Kahayan which joins it at Palangkaraya. By speedboat to Tumbang Jutuh ($15) it takes about 5 hours; by slowboat ($6), much longer. From Tumban Jutuh, it's 8 km. (5 mi.) by foot, motorcycle, or motorboat (*alkon*) to the Tumbang Malahoi longhouse.

You could also travel overland by paved road (about 1.5 hrs.) to Kasongan on the Katingan River. From there, a speedboat ($6) or slowboat to Tumbang Samba. There are also 3 flights a week from Palangkaraya to Tumbang Samba ($22). From Tumbang Samba, it's a day and $45 to charter an *alkon* through the rapids. Wonderful scenery and villages with carved coffins to either Tumbang Senamang or Pendatangaring, the drop-off points to the 6-km. walk leading to the (rebuilt) longhouse at Tumbang Gagu, just south of a range of hills. Check to find out which is the easier walk. The 50-meter (160 ft.) longhouse is on the Kalong, a tributary of the Mentaya River.

The region of Puruk Cahu on the upper Barito River and the area near the border with Kalbar, northeast of the upper Lamandau River, all have Dayak longhouses. For the latter area, it's best by motorcycle or jeep from Pangkalanbun. The 3 longhouses of this region are supposed to be the most traditional in Kalteng. For the upper Barito, there is one at Makunjung, on the main river just before Puruk Cahu. Another, at Parici, can be reached via the tributary heading north from Muara Laung.

WEATHER

Unpredictable in recent years. Formerly, the rain peaked in March with a second peak in November. The driest month was July, followed by January. River travel far inland depends on just the right amount of water, hard to predict.

Kalteng Interior

There may not be a thousand rivers in Kalteng, as claimed, but there are lots of them. Seven major rivers, all running generally from north to south, serve as the major highways to the interior. Regular daily speedboats, usually with 85 HP outboards, travel quite far inland.

On a regular passenger basis, these speedboats are quite reasonably priced. Sitting up front gives a better view (unless too much bag-

gage is piled up around the windshield) but you hit harder when the speedboat bounces on the waves of other river craft. Beyond the route of the regular speedboats, downstream from the hairier rapids, one travels by chartered *alkon*, a motorized canoe. Costs depend on engine size, availability, gasoline supplies and bargaining.

Hopping from one watershed to another is usually accomplished by plane, with a couple of exceptions. There is an 85-km. paved road from Palangkaraya on the Kahayan River to Kasongan on the Katingan. There are also flights from Palangkaraya to Tumbang Samba, upriver from Kasongan. You can also fly from Buntok on the Barito River to Palangkaraya. Alternatively, downriver, you can cross watersheds from the Barito either by canal to the Kahayan or, at the same point (Kuala Kapuas) head up the Kapuas River.

Travel on dirt roads is dry-weather only and there are no passenger vehicles which run only on the bits of pavement around the towns. Also, no gas stations. Travel on these roads is by motorcycle or perhaps chartered minibus.

ACCOMMODATIONS

Kalteng has a fair number of *losmen,* even in the upriver areas, thanks to logging and gold-mining activities. Most are rudimentary, with no attached bathrooms, ranging in price from $1.50 to $6. A few places offer better rooms, AC and attached bathrooms for $5 to $15.

Buntok, the principal town on the Barito River, offers 7 *losmen*, all with lower-priced rooms at $1.50-$2 and better rooms, $2.50-$5. Downriver from Buntok, only Jenemas has a *losmen*, the **Imuh**, $1.50-$2.50. Buntok is connected by paved road with Ampah to the west. Three *losmen* there, all cheap.

Upstream on the Barito from Buntok, the district capital of Muara Teweh has 6 *losmen*. The **Gunung Sintuk**'s best rooms go for $14. Further upriver, there are 4 *losmen* at Puruk Cahu. The **Tepian Barito** is the cheapest ($1-$1.50), with the others slightly higher. The last place of (relatively) easy access on the Barito, the small town of Tumbang Kunyi, has *losmen* as there are gold works close by.

Kuala Kapuas, the principal town on the lower section of the Kapuas River, has at least 7 *losmen*. The cheapest, the **Sinar Harapan**, has rooms in the $1.50-$2.50 range. The most expensive rooms are at the **Kapuas City** and the **Slamet Riyadi**. On the uppermost reaches of the Kapuas River, just before it meets the Barito, gold mining is again behind a *losmen* at Tambang Lahung.

On the Rungan River, which reaches the Kahayan just north of Palangkaraya, **Tumbang Jutuh** provides 2 *losmen*, surprisingly expensive at $3-$6. The **Jakatan Jaya** has cheaper rooms, while **Sari Manis** has only the $6 kind.

On the Katingan River, there are 4 *losmen* at Kasongan and 4 more in Tumbang Samba with the best rooms at the **Colombo**, $6. Way upstream, there is one at Tumbang Senamang.

A wide range of accommodations is found in Sampit, the second largest city in Kalteng. There are 11 hotels and *losmen*. The best of the lot is the full AC **Purnama**, ($6-$20). The medium priced *losmen* include the **Rahmad** ($2-$6), the **Priangan** ($3.50-$6.50) and the **Mutiara** ($5-$12). In the lower range, the **Wisata Indah** ($1.50), the **Mustika** ($2) and the **Handayani** ($2.50). Upstream from Sampit on the Mentaya River, there are lodgings at Kuala Kuayan.

Pangkalanbun

The district of Kotawaringin Barat, with a population of some 156,000, has its capital at Pangkalanbun (pop. 30,000), on the river by the same name. About one third of the district's inhabitants are Tumon Dayaks, mostly Christian, who were evangelized in the late 1920s and early 1930s. About 10% of the Dayaks adhere to the Kaharingan faith.

Since the 30-40 funerary rituals (tiwah) held each year have to be cleared with the *camat,* who reports to the *bupati* in Pangkalanbun, you should check there to see if there is a *tiwah* coming up. The owner of the Blue Kecubung Hotel (see below) can also find out for you.

Accommodations

There are 12 hotels and *losmen* here, for wallets big and small. The best ones, **Blue Kecubung** and **Wisma Nadika,** have AC rooms ($10-$24). The next best are the **Andika** ($5-$12), the **Wisma Sampuraga** ($6-$9) and the **Bahagia** ($5.00-$8.50). Cheapest are the **Waringin** ($2.50-$4.50) and the **Kunia** ($2.50-$5.00). Home-stays here are $4. (See "Tanjung Puting" in the Travel Advisory, page 194, for more information on Pangkalanbun hotels.)

Visiting the Dayak areas

One of the district's most traditional areas lies in the Kudangan subdistrict, far upstream on the Lamandau River, near the foothills of the southwest corner of the Schwaner Range. There are perhaps as many as 100 longhouses in use by the 7,000-odd Dayaks scattered in the 19 villages here.

Although it's possible to get to the Kudangan subdistrict from Pangkalanbun, it's long and expensive—$200 and 4 days, via Tapinbini. Easier to fly to Ketapang in Kalbar and from there go up the Pawan River, either by speedboat (4 hours) or *klotok* (1 day) to Tanjung Asam, then by motorcycle (in the dry season, there are occasional trucks and minibuses) over the 150-odd km "road" to Kudangan.

The Kahayan River

Speedboats of 85HP run daily from Palangkaraya to Tewah, about 7 hrs. with several stops along the way (one for lunch) for $15 per passenger. Smaller 40HP speedboats can be chartered for $150. Without stops, these take 8-10 hrs. to reach Tewah. Longboats with about 30-passenger capacity make the trip in some 13 hours going upstream and 9 hours coming down at $6-$9. Charter a speedboat for this one-way run for $150-$350.

At Tewah, there are 3 *losmen*, all charging $1.50, none with in-room toilet facilities. We recommend the 18-room **Batu Mas**, the only place that serves food ($3 for a good meal and a bottle of water). The proprietors have an excellent collection of antique porcelains and gongs.

The **Seindah Tewah** *losmen*, next to the Batu Mas, 14 rooms above a couple of shops; $3 for a room for up to 3 bodies. There are 2 toilets and 5 ladle bathrooms along with a billiards room. The *losmen* **Nusantara** is above the movie house by the same name. There are 8 rooms on the third floor, for up to 3 people apiece, $1.50/head. One upstairs and one downstairs toilet/bathroom. The *losmen* is usually full whenever a government team comes through. Electricity in Tewah now comes on all over town at dark, and is cut off at 11:30 p.m.

From Tewah upriver, logistics become more complicated. There are no *losmen* so you have to stay with a government official (usually the *kepala desa*), a schoolteacher or a family. Pay about $3 for bed and board, which includes supper and a light breakfast. There are usually no spare mattresses or pillows. For gifts, bring *kretek* cigarettes, sugar, biscuits plus whatever food you need for yourself beyond rice, chicken, fish and (sometimes) vegetables. In season, December to February, there is plenty of fruit.

From Tewah to Tumbang Miri, travel by chartered speedboat, about 1.5 hours and $60 one-way, $90 round-trip. You have to stop in Tumbang Miri to see the *camat*, and he can help arrange transportation further by *alkon*.

There are no public river taxis above Tewah, so you must charter a speedboat, a small *alkon,* or ask around and wait a few days until there is some kind of boat going to Tumbang Miri or beyond. If the water level is high enough, a speedboat can take you as far as Tumbang Hamputung ($90-$110 r/t) or even all the way to Tumbang Kurik ($125-$200 r/t). Alternately, you can travel all the way by *alkon*: Tewah to Tumbang Miri (3 hrs., $30-$40); Tumbang Miri to Tumbang Hamputung (2 hrs., $30); Tumbang Hamputung to Tumbang Kurik (2.5 hrs., $20-$25). Ask the *camat* or the *kepala desa* for help finding a boat.

Tanjung Puting Reserve

See "Tanjung Puting" page 194 under Nature Reserves in the Travel Advisory for a map and practical information. See also "Agency Tours" page 143 in Kalsel Practicalities for organized tours to the orangutan rehabilitation center.

PART VII

West Kalimantan

West Kalimantan, or Kalimantan Barat—Kalbar—is a huge province consisting chiefly of the Kapuas River basin. The province covers 146,807 square kilometers (56,682 sq. mi.), and has a population of 4 million. The Kapuas River, Kalbar's geographical landmark, is the longest river in Indonesia. The region, having received almost no tourist promotion, is largely unknown.

In the 19th century, the situation was quite different, and the western part of Dutch Borneo was more visited than the now popular East Kalimantan. Englishman James Brooke, who received the territory that is now called Sarawak from the Sultan of Brunei, was perceived as a threat to Dutch sovereignty in their territory. The Dutch reinforced their presence around Pontianak—the current provincial capital—and its environs, in order to keep the "White Raja" in bordering Sarawak at bay.

Diamonds and the Dutch

Shortly after their arrival in the archipelago, the diamond fields in western Borneo aroused the interest of the Dutch. Warehouses (then called "factories") were established at Sambas and Sukadana, but these were soon evacuated because of dwindling diamond supplies and Holland's concentration on Java and the spice-rich Moluccas.

In 1698, almost a century after they first arrived in the archipelago, the Dutch intervened to force the Malay rulers of West Borneo to recognize the suzerainty of the sultan of Batam in Java, already under Dutch control. To reinforce her claims, Holland supported the efforts of Abdul Rahman, an Arab adventurer who founded the trading center at Pontianak. (See "Islam and the West," page 30.) The Dutch helped Abdul Rahman crush the local rulers who refused to accept the newcomer's supremacy, and established a Dutch presence at Pontianak.

Although all the region's trade was supposed to be funnelled and taxed through Pontianak, the profits to Holland were not enough to justify continuing the expense of garrisons and offices, and the Dutch withdrew in 1791. Economic and political conditions were to draw them back soon.

Beginning in the 18th century, a gold rush hit the west coast of Borneo and thousands of poor Hakka peasants flocked to the rich alluvial gold deposits which were eventually to produce one-seventh of the world's yearly supply of the precious metal. The Dutch, always on the lookout for economic opportunities, wanted a share of the financial boom. But by the time their military forces defeated the independent-minded Chinese, the gold deposits had been nearly panned out, and the gold was all in China.

Then, for a short while, one of Holland's two principal administrative centers in Dutch Borneo was established at the upriver town of Sintang. This administrative push inland, backed by the military when necessary, opened the way for the exploration of the immense, unknown interior of the island.

The Chinese in West Kalimantan

Today, West Kalimantan holds one of the highest concentrations of ethnic Chinese in all of Indonesia. The estimated 450,000 Chinese-Indonesians here make up about 11 percent of the province's population. These numbers include descendants of Chinese-Dayak marriages.

Large numbers of Chinese arrived in the archipelago beginning in the 1720s to work the abundant tin deposits on Bangka Island. Following this lead, Malay ruler of Sambas

Overleaf: *"The Pontianak River," by Paulus Lauters, a Belgian lithographer. He produced the plate based on sketches drawn by Dutch naval officer C. W. M. van de Velde from 1838-1841.*
Opposite: *An elderly Maloh woman selling vegetables in the Putussibau market.*

invited the Chinese to work the alluvial gold deposits found on his territories, and the migration began on a small scale in the 1750s, picking up speed around 1790.

The invitation to work the gold fields was not a humanitarian gesture. The Chinese were forbidden to farm or to trade, so they would be forced to buy everything necessary from the sultan at highly inflated prices. Plus they had to pay tribute.

When they became strong enough, the Chinese rejected all demands and set up independent units called *kongsi,* patterned after their clan-based organizations back home. These communities flourished during the height of the gold boom, 1790–1820. By the first decade of the 18th century, more than 40,000 men had arrived.

Most of the Chinese settled around the gold fields of Mandor and Montrado, both quite close together, located between Sambas and Pontianak. The *kongsi* formed two federations, one controlling the fields of Mandor, the other those of Montrado. Each had an agricultural arm which grew irrigated rice and other foodstuffs to feed the miners. Other groups built and maintained the water channels which fed the sluices where the precious metal was washed out of the auriferous clay. The West Borneo gold fields were rich, with the quality of the metal running from 18 to 21 carats, but all observers agree that their success was mostly due to the Chinese

propensity for intensive labor and skillful handling of water resources.

When the yields began to diminish, feuds and violence weakened the Chinese community. All-out battles between federations somewhat fragmented and dispersed the Chinese. Facing a determined Dutch military, the Mandar area quickly submitted.

The Montrado Chinese had retained enough cohesion to defend themselves, and kept trading through Singkawang. Since the Java Rebellion of 1825–30 required all available Dutch soldiers, Borneo and the Chinese were left alone. Until, that is, Raja Brooke's empire in Sarawak began to attract Holland's interest once again.

Dutch measures included the administrative reorganization of West Borneo, and a major military expedition—which ended Chinese intransigence at Montrado. The feuding *kongsi* were dismantled, but by then large-scale gold mining had ended. Since most of the Chinese could not afford passage home, they settled in West Borneo.

Visiting West Kalimantan

Pontianak, the provincial capital, is graced with busy docks where Bugis schooners tie up, a regional museum, the Jami Mosque and the old sultan's palace. The coastal area to the north of Pontianak has some nice beaches, and near Singkawang are the clay works where huge ceramic ovens produce copies of ancient Chinese jars, formerly an essential trade item for the Dayaks of the interior.

Weavers in the town of Sambas create beautiful cloth, integrating gold and silver threads into ancient patterns. There is the sultan's mosque in town, and on the way to the city from Pontianak, one passes several Chinese temples.

The landscape of West Kalimantan is dotted with high, steep-sided rock formations, which offer a challenge to the rock climber and a rare view over the jungle canopy from their heights. The most dramatic of these peaks, Mount Kelam, rises from the forest quite close to Sintang.

Up the Kapuas River

To get upriver to Kalbar's remote interior, there are three possible departure points on the Kapuas River. From Sintang, 450 kilome-

Opposite: *The Mesjid Jami at Pontianak just after a rainfall. The mosque, in its time one of the world's largest, is part of the old sultan's palace, on the site where the city was originally founded.*

ters (280 mi.) from Pontianak, one can motor up the Kapuas, then the Kayan or the Pinoh.

Either Semitau or Selimbau, further up the Kapuas, can serve as a departure point for the extensive lake region to the north, which is connected to the Kapuas by river. This unusual ecological zone is the home of Iban and other scattered Dayak groups.

Putussibau, the last town of importance on the Kapuas, lies almost 900 kilometers (560 mi.) from Pontianak. Here Kayan and Maloh Dayaks live in traditional longhouses. From Putussibau one can also cross the island, by traveling to the far reaches of the Kapuas and then trekking through almost uninhabited mountain forest to the Mahakam watershed in the east.

The Dayaks of Kalbar

"Land Dayak" is a catch-all term that dates from the last century, invented to differentiate the Dayaks of the island's interior from the so-called "Sea Dayaks," or Iban. The name Land Dayak, which comes from Sarawak, has been applied to the peoples of West Kalimantan living in the lower and middle Kapuas River basin: the Selako, the Singgi, the Jagoi, the Sadong, and various groups living upstream on the Sanggau and Sekayan Rivers. These groups, as well as the Iban, who live chiefly in Sarawak although there are some 7,000 in Kalbar, speak languages related to Malay.

For centuries, the Kapuas River Dayaks have faced outside influences. There are remains here of a first-millenium A.D. Hindu culture, and the Majapahit Empire of Java established spheres of influence on the coast. It is thought that the presence of these Javanese triggered migrations of both the Iban and the Land Dayaks from southwest Borneo to their present locations.

Not long after the fall of the Hindu Majapahit to Islam in the 14th century, the Land Dayaks came under the influence of the coastal Muslim sultanates which controlled trade, often exploiting and attempting to proselytize the Dayaks. When the Dutch presence was felt in the region, they put an end to Islamic proselytizing, but supported Christian missions among the Land Dayaks.

The Land Dayaks lived in longhouses, but their villages also contained a distinctive men's house. This circular building, topped by a high, conical roof, was both a ceremonial center and a meeting hall. Some of these structures were as high as 10 meters (33 ft.) off the ground, with a trap-door entrance. The men's houses have disappeared today.

In the old days, the war god required offerings of dog meat smeared with human blood, and successful warriors ate a kind of porridge made from human brains and rice wine. When a chief died, his likeness was carved onto a thick post, and the statue was offered a freshly cut head.

PONTIANAK

Thriving City of Ghostly Origins

A few kilometers from the sea, away from the coastal mangrove swamps, the city of Pontianak lies on the junction of the Kapuas and Landak Rivers. It is on the edge of the 5,400 square-kilometer (2,100 sq. mi.) Kapuas delta. A thriving urban and trade center of 360,000, of whom around 30 percent are Chinese, Pontianak owes its prominence to its strategic location and a history of feuding West Bornean sultanates. And to a certain unsuperstitious Arab.

In 1770, Syarif Abdul Rahman Al Gadri, who had earned quite a reputation for his rather dubious activities on the high seas, decided to go respectable and settle down. The spot he chose was deserted, and had no claimers, because it abounded in the evil spirits called *pontianak* by the Malays. Our Arab was a man of common sense, and eliminated the *pontianak*s just as he did his earthly enemies, with a sustained cannon barrage. The spirits fled, but the name stuck.

There were several sultanates then competing for the area's control, including Sukadana, south of Pontianak, although it was fading after its heyday as Borneo's most important power and diamond center. Sambas, an established sultanate to the north, represented a serious rival for Abdul Rahman. So did Mempawah, on the coast, a center of power then recently founded by a Bugis nobleman who had been expelled from the Riau Islands by the Dutch. Rahman's move, and subsequent success, was due in no small part to the support of the Dutch authorities who helped him against the sultans who refused Holland's "protection."

When the 18th-century gold rush made the west coast of Borneo look attractive to the colonial power, and the British in Sarawak seemed to take an increasing interest in the territory to their south, Pontianak took on strategic importance in the eyes of the Dutch. It grew from a modest outpost to its current dominant status in the region.

Syarif Abdul Rahman's original settlement began on the confluence of the Kapuas and the Landak. A century after Syarif Rahman settled the land at the confluence of the two rivers, a large Malay village had grown up behind the mosque and the sultan's palace. The embryonic Dutch administration, the Chinese and some Malays occupied the riverbank across from and just below the main mosque. (See map below.) Although not on the coast, the town's low, swampy ground flooded daily at high tide wherever no dikes were built. Drainage canals helped, but mud was a fact of life here.

Pontianak's Quarters

The city is made up of quarters which were once independent settlements, or *kampungs,* until the city grew around them. The original town is the area around the Jami Mosque and the sultan's palace or *kraton.* The area nearby is the Kampung Dalam, an inner village that in the past sheltered the sultan's friends, court and retainers. The Kampung Saigon testifies to old relations with Vietnam. A large overall area, which includes all the mentioned *kampungs* now fused together, reaches towards the east and is called Kampung Bugis. Kampung Bugis is linked to the rest of the city by two bridges, one crossing the Kapuas River, the other the Landak.

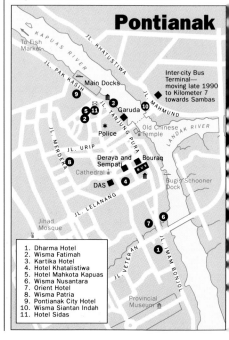

Pontianak

Inter-city Bus Terminal—
moving late 1990 to Kilometer 7 towards Sambas

Main Docks

Garuda

Police

Old Chinese Temple

Deraya and Sempati

Bouraq

Cathedral

DAS

Bugis Schooner Dock

Jihad Mosque

Provincial Museum

1. Dharma Hotel
2. Wisma Fatimah
3. Kartika Hotel
4. Hotel Khatalistiwa
5. Hotel Mahkota Kapuas
6. Wisma Nusantara
7. Orient Hotel
8. Wisma Patria
9. Pontianak City Hotel
10. Wisma Siantan Indah
11. Hotel Sidas

Opposite: *The Bugis schooner dock at Pontianak.*

To the north of Kampung Bugis, across the Landak River, is a quarter called Siantan, the southern terminus of the province's paved road system. The main part of Pontianak, the commercial sector, follows the southwest bank of the Kapuas, around an extended market area and the old Chinese quarter. Jalan Tanjungpura is the heart of this area.

Just in the last decade, a new quarter—Kota Baru—has been developed. Located southwest of the downtown, Kota Baru is strictly for government offices and housing.

Touring Pontianak

Most of Pontianak's highlights are concentrated in a relatively small area, and in a day or two you can explore the city's various points of interest. You can cover everything on your own, walking and taking a couple of rides across the Kapuas River.

The mosque and palace complex is a short boat ride across the Kapuas from the market area, or you can take the roundabout land route over the Kapuas bridge. The Mesjid Jami was first erected a couple of centuries ago, and the various reconstructions have remained faithful to the original layout. The mosque was huge for the time it was built, the late 18th century, and has a triple roof and stained glass windows. You are welcome to enter (after removing shoes, of course) for a look. Don't miss the wooden sculptures of the *mimbar* (pulpit).

The sultan's palace, an impressive wooden structure, is just 100 meters away, and like the mosque, was built by order of Syarif Rahman. The cursive Arabic script on the front of the Istana reads "Al Gadri," the name of the founding family. A part of the palace is still inhabited by the descendants of the sultans. They will open the main hall for you, which included two elaborate thrones, fading photos, Chinese ceramics and Western statues. The furnishings go back to days, if not of glory, at least of better than the current financial circumstances. A contribution, say $1 per person, is appreciated.

Around the market area and old Chinese quarter, there are several *pekong* or Taoist temples, which carry various Buddhist labels so as to qualify as an officially accepted religion. You are welcome to enter and look around any of them.

A short ways downstream from the market area, freighters berth at the Dwikora docks, while the more exotic Bugis schooners tie up opposite the sultan's palace. No one objects to foreigners sauntering around here, snapping shots of the human ant-armies loading or unloading the cargoes of the (motorized) schooners.

From the docks, it's a long walk to the state museum, the Musium Negeri. Better to hop on a minibus (ask which one goes there) from downtown for 15¢. The museum is worth a visit. There is a wealth of items here

relating to the local Malay culture, a fair number of Dayak pieces, and almost nothing on the Chinese, except a few examples of export porcelain. Gigantic relief sculputres cover the museum's front, with one side depicting scenes from traditional Dayak life, and the other side showing that of the Malays.

Close to the museum, just off A. Yani St., check out a full-scale replica of a longhouse which may be opened someday to the public.

In the same part of town, but not too close, is the Jihad Mosque, just off Jl. Sultan Abdul Rahman. It's a new wooden structure with a very distinct style, far from Islamic norms. Shoes off and you can look inside.

The equator monument

Crossing the Kapuas on the ferry, you can then catch a minibus heading northeast out of town to the equator monument, called Tugu Khatulistiwa, from the Indonesian word (borrowed from Arabic) for "equator." The monument is curious: a pair of tall, dark, columns holds up a jumble of metallic circles and an arrow, much like an old astronomical instrument. The Dutch word for "equator" can be made out, as can the longitude, 109° 20' 00" East. This thing has become something of the symbol of Pontianak, and one can find miniatures of it in shops all over town.

Close to the monument, a road to the left off the highway reaches the Kapuas River at a place called Batu Layang. There used to be a small riverside fort here, built by the sultans, but it was taken over by the Dutch and then leveled by the Japanese during the war. The sultans' necropolis and ornate tombs go all the way back to the dynasty's founder, Abdul Rahman, who died in 1808.

Northwest Kalbar

A good system of paved roads links Pontianak to the principal coastal towns to the north. Public buses are frequent, and a sedan taxi can be hired in town. The main road out of Pontianak cuts through coconut plantations along the Kapuas River, then follows the coast. At Sungai Pinyuh, a road, currently in good shape, leads to the interior as far as Sintang, and soon to Putussibau.

From Sungai Pinyuh, a branch of the paved road reaches Mempawah, 67 kilometers (41 mi.) from Pontianak. A Bugis prince settled this area at just about the time the Arab pirate settled Pontianak. Rahman later married his son to the sultan of Mempawah's daughter, gaining control of the area. The royal tombs of Mempawah, fashioned of carved and painted ironwood, are excellent examples of Islamic art.

The Chinese ceramics works

Continuing north along the coast, there are several beaches off the main road between Mempawah and the Sambas River. There is nothing special about the beaches here, and

hey are mostly frequented by locals. Save your time to visit the pottery works.

The ceramics center is at Saliung, just off the main road, 7 kilometers (4 mi.) before reaching Singkawang. There are no signs, so you have to ask where to turn off. Here a huge oven, some 30 meters (100 ft.) long, provides the high temperatures needed to fire the fine ceramics. Craftsmen here make both utilitarian objects and fine copies of Chinese export ware from dynasties past.

In the past, there was enough business to keep several operations going, as large jars and other items were made for sale in the interior of Kalimantan. Some ceramic pieces were traded on a regular basis for salt brought by local boats from Madura Island, off eastern Java. Today, competition from plastic products and low-quality ceramics from mainland China, as well as a factory with modern gas-fired kilns, located just outside Pontianak, has cut into the market. Besides, bricks are easier to make and have a higher profit margin. But the two ceramics works still remain.

Singkawang, 145 kilometers (90 mi.) from Pontianak, is the capital of the Sambas district. The town was founded by the Chinese during the gold rush era, and served as a supply entrepôt for the gold fields of Monrado. In the 1830s, British naval captain George Earl described the town in full boom, full of Chinese men and Dayak women.

Because of Imperial edicts, Chinese women were rarely allowed to go abroad. Montrado fiercely resisted Dutch interference with its independent status, which lasted until 1856. Recently, the Montrado Mas mining company started production in the former Chinese gold-rush area.

Continuing north on the main road, keep an eye out for a Chinese temple at Sebangkau—it is harmonious and colorful, and is beautifully reflected by the river. The road here cuts inland from the coast and follows the southern shore of the Sambas River to the town of Sambas, 225 kilometers (140 mi.) from Pontianak. There is an ancient sultan's palace here, inhabited by his descendants, and a mosque next door.

Sambas is still well known for a special type of cloth woven here. Lots of silver—and occasionally gold—threads are woven into the surprisingly pliant cloth called *kain* Sambas, or *kain songket,* sold in West Kalimantan as well as the rest of Indonesia. At the Sambas market you can buy handsome weavings, but unless you bargain well you could end up paying more than you would in Pontianak. By asking either at the market or the "palace," you can find someone to take you to see a local weaver at work .

Opposite: *Fine copies of old Chinese dynasty jars are fired in a huge kiln at Singkawang.* **Below:** *Heading up the Kapuas in a crowded riverboat.*

SINTANG

Halfway Up the Huge Kapuas River

Some of West Kalimantan's most traditional Dayak groups live in *kabupaten* Sintang. The riverside city stretches along both sides of the Kapuas at its junction with the Melawi River. With its government offices, markets and Chinese-run shops, and population of 20,000, Sintang dominates the middle stretch of the Kapuas River. Sintang was then, and remains today, the key to the interior of West Kalimantan. Its position at the confluence of the Kapuas and the Melawi made it the center of Chinese trade with the interior.

During the last years of the 19th century Sintang was three separate but interdependent enclaves. Facing up the Kapuas River, the Malay *kampung* was located on the left shore, on either side of the sultan's mini-palace. There was a well-built Chinese encampment on the right shore. What had been the Chinese quarter has become the town's hub today with the principal docks, bus terminal, cinemas, shops and commerce all still largely under ethnic Chinese control.

Upstream from the Chinese, just across the Melawi River, the Dutch had built a small fort surrounded by a black palisade. The Europeans lived just beyond the fort, now the location of government offices and housing.

The Dara Juanti Museum, built on the site of the former palace in 1937, contains heir looms, state regalia and Hindu-era artifacts. There is also an army museum here called the Alambhana.

Dayaks of the Sintang area

Several traditional Dayak groups live along the upper courses of the Melawi, Kayan and Pinoh Rivers. Some still live in longhouses and occasionally hold an elaborate funeral where the bones of the deceased are placed in a carved wooden mausoleum. Some Dayak groups here also hold planting festivals called *gawai* (around July) during which most of the participants dress in traditional clothes.

The Pinoh River begins in the Schwaner Range, which forms the natural boundary between the provinces of Kalbar and Kalteng. The Pinoh joins the Melawi at Nanga Pinoh, and the Kayan reaches the Melawi 70 kilometers (40 mi.) southeast of Sintang, and then the Melawi River heads northwest for Sintang, where it meets Kalbar's major river, the Kapuas. Thus Sintang is the gateway to

these three rivers, and from here one can catch speedboats or longboats.

There are still animists in the upriver areas although American Protestant missionaries are making inroads into some isolated regions. These fundamentalist preachers require almost complete abandonment of traditional practices, while the more tolerant Catholics, who arrived earlier and proselytized in relatively more accessible areas, allow much of the traditional culture to remain. In the most remote regions, many Dayaks are followers of the Kaharingan religion, which to a certain extent stymies the efforts of the Protestant fundamentalists.

Members of more than 20 different ethnic groups inhabit the Melawi basin's 20,000 square kilometers (7,700 sq. mi.). Almost all are subsistence farmers, although they sell a little rubber and rattan.

The Dohoi branch of the Ot Danum are the most conservative of the region's Dayaks. Numbering some 10,000, the Dohoi live along the upper Melawi River and its tributaries. Their relative geographical isolation has helped keep them free of Islamic influences, and of all the groups they remain the most distinct—culturally and linguistically— from the coastal Malays.

Some of the Melawi Ot Danum adhere to the Kaharingan faith, as do others of the same tribe who live south of the Schwaner Range. Footpaths over the mountains from the upper Barito and the Kahayan rivers connect this region of Kalteng with the Melawi area. The Barito and Kahayan Ot Danum culture has influenced the Dayaks of the Kayan and Melawi rivers, especially in the adoption of secondary funerary practices.

The Kebahan, some 8,000 strong, live on the upper Kayan River in a *kecamatan* centered at Nanga Tebidah. They have always been a pretty independent group, and never paid tribute to the sultan of Sintang. It was not until 1891, when the Dutch sent a military expedition against the nearby Tebidah Dayaks, that the Kebahan were brought under a measure of outside control.

Climbing 'Dark Mountain'

A stone slab of a mountain rears out of the jungle near Sintang, and the naked rock is the most conspicuous feature of the landscape, whether you arrive by river or plane. Mount Kelam is a huge outcropping reaching 900 meters (3,000 ft.) above the surrounding plain. In the local language, Mount Kelam means "Dark Mountain."

The top of Mount Kelam opens an incredible panorama: to the south, the Melawi River valley from Sintang to Nanga Pinoh, and a section of the Schwaner Range; to the north, the serpentine course of the Kapuas River across the huge plain. As a bonus, the view includes two other outcroppings, Mount Saran, 1,758 meters (5,768 ft.), and Mount Kujau, 1,355 meters (4,446 ft.).

"Mt Kelam deserves a reputation for affording a capital and interesting bit of mountaineering, yet it presents no real dangers to any one at all skilled in the art," writes Dutch geologist G. A. F. Molengraaff in his 1893-4 *Borneo Expedition*. "[I]t appeared to me most imposing and most worthy of its name 'Dark mountain,' when a thunder-cloud enveloped its crest and the ragged clouds swept wildly along its bare surface. One's imagination might almost fancy the rumblings of the thunder which seem to proceed from the very bowels of the mountain, to be the groaning of spirits (hantus) which are supposed to inhabit it. No wonder the mountain is held sacred in the district."

Recent information suggests that it is possible to arrange a climb. Check at your hotel in Sintang for help obtaining guides.

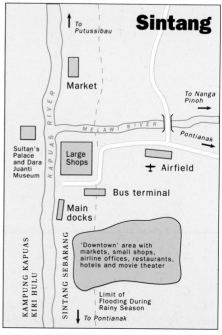

opposite: The main Chinese temple at Sintang, surrounded by the flooded Kapuas River. This is a common rainy season bother, and people simply replace their cars and motorcycles with canoes.

PUTUSSIBAU

Remote Outpost on the Kapuas

In the late 19th century, the tiny outpost of Putussibau—from *putus* Sibau, "cut off (of river traffic) at Sibau"—was a village living in constant fear of head-hunting raids from the fierce Batang Lupar Iban of Sarawak. The Chinese traders in town lived aboard their large *bandung*s, covered trading vessels, with which they could escape from invaders at a moment's notice. The Malay *kampung* was near a small fortress, manned by a garrison of Javanese soldiers employed by the Dutch. The Maloh Dayak living in the the town surrounded their houses with palisades topped with sharp bamboo spikes.

The Dutch established Putussibau as a colonial outpost in 1895, to help curb head-hunting and provide a visible presence in the interior of western Dutch Borneo. Today, Putussibau remains the economic and administrative center of this region. A town of some 7,000, it is the head of *kabupaten* Kapuas Ulu (Upper Kapuas), a huge district holding just 157,000 people. The small town can be reached by daily flights from Pontianak (90 minutes) or by river boat (four to six days).

The timber industry is the leading contributor to the area's cash economy, and the traditional trade goods—raw rubber and salted river fish—have been diversified with the recent introduction of pepper and cacao. In the late 1980s, the uppermost reaches of the Kapuas saw the beginnings of a small gold rush, with hundreds of small-time operators and a joint-venture company setting up shop.

The people of the upper Kapuas

More than a dozen Dayak groups live in the upper Kapuas region. During the centuries before the arrival of the Dutch, a slow process of Islamization along the Kapuas assimilated many Dayaks so that they have now become "Orang Melayu," that is, from a cultural standpoint, Malays. The Orang Melayu are the majority in the region, and most of the upper Kapuas Malays descend from local Dayaks converted to Islam.

The Kayan and the Maloh Dayaks, along with the Iban, are the most traditional people in the region. The Kayan on the Mendalam River, easily reached from Putussibau, preserve some of their old carvings and rites.

The Taman Dayaks (a subgroup of the Maloh) still live in longhouses, quite close to Putussibau, on the Kapuas River. They celebrate the *gawai,* a kind of thanksgiving festival, sometime in May or June and—occasionally—hold elaborate secondary funerals for their aristocrats.

Most of the foreign visitors who make it to Putussibau (not very many do) travel to the Taman village of Melapi I, where it is possible to make arrangements to sleep in the longhouse. With luck, one may also have a chance to see some fine traditional weavings. It is possible here to commission a dance performance in the longhouse.

The Taman and Kayan groups, while maintaining some of their old ways, have been the most successful in the region in entering the modern world. Members of these groups include university graduates and government officials. The education system and tolerant attitude of the Catholic missionaries who proselytized the Taman and Kayan are largely responsible for this happy state of affairs.

The Iban were formerly the region's most ferocious head-hunters. Although they m

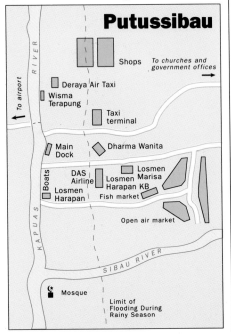

Putussibau

To airport

RIVER

Shops

To churches and government offices →

Deraya Air Taxi

Wisma Terapung

Taxi terminal

Main Dock

Dharma Wanita

Boats

DAS Airline

Losmen Marisa

Losmen Harapan KB

Losmen Harapan

Fish market

KAPUAS

Open air market

SIBAU RIVER

☪ Mosque

Limit of Flooding During Rainy Season

longer demonstrate their skills in lopping off heads, the Iban are still famous weavers of a prized cloth called *pua*. Most Iban live in Sarawak, but about 7,000 live in the lakes region east of Putussibau, near the border with Malaysia. Kantuq Assam (in *kecamatan* Empanang) is said to be the most traditional of the Iban settlements. The people of Kantuq Assam are reported to still live in longhouses and weave *pua* cloth.

To reach the Iban areas, head to Semitau on the Kapuas River, quite a ways downstream from Putussibau. From Semitau, go to Nanga Kantuq, which is the *kecamatan* seat of Empanang, then to Kantuq Asam. Some Iban here, as well as some Maloh Dayaks, live in island-villages.

The large, shallow lakes around this region—Sentarum, Sumpa and Luar—are worth visiting, for their waters sometimes turn jet-black with tannins. An arm dragged in the water disappears. Some who have been there say the effect is extremely eerie.

Although traditional enemies of the Iban, the 15,000 strong Kantuq tribe is close both historically and culturally to their former antagonists. There has been a considerable degree of intermarriage between Maloh, Iban and Kantuq, and this has gradually led to some measure of cultural assimilation and mutual acceptance.

Furthest upriver on the Kapuas, and in the mountainous region beyond, live the Punan and other scattered nomadic groups. These people, who never settled or farmed, living entirely off the forest, are the "least advanced" according to the government, which has encouraged them to settle in stable communities, chiefly in far western Kalim. What the Punan of Kalbar had in the way of traditional culture has been pretty much wiped out by the heavy hand of American Protestant missionaries.

The Maloh Dayaks

Thanks to their skills as smiths of gold and silver, the Maloh were the only group to be welcomed by the Iban, formerly the scourge of western Borneo. The precious metals plundered by the Iban during their raids were shaped and worked by Maloh smiths.

Safe under the wing of Iban, the Maloh were the trade link to the rest of the island for Iban textiles. In exchange, the Maloh did smith work, and crafted fine jackets and skirts from beads.

Although individuals could sometimes travel unmolested among the Iban, the Maloh as a group were not exempt from Iban hostilities. Frequent attacks from the north forced the Maloh into concentrated settlements and impressive, heavily fortified longhouses which helped them (up to a certain point) to keep their heads and lives. Intermarriages between Maloh and their fierce neighbors also contributed a slight degree of safety relations.

While their head-hunting proclivities, longhouses and rice staple make the Iban and Maloh superficially similar, the two cultures had many differences. The Iban were perhaps the most individualistic, classless group in Borneo, while the Maloh's social structure was characterized by a strict social hierarchy. The Iban grew their rice on *ladang* cut and burned out of forested hillsides; the Maloh farmed the rich, relatively flat alluvial plains of the upper Kapuas River.

Although the Maloh also organized head-hunting raids, their frequency and extent were nothing compared to the great and terrible Iban raids. The Iban combined head-hunting expeditions with pillage, whereas the Maloh preferred trade.

The Maloh were the region's greatest traders, exchanging precious metal ornaments and beaded clothing created by their

Right: *A woman from Tanjung Lokang on the upper Kapuas. She sports Islamic dress, but also large tin earrings and betel-stained teeth.*

members for fretted and inlaid Kayan *mandaus,* excellent Kantuq mats of split bamboo, Punan baskets, and fine Iban cloth.

Trade with the coast

In the 15th century, Islam swept through coastal Borneo's centers of power at Sambas, Sukadana and Landak. From here Malays were sent to establish trading centers upriver. Having access to goods desired by the Dayaks, these "river-states" brought salt, tobacco, cloth, iron and beads into the interior, and brought out local rice and forest products: timber, rattan, illipe nuts, palm sugar, damar, honey, fish, mats and baskets.

Trading contacts between Malays and Maloh led to intermarriages between the upper classes of the two groups. The sultans gained allies and exclusive trading rights, and the Maloh noblemen gained a favorable position in the Dayak trade network, enhanced political and economic status within their own group, and the protection offered by superior weapons. These relations also led to some Maloh converting to Islam.

The Dutch in the upper Kapuas

In 1822, Major George Müller became the first European to travel the Kapuas River, reaching the Sibau River, the present location of Putussibau. He wrote the earliest account of the Maloh. The next year, another Dutchman, L. C. Hartmann, made his way to the Kapuas Lakes. It was not until 1843 that O. von Kessel could complete the first general topographic and ethnographic survey of the Kapuas region.

In spite of two Malay rebellions, one in Sintang in 1859 and another five years later in the Melawi region, the Dutch maintained their military and administrative presence in the middle Kapuas.

Holland established military posts along its northern Borneo border to stem the tide of Iban warriors from Sarawak. The soldiers staffing these outposts were mostly Javanese, who received supplies from the coast. To lessen Iban temptation, the Dutch also moved various Maloh groups out of this border area and, in 1885, supplied them with firearms and ammunition to defend themselves against the Iban.

By 1887 Holland was able to impose her Pax Neederlandica on the upper Kapuas. By this time the colonial power had curbed most of the head-hunting in the region, slowing Iban migration into Maloh lands and forcing peace between Iban and Maloh. Official government policy also checked the spread of Islam and, indirectly, Malay culture, into the upper Kapuas region.

In 1895, a Dutch controller was appointed to head the newly created upper Kapuas administrative subdivision with its capital at Putussibau. Maloh aristocrats were integrated into the colonial framework as low level officials in charge of collecting taxes and meting out local justice. The Maloh had to pay some taxes and provide (paid) labor for road construction and other works.

Catholic missionaries

In keeping with the policy of assigning separate areas of the colonies to Protestants and Catholics, the former were encouraged to proselytize in southern Dutch Borneo, and the latter in the western part of the territory. In 1908, the Capuchin Order attempted to convert the Iban at Lanjak, with negligible success. By the 1920s, the Capuchins were focusing on the Maloh. The Maloh accepted Catholicism, largely because this was the religion associated with the Dutch, who were respected by the Maloh aristocrats as the paramount power in the region.

The Roman Catholic priests and the Dutch administration combined to stop external threats to the Maloh, who were menaced by the Iban, the Kayan, and the Islamic Malays. But the new religion at first undermined, then nearly wiped out basic cultural institutions and animistic rituals. When the Catholics abolished slavery among the Maloh, the aristocrats lost most of their power.

The Catholic Church also provided an educational foundation which led to the questioning of traditional authority and the automatic privilege of rank. In addition, schooling

Above: *The Maloh Dayaks are known for their fine beadwork, but the art is dying out. This detail is from a ceremonial shirt.* **Opposite:** *A Maloh longhouse just upriver from Putussibau.*

gave the Maloh opportunities to work in the government or teach. The priests tried to eradicate such sinful practices as premarital sex, abortion, heavy drinking, and cockfighting and its associated gambling.

Although all of these practices still take place today, albeit to a lesser extent, what remains has been largely divorced from its former religious context. The *belian* or native healers are still at work, but this is due at least in part to the Maloh's lack of access to doctors and modern pharmaceuticals.

Even though the traditional religion is mostly gone, an occasional elaborate funeral is still held when an aristocrat dies. In these rare cases *kulambu,* small stilted ossuaries, are constructed to hold the remains of the deceased. One of these *kulambu* was erected with due ceremony in 1973 on the Palin River, a tributary of the Kapuas.

The Maloh today

Rubber trees were introduced in West Kalimantan in 1909, and the crop spread along the Kapuas thanks in part to the Capuchin fathers, then those of the Montford Order, who replaced the pioneers in the upper Kapuas after World War II.

In addition to jobs in the timber industry, raw rubber constitutes the main source of revenue for the Maloh. Occasional harvests of illipe nuts, whose oil is exported for processing into cosmetics, provide extra income for the community.

World War II did not greatly affect the Maloh, as the Japanese mostly stayed out of the upper Kapuas, only extracting periodic tributes of rice and maintaining a small presence in Putussibau. Since independence, changes have come in the form of a vastly expanded educational system and increased population and pressure on land resources.

Today, most of the 12,000 Maloh Dayaks live in the Kapuas Ulu district around Putussibau. The population is growing slowly, in spite of disease and encroachments on Maloh lands by the Iban from the north and the Kantuq from downriver to the west.

The Malohs' proximity to the border with Sarawak has been both a boon and a bane. Because of Sarawak's more developed economy and cheaper goods, some of the Indonesian Malohs have begun migrating there to work or to purchase goods.

A 1965 communist uprising in this border area, headed by discontented ethnic Chinese, led to strict Indonesian military control of the zone, which restricted traditional tribal movements. The military also forced some Maloh to abandon their traditional longhouse way of life, though this policy has not been enforced in recent years.

In fact, today many Maloh along the Kapuas River are living in partially modernized communal longhouses, and are relatively free to live according to the old ways.

Kalbar Practicalities

Unless otherwise noted, prices in US$; city code for Pontianak, 0561.

Traveling in Kalbar requires some initiative, an elementary knowledge of the Indonesian language, and the ability to adapt to local conditions. It also helps to bring along a sense of humor, and be prepared for inevitable delays. The region is very rarely traveled, and while you may encounter difficulties, the satisfaction of seeing the Dayak way of life and the forests and rivers of Kalbar more than makes up for these hardships.

Pontianak

Supadio International Airport, just outside Pontianak, the capital of Kalimantan Barat, receives 3 flights a week from Singapore (Garuda; $111), 2 a week from Kuching, Sarawak (Merpati, MAS; $60). The airport is located 18 km. (11 mi.) from the center of town, which is about a $3.50 (shared) taxi ride. The airport bank offers good exchange rates.

There is also an international road crossing between Indonesia (at Entikong) and Sarawak, but you need the appropriate Malaysian and Indonesian visas. You can also get there by boat—Pelni Lines has a very comfortable passenger liners leaving every two weeks for the 2-day trip from Jakarta.

ACCOMMODATIONS

Few Westerners—and hardly any tourists—stay in Pontianak. English-speaking staff is scarce, even at the better hotels, except for the Mahkota. There's not much to see here; a night or two at the most should be enough for a quick look around and for making onward travel arrangements. There are no hotels in the international class but there is a good range of accommodations. All the better hotels have AC, color TV/video and ice boxes in the rooms.

Mahkota Kapuas. Jl. Sidas 8, Tel: 36022, 36023, 36024, Telex: 29181 NH. 105 rooms. This highrise hotel dominates the downtown area. Good lobby, restaurant, all rooms AC. $28 S; $33 D.

Kapuas Palace. Jl. Imam Bonjol, Tel: 36122, 36123, Telex: 29230 HKP PYK IA. 67 rooms and an Olympic-sized pool that can get very crowded on afternoons and weekends. Not conveniently located for those without their own transportation. Sometimes there are taxis waiting outside, but not always unless you make prior arrangements. Restaurant, coffee shop-cum-nightclub (very tame). $28 S; $31 D.

Kartika. Jl. Rohadi Usman, Tel: 34401, 32012, 32412, Fax: 38457, Telex: 29256 KARTEL IA. 45 rooms, right on the Kapuas River, near the docks and the Landak River. Ask for a room with a view of the waterfront. Coffee shop, restaurant, tennis court. Clean and just renovated. $25-$30 S, $28-$32 D. Discounts of up to 20% are available.

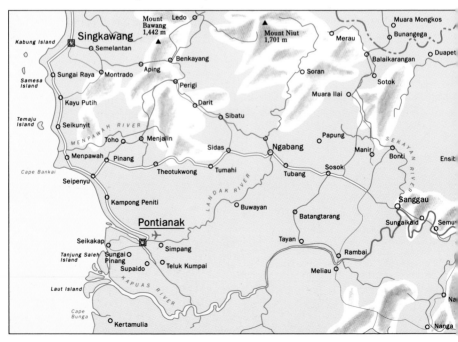

Wisma Nusantara. Jl. Suprapto, Tel: 34217. $12-14.

Pontianak City. Jl. Pak Kasih, Tel: 32495, 32496. $12.

Dharma. Jl. Imam Bonjol, Tel: 34759, 32860. 90 rooms. Formerly the best in town, the Dharma has in recent years been somewhat neglected. Near the bridge over the Kapuas, away from downtown, on the road to the airport. $10-$19.

Orient. Jl. Tanjungpura, Tel: 32650, 36162. $10-$15.

Sidas. Jl. Sidas 11A, Tel: 34337. $9-$12.

Wisma Siantan Indah. Jl. Puring Siantan, across the Kapuas River from the Kartika. 48 rooms. $6-$9 S or D; $10-13 Suite.

Wisma Patria. Jl. Cokroaminoto 497, Tel: 36063. 37 rooms. $6-10.

Wijaya Kusuma. Jl. Muai No. 51-53, Tel: 32547. 68 rooms, near the ferry and busy waterfront area. $5-$12.

Khatulistiwa. Jl. Diponegoro. Cheapest in town. $2.50 to $6.

Accommodations in Singkawang

The **Palapa** (Jl. Ismael Tahir 152), the **Kalbar** (Jl. Kepol Makmud) or the **Khatulistiwa** (Jl. Selamat Karman). All of these places are reasonably priced.

DINING

For a good cheap meal, try one of the open stalls at the night market along Jl. Diponegoro after 6:30 p.m. A filling plate of wok-cooked vegetables, meat, and seafood tidbits served over rice comes to all of 75¢, including tea. You can have more seafood by paying a little bit extra.

THE MARKET

Pontianak's Flamboyant Market specializes in fish and meat, with vegetable and fruit sellers scattered along muddy walkways. Get there early, 6-6:30 a.m. (already well past daylight here) to see a variety of strange fish. Things wind down with the fish sales by 7:30 a.m. The market lets you see some of Pontianak's character (and characters) in the little back alleys. There is a special section for pork (lots of Chinese and Christians in Pontianak), well away from the beef/goat butchers.

SHOPPING AND SOUVENIRS

Lots of antique—both genuine and fake—Chinese porcelain, old trade beads, woven baskets, awful woodcarvings and woven *songket* cloth from Sambas here. Shops selling these items are concentrated in the Pasar Nusa Indah and the Sudirman market next door. Try the **Leny Art Shop**, Nusa Indah III, Blok 191A, **Fariq Art Shop**, Nusa Indah I, Blok C, No. 3, or the **Borneo Art Shop**, Nusa Indah I, B24, among many others.

AGENCY TOURS

P.T. Insan Worldwide Tours and Travel. Jl. Tanjungpura 149, Tel: 32841, 34257. Their city tour includes the provincial museum, a ceramics factory and a speedboat ride on the river ($8). Museum hours, theoretically, are 8 to 11 a.m. daily, and 1:30 to 5 p.m. on Friday. Their day tour to the Singkawang ceramics works

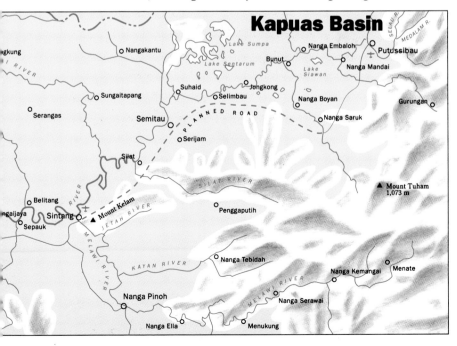

includes a couple of beaches and the chance to observe traditional fishing ($12/person). Their 2-day tour includes Singkawang; the Sambas *songket* cloth weaving; and the sultan's palace ($20/person). Prices negotiable for smaller groups. They have 6-10 day tours to Putussibau (depending on whether you fly one-way or round-trip)—$500 for the hotel in Pontianak, all meals, the works. For large groups, or $100 extra, a traditional dance can be arranged.

Citra Tours. Jl. Pak Kasih 6, Tel: 34284, 34270. A swing around Pontianak is $6 if there are enough people to fill a minibus. The fewer people, the more the cost per person. Day or overnight trips to the coastal region, $45/person in a group of 2, less for more people.

Ateng Tours and Travel. Jl. Gajah Mada 57, Tel: 32638, 36615, 36620, Telex: 29347 ATENG IA. This dynamic new agency, whose guides speak excellent English, offers city tours, the northern circuit to Singkawang and Sambas, as well as a taste of the jungle with a bonus waterfall at Sangan Ledo. They are making surveys to determine the potential of various areas of Kalbar. Given sufficient notice, they can arrange for a 5-day-plus tour to the Gunung Palung Reserve.

On your own

You can also hire a sedan taxi, usually found parked by the better hotels. They are available for hourly rentals at $4/hr., 2 hrs. minimum. The drivers' English is usually limited to smiles. For a tour of the area to the north of Pontianak, taxis can be hired for $60/day.

REGIONAL TRANSPORTATION

Bouraq. Jl. Haji Juanda 169, Tel: 38377. Daily to Jakarta ($52); Surabaya, Java, daily ($95).

Garuda. (includes Merpati). Jl. Rohadi Usman 8A, Tel: 34142. Balikpapan, 3 times a week, ($80); Batam, twice a week, ($62) continues to Medan, Sumatra ($128); Jakarta, 5 times daily, ($70); Kuching, Sarawak, once a week ($69); Singapore, 3 times a week, ($117).

Sempati. Tel: 34840 (See Deraya below.) To Jakarta daily ($53).

By air inland

DAS and **Deraya Airlines**, several times a week, fly to Putussibau ($41), to Sintang ($27), to Ketapang (($26), to Pangkalanbun, Kalteng, ($45), to Semarang, Java ($72). DAS, a bit higher-priced than Deraya, also flies to Nanga Pinoh, two or three times a week, ($46). These airlines use small planes. Book early. If not enough passengers, flights may be cancelled.

DAS. Jl. Gajah Mada 67, Tel: 34383, 32313.

Deraya. Jl. Sisingamangaraja 145, Tel: 34840 (also Sempati) or 32174.

By surface road inland

From Pontianak to Sintang it's 8.5 hours for 395 km. (245 mi.). There are things to see along the way, but of course the bus won't wait. And the next bus might not have any seats left by the time they pick you up.

The roads head north out of Pontianak, along the coast to Sungai Pinyuh, then inland to Mandor, 80 km. (50 mi.) from the capital, where there is a monument to the people of Kalbar who were slaughtered by the Japanese—21,037 in all.

A bit under 200 km. (120 mi.) from Mandor is the town of Ngabang, which was the last capital of the Landak sultanate. The sultan's palace at Landak has been converted into an official museum. Not a whole lot here except for two excellent small cannon with baroque decoration.

From Ngabang the main road continues 90 km. (56 mi.) to Sanggau, crossing palm oil plantations. Not much in Sanggau, but if you are tired of the bus ride, there are a couple of *losmen* here: the **Narita** (Jl. A. Yani 31) and the **Carano** (Jl. Sudirman 7). From Sanggau, it's some 130 km. (81 mi.) by land to Sintang. The road occasionally floods, but the buses can still get through, albeit slowly. You could also get off here and take a boat, 2 days from Sanggau to Sintang.

Crowded, hot buses:

Sintang	8-12 hrs	$4.50
Singkawang	3-4 hrs	$1.50
Sambas	3.5-4.5 hrs	$2.25
Entikong	6-8 hrs	$3

Twice a day (7 a.m. and 7 p.m.) an AC bus leaves for Sintang ($5.50). Take this one.

By boat inland

By passenger boat, called *bandung*—wooden ships, closed like a house but with moveable panels for ventilation—you have 4 or more days traveling before you reach Putussibau, plenty of time to practice your Indonesian but the scenery on the lower Kapuas gets a little monotonous. A combination of road and boat travel might be better—overland to Sintang, then by boat for the last leg to Putussibau, the last segment taking 36 hours. Tourists are few and almost no one speaks English.

One or two passenger/freight boats head upstream daily from the dock near the ferry crossing, leaving around 3 pm. To Sintang, 2 days and 2 nights ($7); to Putussibau, 4 days and 4 nights ($13). Prices include very basic meals. Travel times are, of course, approximate. Depending on river conditions it could be 6 full days to Putussibau.

WEATHER

Being on the equator, seasons are generally quite unpredictable in Pontianak and Kalbar. Generally, there is a light rainy season from March through May, and a heavy one from November through January.

Sintang

Sintang can be reached from Pontianak by air ($28) or by bus, 8-12 hrs. if the road is not too muddy. Heavy rains add 1-3 hrs., but by the time you read this the paving should be complete. This road extends to Putussibau, all paved, and the bridges are *planned* to be completed by the end of 1990. You can also travel to Sintang from Pontianak in a river boat, 2 days, for $7.

Facing downriver, the left bank is the commercial section, holding most of the shops, Padang-style restaurants, and *losmen*. The government offices and housing are also on the left bank (this area is called the *Kompleks Pemerintah*) but cut off from the downtown *Pasar Seberang* by the Melawi River. The right bank, Kampung Kapuas Kiri Ulu, is lined with stilt-perched houses. (See map page 175.)

ACCOMMODATIONS

There are two fairly good *losmen* in Sintang, the **Sasean** on the riverfront and the **Flamboyan**, opposite the bus station. The Sasean, with a good view of the Kapuas from its second floor balcony, has 32 rooms, $3-12. The Flamboyan's 20 rooms are $4.50-10. The higher-priced rooms in both *losmen* have ACs and attached, sit-down toilet facilities. For cheaper digs, try the **Ekaria**, ($2.50) but no in-room facilities. All the *losmen*, as well as *warung*-type and Padang-style restaurants, are concentrated in a small "downtown" area just off the Kapuas River at the end of the road from Pontianak.

LOCAL TRANSPORTATION

River taxis run frequently between the Pasar Seberang downtown area and the government offices section on the other side of the Melawi river. The ride costs 10¢ as one of several passengers, 75¢ to $1.20 for a charter.

REGIONAL TRANSPORTATION

For a chartered longboat trip up the Kayan from Sintang, count on about $200 and somewhere over 6 hours with a 40HP motor. For the Pinoh river and the upper Melawi River, head first to the town of Nanga Pinoh, 12 hrs. by longboat from Sintang ($3). The same trip by speedboat, 3 hrs. and $10 or more. DAS also has several flights to Nanga Pinoh from Pontianak.

Nanga Pinoh has several *losmen*-type accommodations and food stalls. From this town, try to find a boat going further up the Melawi or the Pinoh. If you hop on as a regular passenger, fares run $12-$20, depending on distance. For a charter, count on 10 hrs. or more and $300 to the upper Melawi; perhaps 12 hrs. or more and $600 to the upper Pinoh. This last trip crosses 20 sets of rapids. Prices and times vary greatly with the size of the boat and motor, the state of the river, the availability of boats, and your bargaining skills.

The best time to travel on the upper rivers is during the rains, September to January, worst during the dry season, July-August.

Putussibau

DAS and Deraya fly daily from Pontianak to Putussibau on a mixed bag of small aircraft ($40 one-way). The landing strip is on the other side of the river, at Putussibau Seberang, and the airlines provide transportation to and across the Kapuas—$1.50. Crowded riverboats, 50 to 100 tons and often overloaded, leave Pontianak every day for Putussibau, taking on average 5 days to get there. The trip, with simple meals, costs $15.

Putussibau is concentrated in a small strip along the river. The *losmen* and *wisma* are very close to the main boat landing, as are the principal stores, taxi terminal, mini-restaurants and the two airline offices (See map page 176.)

Just upriver and inland a 100 meters or so, the *pasar pagi* offers a variety of fish, vegetables and dry goods. A picturesque ambience, with a peaceful mosque just over the Sibau River from the *pasar pagi*.

ACCOMMODATIONS

Two *losmen* worthy of the name plus a semi-floating *penginapan*. Both *losmen* are very close to the cross-river ferry landing. The **Marisa** has 7 rooms ($3.50) above a restaurant, the only place in town for beer. The **Harapan Kita Bersama** has 24 rooms, ($3.50). Both provide outside ladle bath and squat toilet facilities. The **Harapan** planned to add 4 rooms w/attached facilities, $6 a night. The **Wisma Terapung**, docked on the river, requires a sense of balance to reach by climbing a slippery plank. 8 seedy rooms, $1.25.

Not much in the way of restaurants (unfortunately, there are no Chinese here). There are three around the Marisa. Basic Indonesian food, 75¢ to $1.75. You must order the good fresh river fish a day in advance.

REGIONAL TRANSPORTATION

All 16 *kecamatan* centers on the upper Kapuas, as well as the more important villages, are linked to Putussibau by the big river and its tributaries. No schedules. If there is a craft already planning to go your way, it's cheap. Ask around. For chartering, either try the boatmen or Pak Hasim, the owner of the *losmen* **Harapan Kita Bersama**. He owns a 10-passenger longboat and a 4-passenger speedboat. Same price for either boat:

Taman Dayak longhouse at Melapi I	$15
Semangkok (Kayan village)	$15
Bungan River (rapids)	$260
Tanjung Lokang (on the Bungan)	$360

Tanjung Lokang is a takeoff point for treks to the Mahakam region.

Travel Advisory

There is no perfect time to visit Kalimantan. The worst of the rainy season—December and January—makes travel unpleasant. But during the "dry" months, July and August, river levels inland drop too low for most boats except for the local canoes. To complicate things, the weather has in recent years, probably because of logging, become even more unpredictable. Most Dayak planting festivals take place around October, and the harvest rituals around February-March, making these good times to come. Funerary rites can happen any time except during the worst rains.

If forced to choose, October and November, and March through June, are perhaps the best times to visit Kalimantan, but this can be considered a general rule only.

Planning a first trip

The best place to begin in Kalimantan is Banjarmasin in Kalimantan Selatan. There are frequent flights here from Jakarta, and the city has enough facilities that you can ease into things. In addition, it is a very charming town, with its floating market, diamond fields and monkey islands to visit. If you are particularly interested in the orangutan, you could visit the Tanjung Puting rehabilitation center from here. This is about the only reserve which has facilities for visitors

After a few days in Banjarmasin, grab a flight to Balikpapan, or take one of the cheap (but long, 12-14 hours) buses to Balikpapan, the New York City of Kalimantan. If you are short of time, skip Balikpapan and head straight to Samarinda, which is the departure point for the Mahakam River.

From here, how far upriver you go depends on your time and budget. Really just your time, as the expense of river travel on regular boats is minimal. One possibility would be to head for Kota Bangun, perhaps spend a half a day there looking at wildlife, and then on to Tanjung Isuy to get a glimpse of Dayak culture on a 3-5 day package ($50-150) from Samarinda.

If more time is available, take a riverboat all the way to Melak and Long Iram. This is far enough upriver for you to get a real taste of the Dayak way of life, and by asking around, you might very well locate an authentic ritual (*upacara adat*) to witness. Or, in Long Iram, you can arrange to have a dance staged for you. For this trip, figure 7-10 days from Samarinda.

If you are particularly interested in wildlife, especially orangutans, although these are notoriously difficult to see, the Kutai Game Reserve

offers the best possibilities. Kalimantan's gam reserves are almost completely undevelope for visitors. (See "Game Reserves" below.) the Kutai Reserve, figure at least 4 days out Samarinda or Balikpapan (via Bontang).

DEEPER INLAND

The further inland you go in any province, th more traditional the way of life, except for th north coast of Kaltim. But don't expect to ste into the wild Borneo of 19th-century Weste imagination. Even in remote villages, most pe ple wear shorts and T-shirts. This does n mean, however, that the ritual and spiritu aspects of Dayak culture have disappeared.

East Kalimantan

Regular passenger boats take 36 hours Long Iram, and if you can find a connectio another day or two on the Mahakam brings y to Long Bagun, just below the rapids. If y want to add a visceral thrill to your cultur adventure, spring for a longboat and run th rapids into the upper Mahakam. Otherwis save a heap of money and time and take on of the three weekly flights from Samarinda Data Dawai, past the rapids. Giver yourself least a week to explore the upper Mahaka and if you go by river, at least two weeks.

South Kalimantan

The Barito River basin is the home of son very traditional Dayak groups, and althou they are harder to visit than the groups alo the Mahakam, you will find yourself in a regi that tourism almost never reaches. Here t people have maintained a great deal of th way of life thanks to the Kaharingan religic Begin in Banjarmasin, and take a speedboat fly to Muara Teweh on the Barito River. If t river is high enough, keep going to Puruk Cah the last upriver town on the Barito. Give yo self a week—better, two—to explore the upp Barito. To up the ante a little more, plan a tr from the Barito Basin to the Mahakam, by h ing from the upper reaches of one to the oth You can do this from Muara Tewah (easier) Puruk Cahu (harder).

Central Kalimantan

Many Dayaks of Kalteng follow the Kaharing faith, and the region is perhaps the mc traditional in all of Kalimantan. But it is hug and there is little infrastructure for touris Plan your trip from Palangkaraya (fly there fr Banjarmasin) up the Kahayan River. Regu river traffic will take you to Kuala Kurun, a from there you can hitch a ride with an upri boat, or hire one yourself, The Ot Danu Dayaks in this region still live in longhouse and the funerary carvings here can be seen their natural setting. Figure on a week 1 exploring the area.

West Kalimantan

utussibau in Kalbar is the center of a tradi-
onal area, and flights land there are least
nce a day from Pontianak on the coast. If this
your only visit, you could also take a boat, to
et a sense of river travel, in this case the
reat Kapuas River. A boat from Pontianak
akes about 4 days. You can spend an interest-
g week exploring the Putussibau area. Fur-
ler upriver is quite tricky, involving good
ck—a boat is leaving anyway—or money—an
xpensive longboat charter.

Another possible itinerary would be to travel
) Sintang either by boat, bus or plane from
ontianak and from Sintang, to explore the
ayak areas around the Kayan, Melawi or
noh rivers. Give this trip two or three weeks.
you are stuck in Sintang waiting for a boat,
ou can always climb nearby "Dark Mountain,"
lount Kelam.

he Basics

VISA FORMALITIES

ationals of the following 30 countries are
ranted visa-free entry to Indonesia for 60
ays. For other nationals, tourist visas are
equired and can be obtained from any
idonesian embassy or consulate.

Australia	Austria
Belgium	Brunei
Canada	Denmark
Finland	France
Greece	Iceland
Ireland	Italy
Japan	Liechtenstein
Luxembourg	Malaysia
Malta	Netherlands
New Zealand	Norway
Philippines	Singapore
South Korea	Spain
Sweden	Switzerland
Thailand	United Kingdom
United States	West Germany

To avoid any unpleasantness on arrival,
heck your passport before leaving for
idonesia. You need at least one empty page
or your passport to be stamped. Passports
1ust be valid for at least six months upon
rrival and you should have valid proof of
nward journey, whether return or through tick-
ts. Employment is strictly forbidden on tourist
isas or visa-free entry.

Visa-free entry to Indonesia means not stay-
1g over 60 days. This is not extendable and is
nly valid when entering via the following air-
orts: Medan, Batam, Pekanbaru, Padang,
akarta, Bali, Manado, Ambon, Biak, Kupang,
alembang, Pontianak and Surabaya, or the
eaports of Medan, Batam, Jakarta, Surabaya,
iemarang, Riau, Bali, Manado and Ambon.

If you plan on traveling to Kalimantan from

Malaysian Borneo, you need a visa prior to
arrival. You can easily obtain one from
Indonesian consulates—in Sarawak, at Kuching;
in Sabah, at Kota Kinabalu or Tawau. Most people come to Kalimantan from elsewhere in
Indonesia, so no special papers are needed.

Tourist visas can not be extended. There
are immigration offices dealing with other kinds
of visas in Balikpapan, Samarinda, Tarakan,
Banjarmasin and Pontianak.

CUSTOMS

Carrying narcotics, arms and ammunition, TV
sets, pornographic materials, printed matter in
Chinese characters and Chinese medicines is
prohibited. Advance approval is necessary to
bring transceivers or large movie equipment. All
films and video cassettes have to be reviewed
by the Indonesian Film Censor Board.

On entry 2 liters of alcoholic beverages,
200 cigarettes, 50 cigars or 100 grams of
tobacco are allowed. Perfume in reasonable
amounts is also permitted. There is no restric-
tion on import and export of foreign currencies
in cash or travelers' checks, but there is a limit
on the export of Indonesian Rupiahs—no more
than Rp 50,000.

POLICE

You no longer have to report to the police with
your passport (or a photocopy thereof) in Kalimantan, but this is a recent change, and it
may be a few more years before the news gets
around. All the better hotels make their report
from your registration form. Some of the cheap
places refuse foreigners because it is not
worth the hassle with the police.

Inland, whether required or not, it is a good
idea to check with the police and tell them of
your travel plans. Usually they are helpful, welcome the chance to practice their English, and
can help find you a place to sleep if there are
no *losmen*. When traveling inland, carry photo-
copies of your passport, leaving the original at
your hotel on the coast, preferably in a waterproof bag.

MONEY EXCHANGE

Change whatever money you will need (plus
some reserves) in Balikpapan, Tarakan, or any
of the provincial capitals. There are no banks
or money changers in the interior. The problem
for long-term travel in the interior is that the
largest denomination of bills is Rp 10,000,
about US $6. Use a money belt or have a safe
place for carrying your bills. Many places, especially in the interior, cannot change large bills.
Stock up on Rp 1,000 notes.

Bring your money to Kalimantan in US$
denominated travelers checks from well-known
companies. It is a good idea to carry checks
from two of these, just in case. The only notes
you can count on being able to change are
US$, and these only if in perfect condition.

HEALTH

It is a good idea to have a thorough medical (and dental) checkup before leaving. Ask which inoculations your doctor recommends—tetanus, definitely, and cholera, although it is painful and doesn't eliminate the risk, can help. A gamma globulin shot, effective for about six months against some strains of hepatitis, may also be worth getting.

Get another medical checkup when you get back home, including blood and stool tests, to see if you picked up any microscopic tropical creatures. Another good idea is to buy most of your basic pharmacy and medical kit before you leave home.

Malaria

Taking malaria pills is essential for travel in Kalimantan. Since some strains of malaria have developed a resistance to the usual cloroquin phosphate, it might be safer to also take a non-chloroquin based prophylactic sold locally under the name "Fansidar." You cannot get these pills in the United States without a prescription, and it is unlikely that your local pharmacist will have them. Best (and much, much cheaper) to buy them over the counter in Indonesia. (See "Basic items" below.)

Use mosquito coils, those green intertwined spirals of incense that are so hard to separate and were banned in the United States sometime back. Light one before you go to bed, and it will work for about 8 hrs. These *obat nyamuk bakar* are cheap and widely available, and you'll get used to the smell. For the best protection, bring or buy a mosquito net.

In the tropics, a scratched mosquito bite or other tiny abrasion can quickly turn into a festering ulcer. You must pay attention to these things here. Before you scratch, apply Tiger Balm or some imitation thereof. This camphorated salve relieves itching. Treat any broken skin with strong disinfectant and/or antibiotic powder, and change bandages at least daily.

Stomach problems

Drink only boiled or bottled liquids. Bottled water—"Aqua"—is widely available, if a bit expensive. Try not to even brush your teeth with river water. It is likely that you will have either constipation or loose bowels, so take remedies accordingly. For constipation, eat a lot of fruit.

Diarrhea is a frequent problem, and it does not necessarily come from bad food. Most cases can be traced to a combination of climate, fatigue, change of food and culture shock. Your system has to get used to a new set of bacteria in Kalimantan. This is not widely known, but Indonesians or Mexicans often come down with diarrhea when visiting the United States or Europe. Whatever you do for relief, *don't* take Enterovioform. Better try Kaopectate or Lomotil in recommended dosages. Put a cold water compress on your stomach and change it often.

While affected, drink plenty of water with a bit of salt and some sugar, and keep your diet simple. No meat, spicy foods or milk products. Start with plain boiled rice or dry biscuits, then papayas and bananas. Remember that you have diarrhea, not dysentery. If you contract the latter, which is much more serious, you must seek medical help. Do this if your stools are mixed with blood and pus, are black, or you are experiencing very severe stomach cramps and fever. To prevent stomach problems, try to eat only thoroughly cooked foods, don't but already peeled fruit, and stay away from unpasteurized dairy products.

Exposure

Visitors insist on instant suntans, and overexposure to the heat and sun are frequent health problems. Be especially careful on long river boat rides where the roof gives a good view. The cooling wind created by the boat's motion disguises the fact that you are frying like an egg. Wear a hat, long-sleeved shirt, pants, and use a good-quality sunscreen (bring a supply with you). Tan slowly—don't spoil your trip.

To avoid exposure, drink plenty of fluids and take salt. Wear loose-fitting, light-colored cotton clothes. Do not wear synthetic fibers that do not allow air to circulate.

Basic items

A basic health kit should consist of aspirin and multivitamins (bring along a lot of these two for much-appreciated gifts in the interior), an antihistamine, disinfectant (such as Betadine), antibiotic powder, fungicide, an antibiotic eye wash, Kaopectate or Lomotil and sunblock. Also good strong soap, perhaps Betadine or other antiseptic soap. Go easy on the antibiotics unless you know how to use them. For injuries, make up a little kit containing Band-aids and ectoplast strips, a roll of sterile gauze and treated gauze for burns, surgical tape, elastic bandages for sprains. Also very important are Q-tips, tweezers (to remove thorns etc.) scissors, needles and safety pins. Keep your pills and liquid medicines in small unbreakable plastic bottles, clearly labeled.

Pharmacies—*apotik*—in the major cities of Kalimantan carry just about everything you might need, but there could be a communication problem. You can readily get malaria pills here, and an excellent anti-bacterial ointment called Bacitran. Definitely purchase Tiger Balm in Asia, it is excellent for itching bites and lots of other things. Either bring medication for fungal infections or buy Mycolog in Indonesia.

Stock up on tampons as your brand will probably not be available. Also bring condoms. Outside the coastal cities, it's nearly impossible to purchase medicines or first aid supplies.

Doctors

Balikpapan has Kalimantan's best doctors, and some speak English. Elsewhere, the quality varies greatly. Try to find an ethnic Chinese doctor. Many Indonesians seek them out as well. Local doctors are not very skilled in diagnostics, so they cover all possibilities by prescribing everything, combining antibiotics and antihistamines with whatever else comes to mind. Use common sense.

Hospitals

The hospitals in the big cities are adequate, especially in Balikpapan, but there might be a language problem. Once you are away from the coast, forget about hospitals. Local clinics are usually out of medicines and staff training leaves much to be desired. The occasional mission hospital, especially if there are foreign nurses, is the best place in the interior of Kalimantan to be sick.

CLOTHING

Bring mostly wash-and-wear, light cotton clothes. No synthetics, especially underwear or socks. A sweater and rain jacket (with hood) are also essential. Tennis shoes and sandals are basic footwear, but for trekking bring hiking boots. The best weapon against wet, slippery surfaces and leeches are army "jungle boots," with hard rubber soles and a high canvas top. Bring a baseball cap until you can buy a large, wonderfully made native sun-and-rain hat.

It is a good idea to bring one set of "decent" clothes—city shoes, trousers and a batik shirt for men. For women, comfortable shoes (not tennis shoes) and a blouse and knee-length skirt. Foreigners, especially young ones, are usually the worst-dressed in Kalimantan, and Indonesians judge by appearances. You meet more interesting people if you are well dressed. And "decent" dress is advised at all government offices, even to call on a *camat* way out in the sticks.

It is up to you to strike a balance between how much to carry and how well-dressed you want to appear.

ACCOMMODATIONS

While Kalimantan has only one really international-class hotel, the Benakutai in Balikpapan, all provincial capitals as well as Tarakan and Balikpapan have several hotels acceptable to foreign visitors in the $20-$50 price range. There are also simple, inexpensive accommodations in these cities for as low as $5.

The principal town of each *kabupaten* also has commercial lodgings, ranging from $4 to $25. Beyond this, many of the inland commercial centers have rudimentary *losmen* or *penginapan* without private toilets or bath, but cheap at $1.50 to $3 a night for a basic place to sleep and wash up.

Dayak hospitality

Where there are no official lodgings, you have to rely on local hospitality. In the *kecamatan* centers, either the police or the *camat* could help you find a place to sleep. In the villages, you should find the *kepala desa* (village chief) who will help—but remember that basically you are a bother. The Dayaks do not keep guest rooms for foreigners with their strange ways. You should pay about $6 for a place to sleep and the meals to which you will be invited.

Gifts such as sugar, salt, cigarettes or tobacco sticks, batteries, and clothing are always appreciated. Be prepared for lots of tea with lots of sugar—a lot of sugar in coffee or tea is a sign of hospitality in Indonesia.

The woods serve as a toilet. Bring toilet paper, and check out the area before dark. Don't go inland without a flashlight. Bathing is in the river, so pack a bathing suit. This is no problem for men, but women should master the technique of bathing in a sarong, and changing into dry clothing behind the screen of the sarong, otherwise in full public scrutiny. Being the center of attraction while bathing, and at most other times, is part and parcel of traveling in Kalimantan.

FOOD

Western-style meals are expensive ($5-$25), but include items like imported beef. These are available in the largest cities. Chinese and Indonesian restaurants charge $2-$7. Away from the towns, it's Indonesian and local-style food only. This means that meals are no problem if you can eat copious quantities of rice and some hot sauces.

On the lower sections of the rivers, there are plenty of *warungs* (small restaurants) wherever passenger boats stop. A plate of fish and rice, or chicken and rice, is $1 or a little more. Shrimp or large crayfish are also available. You can find lots of soft drinks here, and sometimes beer. Further upriver, the *warungs* are fewer and more spartan: fish and rice, period. In Dayak villages, if someone has been successful hunting, you could buy chicken, wild pig, deer or more exotic game—an armadillo, a monkey or two, or a slow loris.

SOUVENIRS

Antique souvenir shops in the coastal cities are the best places to see what is available and to get an idea about prices. Many of the antiques are fakes, so good that they sometimes fool experienced primitive-art dealers. If you know what you are doing and are really interested in antique Dayak carvings or Chinese porcelain, ask to see what is in the "back room" where the best pieces (even the best fakes) are kept. The highest-quality craft items are the beautifully woven Dayak rattan-strip baskets, also found in Bali and Singapore but at higher prices.

There is some exquisite beadwork on bags and baby carriers but these could run over $150. There are antique beads for sale, but usually only collectors pay the very high prices.

Don't make the mistake of thinking that you will find things cheaper in the interior. Except for Tanjung Isuy cloths in Kaltim and some baskets in the Barong Tongkok area (also in Kaltim), you might not find anything the Dayaks are even willing to sell. Or they will ask for outrageous prices. Don't wait for the last minute to buy something. That piece that you fell in love with at a particular store might well be gone by the time you return.

East Kalimantan, where most tourists go, has the most souvenir shops and the greatest variety. There is much less available in either Banjarmasin or Palangkaraya (with the exception of the locally made ships-of-the-dead).

In Pontianak, there are several antique shops but few crafts. But this is the only place where we have seen fine Iban *pua* cloths. Here you can also buy the *kain* Sambas cloths, woven by the coastal Malays in the vicinity of Sambas. Always bargain. We have bought items for as little as one-third of the asking price.

TRAVEL AGENCIES

Particularly in East Kalimantan, there is a wide range of tour possibilities, from a short ride on an almost luxury-liner-quality river boat to staged Dayak dances to 10 days or more trekking across virgin forest. The drawbacks to a guided tour are the ones you would expect: you have little contact with the people, the performances are sanitized, and your sense of personal accomplishment is much reduced.

For those planning only a few days in Kalimantan, we recommend going through a travel agency in Jakarta or Bali. **Colors of Asia** and **Pacto** in Jakarta specialize in off-beat Kalimantan tours, but all the larger agencies have connections with local tour operators. If your finances permit, a special tour can be set up just for you, but give at least one month's notice and confirm your schedule.

Riverboat Travel

Rivers are the traditional highways of Kalimantan. Although you can fly to many interior towns, you should take at least one boat ride, just for the experience. It is a great way to meet people, practice your Indonesian, and slowly ease into the interior. The scenery can be stunning. The inconveniences will probably put off the fastidious traveler, but it is a great way to get a feel for the land and its people. And, of course, the fares are geared to the local wallet.

Kalimantan's provinces each encompass a great river system, with the capital located on the lower reaches of the most important waterway. Regular upriver river transportation stops at the rapids. From here on, the trip get either time-consuming or expensive.

In South and Central Kalimantan, most passengers move by speedboat, or by passenger ships with bunk beds, enclosed toilets and small kitchen serving cheap, simple meals. On the Kapuas River, most of the boats are fairly large, also with enclosed toilets, and three simple meals a day (bring your own bedding). It is on the Mahakam River and its tributaries that you will find the greatest variety of craft ready to motor you upriver.

SOME PERSONAL LESSONS

Several years ago, I took my first trip up the Mahakam River, with only a vague idea as to where my ship was heading. I knew a little Indonesian, but knew nothing about Kalimantan or river travel. The dozen or so journeys I have taken since have been much more pleasant.

Early one rainy morning, I slid aboard the *Air Bunga* at the dock in Samarinda. I squeezed my body and luggage onto the covered deck, which was already crowded. Lesson one: get there early.

Passengers in these smaller craft usually sit in facing rows, with luggage used as pillows and foot rests. If possible, a space is left in the middle allowing passengers to move fore and aft. But because of overcrowding, this space vanishes quickly. From then on, moving around entails stepping on or around bodies.

Territory

After boarding, I spread my luggage and laid down a newly purchased woven leaf mat. Other passengers will not move your luggage (well, not much), nor will they (usually) step on your mat. When I got on, the 30 or so passengers on the *Air Bunga* made it seem already crowded, but after a few upstream stops, our human load more than doubled.

During the first 36 hours, we continued to pick up passengers. Territory became imperative. A tiny empty spot, just enough space for a man's backside, suddenly expands to fit the man's entire family and luggage. Absolutely amazing. At times I thought of taking a photo every 30 seconds to monitor how this was done. That little bare space somehow borrowed a bit of your room, as well as a bit from every neighbor. Luggage was nudged and slid over a bit. Only stiff mats resisted insidious wiggling and sly maneuvers. Moral: do not leave uncovered space near you.

Of course, when things really get crowded, and they do, all notions of propriety are suspended. You end up trying to sleep with two pairs of feet hovering close to your face, while attempting to keep your own extremities out of your neighbors' private parts.

Before settling in just any open space, I later learned to evaluate it first. These boats are built for Indonesians, so a Westerner of

rmal height often lacks clearance. Areas
en to the outside (most of the boat), offer a
ew and a breeze, but also let in the scorching
n and, unless a canvas is ready, sheets of
ter. Other factors to keep in mind: Where are
e good spots for photography? What about
cess to the toilet? Is there a dining or snack
ea? Most important of all, where is the
gine? The closer you are to the engine, the
re noise, heat and vibration you have to live
h. And the exhaust is smoky and deafening.

Shoving off

passengers settled in, vendors swarmed
oard, displaying last-minute supplies: bottled
ter (buy lots), magazines, eggs, soft drinks,
er, bread, all shapes of sweet rolls, choco-
es, peanuts, hats, rice, cooked bits of chick-
and fish. As vendors hawked, our cargo was
ded in the hold and on the roof: dozens of
otesting chickens, assorted merchandize in
rdboard boxes, toys, umbrellas, drums of
el, a rusting obstetrical bed.

Our ship was typical: 12 tons, 17 meters
 ft.) long with a 2.5-meter (8 ft.) beam.
wered by a Japanese diesel engine, the *Air
nga* could chug along at 12 km. an hour (7
h.) in still water.

Soon after leaving Samarinda, I learned why
 boat was called a Slow Boat—her engines
re strong, but during the first day we
pped every half hour on the average. Pick
 a passenger here, drop off a box or two
ere. The river taxis, by contrast, carry little
go and make fewer stops.

Photography

board etiquette calls for the removal of
otwear, except on the scorching-hot tin roof,
ich is the best vantage point for photography
d a tan. But as we pulled away from the dock
der a steady drizzle, about two hours after
 were scheduled to depart, neither photogra-
/ nor tan looked possible. The weather being
sy, I sat crunched up with the other passen-
s, reading and glancing at the gray sky with
spair. When it cleared the next day, I appro-
ated a spot for myself and cameras at the
nt edge of the roof, close to the bow. Slowly
ng to a crisp, I watched the scenery and
t from dawn to dusk. Fantastic! The sky was
e, and the river ever changing.

Travel on the Mahakam by any type of boat
itself justification for a trip to Kalimantan.
nber mills, coal mines, and small towns and
ages hug the riverside. Houses built on stilts
 common, as are floating platforms tied to
 riverbank. These tied-up rafts usually sport
small hut used as the house toilet, along
h space for bathing and washing clothes.
ong-wrapped ladies are there at all hours,
sy with laundry.

And everywhere, people along the river
end their spare time brushing their teeth.

This is a long, leisurely process wherein lots of
foam is produced. No one seems bothered by
the fact that the river serves as a huge toilet
for those living upstream. (Organized tours for
foreigners provide bottled water for brushing
teeth, a good idea even if you are on your own.)

Rafts of huge logs drift downstream, tugged
and guided by one or more boats. Men live on
these rafts for the weeks that it takes to float
them downstream to the sawmills near
Samarinda. Nearby, paddled canoes glide
serenely—until tossed by the *Air Bunga's*
wake. The Dayak occupants of the canoes
often sport wide, colorful hats, eminently practical in the blazing sun.

Meals

Four hours out of Samarinda brought us to
Tenggarong, where all craft have to report to
the river-traffic control office. Small boats,
laden with pots of steaming rice, fish, meat
and soft drinks, tried to catch the *Air Bunga* as
it began to drop speed to dock. The skilled ped-
dlers in the food-canoes could steer, propel
and vie for our attention as they made a des-
perate grab for some part of our still-moving
vessel in order to hang on as we slid dockside.

They all wanted first crack at offering their
banana-leaf wrapped packets of chow. Other
vendors, working from the dock, carrying their
goodies in baskets, blitzed their way across
several river taxis already tied up. I did not
know it on my first trip, but this is the last
chance to buy many items. Ask your fellow passengers the correct price, as foreign faces
sometimes invite overcharging. Advice: buy bottled water, hard-boiled eggs, biscuits and whatever you fancy that will not smash together into
a disgusting goo in the crucible of the crowded
boat. Buy provisions at Samarinda. Upriver,
about the time you want to be assaulted by
another horde of hawkers, there are none.

Every boat I have ever been on tries to
arrange its schedule so as to stop at meal
hours wherever meals can be purchased. Close
to Samarinda, there is an appetizing variety of
food, even crayfish and sometimes cold beer.
As we progressed further upriver, the food
stalls became much less frequent, and the varieties were reduced to bony river fish, tough
chicken, chili sauce and rice. I became accustomed to the smallest, boniest pieces of battle-
fatigued chicken I have ever experienced.

The Call of Nature

The most difficult part of the trip was becoming
accustomed to the *Air Bunga's* toilet. The contraption hung over the stern like a gang-plank,
1 meter above the rushing water. The sides
were only about 60 cm. (2 ft.) high and the
front, facing the passengers, afforded but 50
cm. (20 in.) of privacy. You aimed for the hole
in the middle of the floor planks.

I learned the technique by surreptitiously

observing some male passengers. First, they pulled their pants off completely. (Along the river, it is no breach of etiquette for males to be seen in briefs.) Next, they climbed into the john, squatted down and pulled their underpants to mid-thigh level. They then bent their heads down, the better to aim or not be seen?

Of course, when any of the Indonesians went to the toilet, no one paid any attention. But when I had the urge, all eyes followed my movements, not even surreptitiously. Once I was in and struggling, with bad knees, to squat low enough to keep my private parts out of the direct line-of-sight of every single passenger, a couple of children sauntered over to the toilet for closer inspection. Foreigners being so different, perhaps the kids expected me to do whatever through my belly button. Or were sent to spy by their parents. My urge and concentration gone, I was constipated until nightfall.

To urinate, I simply stood on the stern facing away from the passengers. The other passengers squat to urinate but there are limits to my wish to conform. Later I observed that at some of the stops along the river, there are enclosed toilets on the mooring platforms. But you have to be quick to get there, as others are obsessed by the same idea.

It's not always this bad. Bigger boats have enclosed toilets so your struggles do not become group entertainment. But unless on a for-tourists-only boat, forget about sitting down. Or reaching for the toilet paper. Either bring this luxury yourself or follow the local technique: use your left hand and river water from the ever-present plastic bucket. This technique is why the rules of politeness in three-quarters of the world forbid eating or receiving things from others with the left hand.

The sustained stares result in a lack of privacy in only our sense of the term. I was the only Westerner on board with a boatload of people who had never had the opportunity to observe such a bizarre creature at close range and for an extended period of time. I was the sore thumb, the circus, the living TV. Anyway, it was a good time to practice my Indonesian.

Of course, my bathing also attracted fellow passengers' undivided attention. It took some careful observations and a bit of practice. One squats next to the toilet in briefs (sarongs for women) and pours water over oneself from an available bucket using a plastic bucket (not the toilet bucket). Stand up, soap all over, and squat to rinse. Then comes the hard part: wrapping a towel or sarong around your waist, and pulling off the wet underpants from underneath. Voila! All is well until the towel comes unwrapped at the critical moment.

Shaving invariably attracted a crowd, as Malays have little facial hair. Kids giggled as I grimaced and scraped. Shaving foam would have been too much. As it was, my act was better than the circus clowns.

Sleeping

During my first Mahakam trip, I slept on the *Bunga,* not knowing any better. We h stopped one night, and I noticed that a few the better-dressed passengers disappear into the darkness, returning refreshed at dav Later, I learned of the *penginapan* in some ri towns. Not exactly The Hilton, but the sm bedrooms with a smoldering mosquito c were cheap at $1 to $3 a night. There are *penginapan* once you get far enough fr the well-traveled portion of the Mahakam. E by then you reach Dayak hospitality.

Trekking

Hiking in Kalimantan can mean trompi through rivers and along slippery trunks, be snagged by thorns, and constantly picking leeches. Your eyes are constantly glued to ground, and you are too tired at the end of day to do much of anything except bathe qu ly, eat an insipid meal on the ground, and th sleep. You are guaranteed to lose weight.

The best way to plan a trek is to first tra inland until you are at or near the last upri village of a tributary or major river. Making initial trip by river gives you a chance to ac matize, but takes time. Flying saves time, results in physical and culture shock, as y skip the several days of winding down from pace and style of the Westernized coas cities to the down-to-earth Dayak way of life.

PLANNING YOUR HIKE

The hard part of organizing a hike is comm cating what you want to accomplish to y guides and porters. Fluency in Indonesian well-nigh essential. You could also bring alc an interpreter from the coast, paying him eit a daily fee ($5-$15) plus expenses or agree a set fee for the whole trip, say $100-200 more or less ten days to two weeks. But i difficult to find a fluent English-speaker w also wants to trek inland and has the time do so. Very likely, you will have to settle someone with a bare knowledge of English. proprietors of your hotel could help you f someone. This is fairly easy in Banjarmas difficult in Pontianak, and just possible Samarinda or Palangkaraya. You could a take a crash course, bring a dictionary, and to communicate with your guides yourself.

Always trek with a guide. Always. Better two porter/guides. Dayaks always like to tra with another of their own. Your guides/port carry your gear, fish, cook, and build overnight shelters. There should be at le one porter/guide for every member of y party, more if there is lots to carry. You sho not lug your own gear unless you are used hiking in a slippery tropical jungle. Before ting out, come to an agreement with y porter/guides as to the payment for their return trip, unless you plan a round trip for yourself. As a general rule, they can return in half the time (or less) it took while accompanying the tenderfoots. Depending on local circumstances, a normal wage might be $3 to $6 a day for each porter/guide.

During the crucial phases of the planting cycle, it can be difficult to find guides/porters and canoes, as everyone is needed in the rice fields. The months during which these activities take place vary, but generally clearing, which takes a few weeks, happens from May to August. Planting takes a few days in September or October, and harvest, which also just takes a few days, from January to April. Even during these times, however, it is likely that if you wait a bit, some guides will be available.

Supplies

You can usually count on buying rice, the staple for any trek, at the last village before your jaunt begins. The same usually goes for salt, although you can carry several-kilo packets from the coast. Unless you want to walk from dawn to dusk (you don't), your porter/guides will have time to catch some fish, which are bony, but welcome. The above are the basic rations, and together with a pot for cooking is all that you will need. But only the most masochistic will not want to invest in at least sugar, coffee and tea and some plastic cups. Morale-boosters include condensed milk, pasteurized cheese, chocolate and a few tins of meat and vegetables. Also toilet paper. These items, as well as cigarettes and raw tobacco sticks for your guides, should be purchased at your point of departure on the coast. Also, bring a bottle of brandy or whiskey for an emergency. You will never have everything you need, but that's part of the experience.

There is plenty of game left in the isolated regions, and if you bring along an extra man with a blowgun-cum-spear and a couple of dogs, you will almost certainly be able to eat venison, wild pork, and other smaller game. A man with a net, given time, will always bring fish to the table. Traveling this way means there will be several Dayaks in your party, and organizing the group might well take several days. But it is always worth it.

A light sleeping bag, sweater, rain jacket, several pairs of socks, bug repellent, canteen, basic pharmacy, hat, boots, sandals, flashlight with spare bulb and spare batteries are all part of your basic personal gear. Large plastic garbage bags, placed inside your knapsack or carrying gear, will keep your personal items dry, but will probably also make them moldy. A large piece of waterproof canvas or tarpaulin could keep you from spending uncomfortable nights in the inevitable rain. The Dayaks can build overnight shelters from leaves, but these can leak in a heavy downpour.

Always carry a walking stick as you never know when a slippery stretch is coming up (soon). Your Dayaks will cut one for you whenever needed. Much of the trekking in Kalimantan follows water courses, meaning many an hour's slog in the waters. Tennis shoes and cheap boots fall apart. Get tough, canvas jungle boots. They dry out fairly quickly and keep out most of the leeches.

Leeches

In some places there are far too many of these to burn out with cigarettes, even for chain-smokers. The natives simply pull the buggers out with their fingers and flick them away, or scrape them off with their *parang* or machetes. Foreigners should follow their example. During rest stops, the Dayaks take a wad of raw tobacco and squeeze the juice out on the embedded leeches who then get out, and fast. The problem with tobacco juice or other repellents is that you quickly sweat it off, or it washes off when sloshing through the rivers.

When trekking in the jungle, it is always single file. Try not to lead or be the last. Keep an eye on the man ahead of you and tell him if you see a leech sucking away. The person behind you will return the favor. You can usually feel the leeches from the knee up on bare skin and flick them off before they start their meal.

Interesting itineraries

Among interesting treks, you could hike from the upper Barito drainage to the Mahakam. Or either the Pinoh or the Melawi Rivers as far upstream as possible, then across the Schwaner Range to one of the rivers of Central Kalimantan. Count on at least a week for walks between the village of departure and the first one on the other side.

There are some trails from East Kalimantan and West Kalimantan into Sarawak. But you should have the proper visas and permits, from both Indonesia and Malaysia if you want to attempt this walk. Lots of time and bother. It has been done without going through the paperwork, but we do not advise it.

Wildlife

Because of the dense cover, trekking is not the best way to see wildlife. Better to hire a canoe (paddled, no motors) and glide quietly along the smaller tributaries.

Nature Reserves

There are many game and nature reserves in Kalimantan, but none—with the exception of Tanjung Puting—is easy to reach or has accommodations for visitors. Some reserves are so difficult to reach that they are not even worth mentioning, and if you travel to the interior, within a day's walk from the village, wildlife is as plentiful (not very) as it is at the reserves.

Tanjung Puting

The 3,500-hectare (9,000 acre) Tanjung Puting Reserve is mostly a freshwater swamp with small stretches of forested dry land. The orangutan rehabilitation center is the most famous attraction, but wildlife can be seen from a boat on the Sekunyer River out of Kumai as well as from a network of trails.

To reach the reserve, one must first go to Pangkalanbun for a police permit, then to Kumai to register with the conservation office.

Arriving by air

From Java: 4 flights a week on Merpati ($96) from Halim Airport in Jakarta. Merpati also offers daily flights to Pangkalanbun from Bandung ($92) and Semarang ($58). Deraya has cheaper daily flights from Semarang ($46).
From Palangkaraya: Daily flight by DAS ($47), and Bouraq ($32).
From Pontianak: Daily on both DAS (except Friday) and Deraya ($48).
From Sampit: Daily on DAS and Deraya ($25). From Ketapang: 3 flights a weel on Deraya ($30), and 4 flights a week on Merpati ($37).
From Banjarmasin: Daily flights on DAS (7 a.m. departure, $45) and Bouraq (9 a.m., via Sampit—$37).

By Boat

The Pelni ship *Krakatoa* calls twice monthly at Kumai from Banjarmasin and Semarang. About $12 and 24 hours from either town, economy fare. Add $5-10 for the better berths.

ARRIVING IN PANGKALANBUN

First, reconfirm your departure date at the airport, if it's already set. Airport taxis charge $4 for the 7-km. ride to anywhere in town. One possibility, for those in a hurry, is to charter one of these taxis for your necessary stop at the police station (Kantor Polisi) in Pangkalanbun (needed: photocopy of the first page of your passport) for your essential police permit. This takes 15-30 minutes. Then you go on to Kumai, about 15 km. away. This trip, including the waiting time at the police station, costs $11. The airport and its 2-km. access road is located about halfway between Pangkalanbun and Kumai.

If you are on a budget you can walk from the airport to the main road and grab a public minibus to Pangkalanbun (15¢). Once in town you can walk to the police station, and take a minibus back to Kumai (30¢).

If you want to spend the first night in Pangkalanbun, there are plenty of lodgings in various price categories. (see below) But if time is a factor, we suggest going to Kumai on your first day. There are a couple clean, if basic, places to spend the night there. This will give you time to obtain the other essential permit you need from the Conservation Office (Kantor

PHPA) in Kumai where you need to present your police permit, passport and photocopy of the first page. Then you have to fill out a form and pay a compulsory $1 insurance fee for every week (or less) that you plan to spend in the Tanjung Puting Reserve.

Accommodations

Blue Kecubung Hotel. The best in Pangkalanbun. 18 rooms, ranging in price from $13 to $19, all rooms with AC, attached facilities, color TV with satellite dish reception (but only Indonesian TV and English-language news and other programs from Malaysia). A good restaurant, with live music and singing some nights, decent selection of Indonesian and Chinese dishes $1-4 and Western dishes such as Wienerschnitzel, spaghetti and steaks in the $3-5 range. Beer is expensive. The hotel has a print film processing service and a taxi ($3 to airport, $4.25 to Kumai), and a little stand for souvenirs and useful knickknacks. Connections for domestic and international phone calls. The staff is helpful, some speaking a bit of English.

The owner of the Blue Kecubung, Pak Yupiter Siemon, alias and better known as Pak Aju, also owns the Rimba Hotel (see below) just across the Sekonyer River from the Tanjung Harapan post at the park. If interested, ask him to find out if there are any *tiwah* funerary rituals coming up. He can help you to find a guide who speaks some English for about $6 a day plus expenses—either to the interior or to the Tanjung Puting National Park.
Andika Hotel. A nice place, basically the same room facilities as the Blue Kecubung. 21 rooms, some AC. $5-18.
Rahayu. Near the market and minibus terminal. 29 rooms. $2.50-4.50 S, $4-8 D.
Rangga Santrek. Near the market and minibus terminal. 31 rooms. Owned by a reporter who has traveled quite a bit and speaks some English. $2-4 S, $4-7 D.
Abadie. On the main street. 18 rooms, clean with small dining room. $3-7 S, $4-8 D.
Yadie Firdana. 14 rooms. The owner also owns a travel agency on the premises and can reserve DAS, Bouraq and Garuda flights. $1.75-$3.00 S, $3-5 D.
Aneka Jasa. Next to the river and speedboat-taxi dock. 20 rooms. $3/person w/attached bath, $1.75/person w/shared bath.
Selecta. Second-floor *losmen* next to the minibus taxi terminal to Kumai. 11 rooms. $2.25 S, $4 D, 3 toilet/baths.

ARRIVING IN KUMAI

Kumai is a small town and you can walk from any of the two "hotels" to the PHPA office, so it's best to register and drop off your gear first, then go for your permit.

Kumai is essentially a two-street town: the main road from Pangkalanbun dead ends at the river, and another street runs parallel to the river. The PHPA office is on this second street, about a half a km. from the intersection with the road from Pangkalanbun.

Accommodations

The **Losmen Kumara**, located on the main road from Pangkalanbun a couple of blocks from the river, has 15 rooms, $3S, $4.50D, fans and 4 shared toilet/baths. The **Losmen Cempaka**, next to the market and above the Bank Rakyat, has 10 rooms, $1.75S, $3D, with 2 toilet/baths and fans on request, if available.

Dining

The Kumara is across the street from a small restaurant and there are plenty of food stalls around the market area near the Cempaka. Only the simplest of meals, 60¢ to $1.25.

Boats to Tanjung Puting Reserve

Once you have the necessary police and park permits, your next task is to find a longboat, locally called *klotok*. There are about 30 of these available for charter at Kumai, ranging in price from $22 to $33 per day (The day starts at dawn—it's not just any 24-hour period). These boats, while not having much headroom below decks, sleep 6-10 comfortably.

Make sure that your boat has lamps, a stove of sorts and cooking utensils, plates, cups, boiled water (or bring bottled water, "Aqua," although it's expensive—85¢/liter) and, hopefully, mattresses and pillows. All the boats are covered, with inboard diesel engines.

Only the boats called *Garuda I* and *II* were planning to enclose their toilets and install seats for weird Westerners. We recommend either of these boats, owned by the Baso family, who live on Jalan Idris street, between the docks and the PHPA office. It's $28 a day for the smaller *Garuda I* and $30 for the *Garuda II*. The boats are spotless, and the owner-crews are polite and helpful. The *Garuda II*, 12 meters long, can carry 5 tons.

Your boatman will help you to make the necessary food purchases. You are expected to feed the two-man crew, but fish and rice will do nicely. Count on about $3-5/day for food for yourself and boatmen. We suggest rice, noodles ("Supermie" or "Indomie"), canned sardines, biscuits, coffee, sugar, salt, vegetables and fruit.

The *klotok*, although somewhat expensive for only 1 or 2 persons, is the ideal way to get around the Tanjung Puting area. They are your transportation, restaurant and hotel all together. You could try to find other visitors heading to Tanjung Puting to share costs. But in 1989 only 300 foreigners came to Tanjung Puting, many of them in tour groups. Anyway, if you have more time than money, hang around Kumai for a couple of days to see if any other travelers show up, willing to share a *klotok*.

There is a more expensive alternative for

those in a hurry, perhaps with only one day to see the park. Speedboats with 40HP outboards, with 4-5 passenger capacity, cost some $55/day. No place to sleep on board of course and the scenery zips by too fast to enjoy but you get there and back fast, less than half time it takes a *klotok*. By *klotok* from Kumai it's 2 to 2.5 hours to Tanjung Harapan, and another 2 hours to Camp Leakey.

For the cheapest one-way ride, hop on a river-taxi (a *klotok*) from Kumai to the gold-rush area of Aspai ($1 to Harapan). These leave at irregular intervals, whenever they fill up with bodies. Get dropped off at Sekonyer village, across from the Tanjung Harapan post, then try to find someone to put you up. Canoe or swim across the river to visit the orangutans.

The **Rimba Hotel**, just upriver from Sekonyer village, was planning on opening in mid-1990 with 15 rooms and more to be added later. $20/person, including meals. Canoe rides across to Tanjung Harapan, $1-2 rt.

However you travel to the park, bring insect repellent, a sweater/jacket and light blanket if you sleep on the boat as it might get nippy during the pre-dawn hours. Don't walk around barefoot: orangutan droppings might carry parasites. And don't wander off into the jungle by yourself—there are poisonous plants, bears, and pigs which could attack, not to mention snakes. Take malaria pills—although they are far from 100% effective—for at least a couple of weeks before arrival, during your stay, and for two weeks afterwards. Bring disinfectants for small scrapes and wounds and treat even the smallest cut or bite immediately.

Other Reserves

East Kalimantan

Kersik Luwai. The most accessible reserve in East Kalimantan is Kersik Luwai (or Padang Luwai) just off the Mahakam River, a short distance from Melak. The 5,000-hectare (12,000 acre) area merits attention for its "drought" adapted vegetation—it is not that it doesn't rain here, but that the sandy soil drains so quickly. Look for orchids, and with tremendous luck, you could glimpse deer or other wildlife.

Kutai Reserve. Visiting this game reserve requires a more firm sense of purpose. From Samarinda, travel to Bontang either by daily boat (some 5 hours, $5) departing from the dock in front of the central Post Office, or by paved road, on inexpensive public transportation. Pelita (an airline belonging to Pertamina, the national oil company) flies paying passengers on a space-available basis from Balikpapan to Bontang, $40 one-way. There are several flights daily, but none on Sunday. At Bontang, there are accommodations in various price ranges, including the Kutai Indah at $10-$25 and cheaper digs, down to $3 a night.

Upon arrival in Bontang, the site of a huge liquified natural gas plant, head for the Nature Reserve Office, known under its Indonesian abbreviation of PHPA. You must report to this office before traveling to the park. The staff, who speak some English and are unusually helpful, will arrange a schedule to fit your time and budget. This includes boat rental and a stay in the park of any number of days. This office will contact their field units by radio, advising them of your time of arrival. The PHPA has several guard-posts in the reserve where you can sleep and (likely) purchase simple Indonesian food.

Daily charge: accommodation $2.50; meals (rice, noodles, fish) $1.50 each; and guide, $5. One guide is required for every 3 visitors. It would be a good idea to bring your own bedding and at least some food unless you are completely used to Indonesian fare. Boat rentals vary tremendously, depending on the type of vessel and time required. A safe, motorized canoe will cost $15 to $25 for a 2-5 hour trip, while the same journey in a sleek speedboat could run $200 or more.

The first PHPA post, Teluk Kaba, is on the coast, some 15 km. (9.3 mi.) from Bontang. The other posts are strung out along the Sengata River, past the village of Sengata and its Pertamina complex. The village has shops with food and other essentials but no film. The PHPA unit is just upriver from Sengata village.

Facilities at the PHPA posts are rudimentary at the moment, but there has been talk of improvements. Plans are also afoot to build a road through part of the reserve, or to go around it, to reach Sangkulirang. For more information, contact the PHPA office: Taman Nasional Kutai, Jl. Mulawarman, Bontang, Kalimantan Timur.

South Kalimantan

In Kalsel, forget about what you might read concerning the **Pleihari Martapura Reserve**. It is just too difficult to see any animals there. If you are in Banjarmasin, definitely consider the 12-km. (7 mi.) river trip to the small Pulau Kaget Island for a very early morning or late afternoon sighting of proboscis monkeys. (For more details, see "Visiting Kalsel," page 137.)

Central Kalimantan

In Kalteng, the **Bukit Raya Reserve** requires too much effort, although it is said to hold many species of wildlife.

West Kalimantan

Of the three existing reserves in Kalbar—Gunung Palung, Mandor and Gunung Nuit—only the botanical park at Mandor is easy to reach. This 2,000-hectare (5,000-acre) reserve is composed of peat swamp and heath, with several varieties of orchids and the red *pinang* palm.

Gunung Palung. This reserve has plenty of wildlife, but getting there is definitely not half of the fun. On the positive side, you can see a fair number of animals without getting out of your rented boat. Locals believe the place haunted, which always aids conservation. This is said to be one of the best places in Kalimantan to see orangutans, gibbons and *sambar,* a kind of large deer with very coarse hair, a short, erectile mane and three-pointed antlers.

To get to Gunung Palung, start from Pontianak with a 10-20 hour boat ride (depends on engine size) to Teluk Melanu through the Kapuas delta's *nipa* palm and mangrove swamps. At Teluk Melanu, switch to a small motor boat to buzz up the Simpanang River, 2 hours to the Mantan River and 2 more hours to the end of the navigable stretch. From there it's a 5-hour hike to Gunung Palung. There is a Harvard University research camp in the park, but visitors are definitely not welcome.

The only accommodations are stilt-perched home-stays at the coastal villages. Plan on 5-7 days for this jaunt if you expect to see anything, but we can't offer any guarantees.

Gunung Niut. This reserve is located to the north of Ngabang, covering the headwaters of the Sambas, Landak and Sekayan Rivers. During the dryer season—April to September—there is a negotiable dirt road from Ngabang to Serimbu, where you will have to find guides. Among the 70 species of mammals here are orangutans, Borneo gibbons, clouded leopards, *sambar* deer and sun bears. There are also 15 species of birds, including 6 hornbills, 53 kinds of orchids, the rafflesia, and pitcher plants. Don't try to visit this reserve on an impulse: it requires careful planning.

Further Readings

Unfortunately for Kalimantan, most of the literature about Borneo in English centers around the former British colonies, Sarawak and Sabah. From the Dutch side, government reports and accounts of explorations remain mostly untranslated and tucked away in back stacks of libraries.

Of the basic Dutch works on Borneo, only one has been translated into English: Dr. G. A. F. Molengraaff's *Geological Explorations in Central Borneo*, published in Leiden in 1902. Much more than a dry tome of geology, this is a true explorer's tale of travels in the west and south of then Dutch Borneo, along with a description of the lifestyle of the area's Dayaks. Not available at every public library, but worth the effort to track down.

Spenser St. John's *Life In The Forests of the Far East,* originally published in 1862, ranks among the earliest and best accounts of Borneo peoples. On several occasions during his 13-year stay, St. John canoed and walked far inland when exploring meant no mechanized transport, no canned food and no malaria pills— and head-hunting. While this book describes only the parts of the island under British influence, its style and content make it a worthwhile read for those interested in Kalimantan.

In the field of literature, Joseph Conrad stands far above other Borneophiles, though his knowledge of the island was limited to the coasts. His masterpiece, *Lord Jim*, was partially set in Borneo, as were *Rescue, An Outcast of the Islands* and *Almayer's Folly.*

Alfred Russel Wallace writes with style of Borneo's startling natural creatures in *The Malay Archipelago*, still a classic in its field. Odoardo Beccari's *Wanderings in the Great Forests of Borneo* is another fine work. Beccari, a first-rate scientist from Italy, spent over two-and-one-half years in Borneo. Landing at Kuching in 1865, he trekked, canoed, climbed and slid through the jungles, describing plants and animals, collecting samples for later analyses. Most of his work remains valid today. John McKinnon's *Borneo* presents a contemporary, magnificiently illustrated overview of the geology, flora and fauna of Borneo. Although the research was conducted in the Malaysian part of the island, most of the contents apply to Kalimantan as well. David Attenborough's *Quest for a Zoo Dragon* is another worthwhile recent contribution to this field of literature.

Carl Bock's *The Headhunters of Borneo* is one of the earliest accounts of travel far in the interior of Kaltim and Kalsel. Currently available thanks to Oxford in Asia reprints, Bock describes his travels (in a somewhat overblown style) up the Mahakam river and down the Barito to Banjarmasin. The merit of this work is largely due to its early (1879) date and the author's ground-breaking explorations.

Three books, all written in the 1980s, describe trips into Borneo with a more modern sensibility than the 19th century explorers. In these, the Dayak guides have names and personalities, and the difficulties and charms of the intercultural experience become part of the book's subject. In the well-written and often riotously funny *Into the Heart of Borneo,* British naturalist Redmond O'Hanlon recounts a short trip into the island's interior with the British poet and journalist, James Fenton.

James Barclay's *A Stroll Through Borneo* recounts five months' walk through Sarawak and East Kalimantan in the late 1980s. Though not as well-written as O'Hanlon's book, Barclay's trip was much more of an adventure. He has an excellent rapport with his Dayak guides (as did O'Hanlon), and there is lots of walking and an amazing attack on his canoe by a huge king cobra.

In a similar vein, Eric Hansen's *Stranger in the Forest* talks about his months of trekking, mostly with Punan guides. More introspective than Barclay, Hansen describes the problems of initiating such a jaunt, often the most diificult part of any journey.

The turn of the century saw several ethnography-cum-travel accounts which focused on the Dayaks. Still a classic today is Hose and McDougall's *The Pagan Tribes of Borneo.* Charles Hose also wrote a book called *Natural Man.* Alfred Haddon's *Headhunters Black, White and Brown* is another worthwhile contribution. A contemporary account of the Dayaks, drier, although more accurate, is *Essays on Borneo Societies* edited by Victor King.

Carl Lumholtz, a tough, intelligent Norwegian explorer-ethnographer, wrote *Through Central Borneo* after two years of travel in the island. The reader rejoices along with Lumholtz when, after a five-month jungle trip on a diet of rice and salted fish, he triumphantly opens up a much-dreamed-about bottle of Margot-Medoc. William Krohn's *Into Borneo Jungles*, focusing on the Mahakam basin, is filled with unusual and interesting information.

Several periodicals offer information on Borneo: the U.S.-published *Borneo Research Bulletin*, and the *Sarawak Museum Journal* and the *Brunei Museum Journal.* Oxford in Asia has reprinted many of the classic Borneo writings.

Bernard Sellato's *Hornbill and Dragon*, a profusely illustrated and authoritative work, is probably the best book to date on Dayak arts.

Arguably the best book on Borneo is Tom Harrisson's *World Within*. No one has written more lively, entertaining and still profound ethnographic account than this book's first chapter (some 130 pages) on the Kelabit Dayaks. The rest of the book sparkles with humor and true adventure as Harrisson parachutes into Central Borneo and organizes native resistance to the Japanese during World War II.

SELECT BIBLIOGRAPHY

Appell, G.N. (ed), *Studies in Borneo Societies*, Northern Illinois University, 1976.

Attenborough, David, *Quest for a Zoo Dragon*, London, 1957.

Avé, J.B., *Art of the Archaic Indonesians*, Geneva, 1981.

Avé, J. and V. King, *Borneo: Peoples of the Weeping Forest*, Leiden, 1986.

Avé, J., V. King and J. de Witt, *West Kalimantan, A Bibliography*, Leiden, 1983.

Barclay, James, *A Stroll Through Borneo*, London 1980.

Beccari, Odoardo, *Wanderings in the Great Forests of Borneo*, Singapore, 1986.

Beeckman, D., *A Voyage to and from the Island of Borneo*, London, 1718, New York, 1973.

Bellwood, Peter, *Prehistory of the Indo-Malay Archipelago*, Sydney, 1984.

Bickmore, A.S., *Travels in the East Indian Archipelago*, London, 1868.

Bock, Carl, *The Headhunters of Borneo*, Singapore, 1985.

Bodrogi, Tibor, *Art of Indonesia*, New York, 1972.

Brown, D.E. et al, *The Penis Inserts of Southeast Asia*, Berkeley, 1988.

Cense, A.A. and E.H. Uhlenbeck, *Critical Survey of the Languages of Borneo*, Leiden, 1958.

Collier, William L., *Social and Economic Aspects of Tidal Swamp and Development in Indonesia*, A.N.U., Canberra, 1979.

Conley, William Wallace, *The Kalimantan Kenyah*, New Jersey, 1973.

Crawfurd, John, *A Descriptive Dictionary of the Indian Islands*, London, 1856.

—, *History of the East Indian Archipelago*, 3 vols., Edinburgh, 1820.

Earl, G.W., *The Eastern Seas*, London, 1837.

Feldman, Jerome, *The Eloquent Dead*, Los Angeles, 1985.

Gill, Sarah, *Borneo Masks*, New York, 1965.

Gittinger, M., *Splendid Symbols—Textiles and Tradition in Indonesia*, Washington, D.C., 1979.

Graham, Irwin, *Nineteenth Century Borneo*, Singapore, 1967.

Hanbury-Tenison, Robin, *Mulu, The Rain Forest*, London 1980.

—, *A Pattern of Peoples*, New York, 1975.

Hansen, Eric, *Stranger in the Forest*, London, 1988.

Harrisson, Tom, *World Within, A Borneo Story*, Singapore, 1984.

Harrisson, Barbara, *Orangutan*, London, 1984.

Hoffman, Carl, *The Punan*, American Amber, 1986.

Holt, Claire, *Art in Indonesia*, Ithaca, 1967.

Hose, C. and Wm. McDougall, *The Pagan Tribes of Borneo*, London, 1966.

Hudson, A.B., *Padju Epat, The Ma'anyan of Indonesian Borneo*, New York, 1972.

Jackson, James, *Chinese in the West Borneo Gold Fields*, University of Hull, 1970.

King, Victor, *Essays on Borneo Societies*, University of Hull, 1978.

Kipp, Rita, *Indonesian Religions in Transition*, Tuscon, 1987.

Krohn, W.O., *In Borneo Jungles*, Indianapolis, 1927.

Lumhotlz, Carl, *Through Central Borneo*, New York, 1920.

MacDonald, David, *Expedition To Borneo*, London, 1982.

McDonald, Malcom, *Borneo People*, Oxford in Asia, 1985.

MacKinnon, John, *Borneo, The World's Wild Places*, Amsterdam, 1975.

Mills, D., *Cutlass and Crescent Moon*, Sydney, 1976.

Mjöberg, E.G., *Forest Life and Adventures in the Malay Archipelago*, Singapore, 1988.

Molengraaff, G.A.F., *Borneo Expedition: Geological Explorations in Central Borneo, (1893–94)*, London, 1902.

O'Hanlon, Redmond, *Into the Heart of Borneo*, New York, 1984.

Piazzini, Guy, *The Children of Lilith*, London, 1960.

Perelaer, M.T.H., *Run Away From the Dutch, or Borneo from South to North*, London, 1887.

Rousseau, Jérôme, "The Peoples of Central Borneo," *Sarawak Museum Journal*.

Rutter, Owen, *The Pagans of North Borneo*, Oxford University Press, 1985.

Rutter, Owen, *Pirate Wind*, Singapore, 1987.

Savage, Victor, *Western Impressions of Nature and Landscape in South-East Asia*, Singapore, 1984.

Schärer, Hans, *Ngaju Religion*, The Hague, 1963.

Sellato, Bernard, "The Upper Mahakam Area," Borneo Research Bulletin, 12:40-6, 1980.

Sellato, Bernard, *Hornbill and Dragon— Kalimantan, Sarawak, Sabah, Brunei*, Jakarta, 1989.

Shelford, R.W.C., *A Naturalist in Borneo*, London, 1916.

St. John, S., *Life in the Forest of the Far East*, London, 1862; Oxford, 1986.

Smythies, Bertram E., *The Birds of Borneo*, Kuala Lumpur, 1981.

Tillema, H.F., *A Journey among the Peoples of Central Borneo*, Oxford, 1989.

Wagner, Frits A., *Indonesia: Art of an Island Group*, New York, 1967.

Wallace, Alfred Russel, *The Malay Archipelago*, Singapore, 1983.

Whittier, Herbert and Patricia, "The Apokayan," Sarawak Museum Journal, 1974.

Weinstock, Joseph A., *Kaharingan and the Luangan Dayaks*, Ithaca, 1983.

Index

Kalimantan

0 10   50   100 km

0   10   25   60 mi

SOUTH CHINA
SEA

Natuna Besar
Island

NATUNA ARCHIPELAGO
(Indonesia)
Sabi Besar
island

Serasam Island

Cape Datu

Sibu

Serikei

Hutan
Sambas
Reserve

Baka
National
Park

Kuching

LUPAR RIVER

Pamangkat

Sambas

Singkawang

Semitau

KAPUAS RIVER

Ngabang

LANDAK RIVER

Sanggau

Pontianak

Sintang

Nanga Pinoh

KAPUAS RIVER

WEST KALIMANTAN
(KALBAR)

SCHWANER RANG

Nanga
Tayap

Karimata
Islands

Sukadana

Gunung
Palung
Reserve

Ketapang

CE
KAL
(K

Kendawangan

Sukaraja

Pangkalanbur

Tanjung
Pandan

Bintung
Island

KARIMATA STRAIT

Cape Sambar

Tanjung
Puting
Reserve

Cape Puting

JAVA